Ghana observed

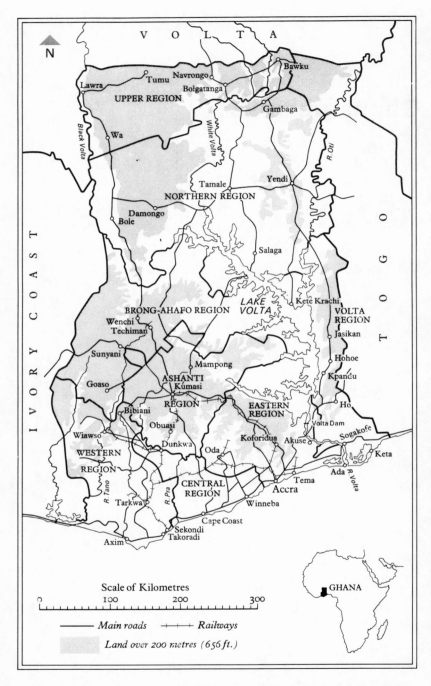

Dennis Austin

Ghana observed

Essays on the politics of a West African republic

MANCHESTER UNIVERSITY PRESS
AFRICANA PUBLISHING COMPANY

© Dennis Austin 1976

Published by
Manchester University Press
Oxford Road, Manchester M13 9PL

ISBN 0 7190 0646 5

North America

Africana Publishing Company
A division of Holmes & Meier Publishers Inc
101 Fifth Avenue, New York, N.Y. 10003

ISBN 0 8419 0278 X

Library of Congress Cataloging in Publication Data

Austin, Dennis, 1922-
  Ghana observed.

  Includes index.
  CONTENTS: The Working Committee of the United Gold Coast Convention, 1947-49.—The Convention People's Party in 1958—The Ghana Parliament's first year. [etc.]
  1. Ghana—Politics and government—1957- Addresses, essays, lectures.
I. Title.
DT512.A85   320.9'677'05   76-15398
ISBN 0-8419-0278-X

Printed in Great Britain by Unwin Brothers Limited
The Gresham Press Old Woking Surrey England

Produced by 'Uneoprint'

A member of the Staples Printing Group

Contents

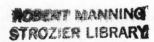

Preface

To write a preface for an introduction is extravagant, but a brief personal note, sketching the background to the origin of these essays, may be of interest.

It was late in 1949 when I first arrived as an extra-mural tutor for what was then the University College of the Gold Coast at Achimota, and I lived for a number of years in Ashanti, the north and at Legon (the present site of the University of Ghana) before returning to England in the summer of 1959 to write about the political events of that critical decade. After *Politics in Ghana* was published I turned to other concerns, although I never quite lost sight of what was happening in Accra. But it was not until the first military *coup* in 1966 and the subsequent election of 1969 that I directly renewed my interest in Ghana when Robin Luckham and I began to put together what became in effect the second volume of politics in Ghana: *Politicians and Soldiers*. The first had appeared in 1964, the second struggled into existence in 1975.

Enough at this point—two bulky volumes on a small West African republic—might well have been thought almost too much. On the other hand, there were still in existence several articles and unpublished essays (I was mildly abashed by their number) which could not be accommodated in the new volume. I had not thought there were so many over so long a period. Almost entirely about politics at a national and local level, they were very much of their time, and they have no claim today to be more than a commentary on what I once thought I saw; but placed chronologically together they tell a tale, and might sensibly perhaps be regarded now as entertainment. The reader will also notice (I hope forebearingly) that at various points of crisis I tried to predict the future course of events. The attempt was not, of course, very successful, and I am doubtful now whether it was sensible to do so in relation to the party and military regimes which then struggled to survive. Very likely in such difficult times

> Men's fates are already set
> There is no need of asking diviners!

But one last word about the essays does need to be said. I am so in debt to numerous individuals and institutions as to be bankrupt of means to repay in proper measure those who helped to bring them together. The least, therefore, I can do is mention some by name. The original suggestion of publication came from Mr Frank Cass, and I do not think that they would now appear in print without the friendly promptings of Miss Elizabeth Rose or the secretarial assistance always readily supplied by Mrs Joyce Ingham. Special financial support was given by my university, with the happy result that it is under the imprint of Manchester University Press, kindly imposed by Mr Martin Spencer (as publisher) and Mr Ray Offord (as editor), that I very willingly make this final appearance on politics in Ghana.

Chronology of events

1947　United Gold Coast Convention formed (Danquah).

1949　Convention People's Party formed (Nkrumah).

1951　First general election, first National Assembly.

1954　Second general election.

1956　Togoland plebiscite, third general election.

1957　Independence.

1960　First Republic, after referendum.

1964　Single-party republic, after referendum.

1966　First *coup d'état:* National Liberation Council.

1969　General election. Second Republic, Progress Party government under Busia.

1972　Second *coup d'état:* National Redemption Council under Colonel Acheampong. Nkrumah dies in exile.

Acknowledgements

For permission to reproduce here the substance if not always the exact form of articles which originally appeared under their auspices the author and publisher are indebted to the editors and proprietors of the *Journal of African History* (chapter I), *Parliamentary Affairs* (chapter III), *Political Studies* (chapter IV), *Africa* (chapter V), *Venture UK* (now *Third World*) (chapter VI), *Government and Opposition* (chapter VII), *New Society* (chapter VIII), *West Africa* (chapters IX and XIII), *Africa Quarterly,* the *International Journal* (chapter XII) and *Minerva* (Epilogue).

Of the making of books on Africa there is no end.

Sir F. D. Lugard, GCMG, introduction to *The Golden Stool* by E. W. Smith, London, 1926

Introduction

Collected and revised, the essays reprinted in this volume have brought
home to the writer the marked inveteracy of a view which he once held of
the events described therein. They begin, as any account of modern politics
in the former Gold Coast must, with the 1948 riots. They end, as perhaps all
accounts of the nationalist years before and after independence will have to
close, with the arrival of the military in 1972 as a recurrent contender for
power. But there was a time in between, of which the details may be seen in
the chronology, when it seemed to the writer that a broad consensus of
support could be formed within a parliamentary framework for the government of this newly independent country. In those formative years there was
a political party—more than one—of national breadth and appeal. There were
also leaders at local and national level whose followers were sufficiently
numerous to take hold of the colonial State, and adequately aware (it might
be thought) of their common interests to make use of the parliamentary
structures which had rather hurriedly been constructed to bear the weight
of the transfer of power from colonial to nationalist hands. After all, free
elections, peacefully conducted, had been held in the early 1950s, and were
held again in 1969. Very many voters had queued patiently under a tropical
sun to cast their ballot between rival candidates. Moreover the colonial
instruments of rule, dependent largely on the civil and judicial service, had
been brought considerably under Ghanaian control, while throughout the
country there was a growing educated class whose members, though clearly
intent on securing the major share of the surplus extracted from the rural
population, could scarcely be seen as brutally exploitative. Land ownership
was widely dispersed among peasant smallholders with whom the least
acquaintanceship was sufficient to persuade a reasonable observer that they
were neither docilely subservient nor sullenly in revolt. Of course there
was dependence: the dependence of the illiterate on the literate, of villages
very often on towns, of the small trader on the large merchant houses (still,
in the 1950s and '60s, under expatriate control), and of the economy as a
whole on distant metropolitan markets and external sources of capital.
There were times when much of the drama of these twenty-five years
appeared as the politics of theatre, of words not deeds, and of rhetoric in
place of policies, when successive governments, in whatever role they cast
themselves, seemed like the actors of a play in which the controlling action
was decided offstage—in the loan agencies and commodity markets of the
developed world. But that was not how the reality of the conflicts within
Ghana appeared to the actors of the time. Nor is it altogether clear why a
large degree of economic dependence should have denied to local politicians
the opportunity to moderate their disputes through representative institutions. There is no universal law of external dependence and internal
collapse even in the world of the newly sovereign. If in the writer's mind
there was a parallel when describing the course of Ghanaian politics it was

perhaps south Asia, where the attempt to maintain colonial States transmuted into independence through parliamentary institutions was still in evidence. The writer was unable, therefore, to accept that the movement in Ghana away from political competition in the early 1960s *via* the single-party State, or in 1966 and 1972 towards military rule, had anything of the inevitable about it. All too often men describe as inevitable what they simply wish and intend to do: necessity is used as a cloak of self-indulgence; and when, as in Ghana, the cloak was embroidered by Nkrumah and others with a token 'Africanness' it seemed still less convincing as an explanation of the overthrow of democratic institutions.

Such is the tenor of many of the essays which record the shifts of political fortune in a small West African republic. How lamentably wide of the mark such beliefs and hopes were became clear in 1972 on the downfall once again of parliamentary government under renewed assault by the military, and, wiser after the event, the writer ought perhaps to be able to describe more closely the ground of failure (for failure it undoubtedly was) of representative government and party rule. But there are other aspects of these years on which it may first be helpful, by way of prior explanation, to comment.

The riots of 1948 are presented in the first essay as having shoved forward, irrevocably, the move towards independence, and certainly the consequences were extensive, not only in the Gold Coast but in neighbouring colonies.[1] A year after the disturbances the Convention People's Party was formed. Two years later a new constitution, locally hatched, was promulgated, under which the CPP and Nkrumah (when released from prison) took office after the first general election in 1951. The particular view of these events in the essay is largely that from the party headquarters with which the writer was always much more closely associated than he was with Government House, but there was also that second side to the story—the 'view from the Castle'—which others have now depicted, most notably Dr Rathbone. (There was also a third side to the triangle of forces by which independence was achieved—the Colonial Office in London—but that has still to be examined.) The story that Dr Rathbone tells[2] adds considerably to what we thought we knew, particularly in respect of the role of the colonial regime, which (as he says) 'was not that of passive and recognised concession ... [but one which] retained considerably more control of the colony's affairs in the crucial period of the transfer of power than usually inferred', and he gives Arden Clarke's very interesting comment (in a letter to his mother in 1953): 'There is no doubt that there is a powerful body of opinion in the highest quarter here [in London] who think that I am going too far and too fast but as no one has been able to put forward an alternative working policy that has the remotest prospect of working I am being allowed to have my own way'.

'Taking a new initiative' was often the rather desperate remedy of a Governor who was caught in the difficulty of trying to maintain his balance at the middle of a see-saw which was beginning to tilt quite unexpectedly and sharply downwards on the populist side. It produced policies of collaboration, notionally defined as 'diarchy', and held only for a limited period, which none the less enabled the colonial government to retain control until the final ceremony of independence. But of course the main weight in the Ghana balance came from the accumulative force of the nationalist party of that time—the CPP. It is described as the writer saw it in the 1950s, before it moved irrevocably, disastrously and inefficiently towards the attempt at single-party rule, and within that account the reader may note that there appears from time to time, as in later essays on the main successor to the CPP which took shape as the Progress Party in 1969, a common theme by which the rise and fall of both parties can perhaps be made intelligible. Because it is more often presented obliquely and descriptively than directly or analytically, it may be helpful to restate what that theme is, since it has been at the centre (in so far as there *is* a centre) of much of the political history of Ghana since 1945.

It has as its primary motif the effect of an expanding 'political nation' which, growing rapidly in number and influence, was actively in pursuit of its interests under whatever government ruled in Accra. It was, so to speak, the news behind the nationalist headlines in the 1950s, and the substance behind the revival of party rule at the end of the '60s. Membership—although such a phrase conveys perhaps too precise an implication of attachment to any single body of organised interest—of this growing political class could be explained fairly simply in the early nationalist years by social origin (non-chief), wealth (less than £20 a month) and education (less than full secondary school). Thereafter, however, because the attractive power of the CPP, as that of the Progress Party after 1969, drew together a wide following behind the party leaders who used the resources of the State to try and entrench themselves in office, it was much less easy to see either the CPP or the Progress Party as the political expression of a particular social stratum. The latter particularly had among its leaders many who belonged to the now relatively broad group of professional interests as indigenous businessmen: a nascent class (it might be said) of *bourgeois gentilhommes*. They were certainly very different from the teachers, traders and clerks who took office under the CPP. Moreover a much greater number had been drawn into politics. At the last election before independence under 700, 000 went to the polls; at the 1969 election there were over a million and a half voters. Yet, even at the time of the second Republic in 1969, much less perhaps had changed than seemed at first to be the case. Below the very dramatic changes at national level, from Nkrumah to the National Liberation Council of the first army *coup,* and from Dr Busia to Colonel Acheampong of the newly constituted National Redemption Council, the broad elite of the not-very-well-educated was still there—deeper, wider, more self-confident, a good deal wealthier, and far more firmly established locally than it had been in the critical and formative years of the nationalist period—yet there still, in 1972. At district level, for example, the constituency executives of the parties which began to be formed, after the first military government made clear its intention to withdraw, contained much the same kind of local leaders as those who once upheld the CPP—some indeed were astute enough to make the transition from one regime to another—and to measure the distance between the party of Nkrumah and that of Busia was not to record any major shift in the social base of power. On the contrary. After talking to many of the local leaders during the 1969 election the writer was quite prepared to conclude not only that the Progress Party was the kind of movement which many of the early nationalists would very probably have liked the CPP to have become, but that Busia and his colleagues were really an 'elite within an elite' whom those who had done well out of the former People's Party were now rather inclined to admire.

It is also worth emphasising that throughout the years covered by the essays there was no sign of a challenge to the dominance of this elite. It was internally divided, and many of its leaders (together with those who supported them) suffered politically—they were imprisoned, or went into exile—but party and military governments alike were drawn from the

English-speaking educated minority of which by far the greater number
were still middle-school-educated and very little more than that. The final
essay raises the question whether the military, too, should not be seen as
the 'last of the elementary school leavers' to arrive in office. That certainly
is arguable, but not the deeply entrenched position throughout these years at
local positions of power of the same ill educated elite from which the CPP
was first constituted in 1949. Despite the grievances of the cocoa farmers
on which the wealth of this elite was essentially dependent, there was no
attempt to draw together a smallholders' party; nor was there any eruption
after 1948 of organised discontent in the towns, despite a good deal of urban
poverty. There had been an earlier history of farmers' protests, and of
'cocoa hold-ups', under the colonial government, and a later essay describes
the farmers' movement which began to take shape in Ashanti in the 1950s;
but it also shows how a dissatisfied section of the CPP, in alliance with a
number of Ashanti chiefs, took control of its complaints and produced the
National Liberation Movement. Throughout the 1960s (as in the 1950s) the
rural population of cocoa and food farmers, much like the rank and file of the
larger trade unions in the mines and railways, turned to and allowed themselves to be represented by the educated elite—and to whom else (it might
be asked), lacking the confidence, one must suppose, in their own ability,
could they turn? It is in such painful decisions that we can understand the
suggestion that the search behind the politics of many African States—a
search which can hardly as yet be described as successful—has not been for
'democracy' as such, of which at least the rural population has direct if
intermittent experience in its day-to-day life, but 'representation'.[3]

It was all the more remarkable, therefore, that hope continued, persist-
ently if not altogether unreservedly, during these twenty-five years. As is
recorded in many of the essays which look at local politics, most Ghanaians
applauded each change of regime. The crowds which gathered to listen
delightedly to the CPP leaders—Nkrumah, Botsio, Gbedemah, Krobo Edusei,
Archie Casely Hayford—danced in the streets to welcome Colonel Kotoka in
1966. They queued patiently—in Accra and Paga, Tsito and Dormaa Ahenkro—
to vote for Busia or Gbedemah in 1969 but were ready again to turn to
Colonel Acheampong in 1972. There was a hopeful acceptance of each turn
of fate, and popular expectation rode high at least until that second *coup*.
There were many, of course, at each turn of fortune who were disadvantaged,
since those who had benefited individually or communally from a particular
structure of power went out of business; but it seemed always to have been
assumed that their time would come again: fortune's wheel would turn,
whereupon those who had been displaced would, if they survived, return to
reward not only themselves but their kinsmen and dependants. What
mattered was to survive each Castle revolution. So the ordinary elector
waited hopefully and patiently while those who claimed to act for him did
what they could to capitalise on the resources they might one day be able
to offer the new rulers. As Achebe makes his hero comment reflectively in
that most political of African novels, *A Man of the People:*

> 'Let them eat,' was the people's opinion. 'After all, when white men
> used to do all the eating did we commit suicide?' Of course not. And
> where is the all-powerful white man today? He came, he ate and he
> went. But we are still around. The important thing then is to stay
> alive: if you do you will outlive your present annoyance. The great
> thing, as the old people have told us, is reminiscence; and only those
> who survive can have it. Besides, if you survive, who knows? It may
> be your turn to eat tomorrow. Your son may bring home your share.[4]

The fatalism of hope illustrated here could as easily be drawn from Ghana as from Nigeria. Expressed at its simplest, it is perhaps the reflection of a conditional allegiance. Each government that begins its term of office is seen as the instrument of disbursement via an intermediary elite to the population at large That was not wholly true of the attitude to the CPP in all the joyous swing of its advance as a nationalist movement in 1950; but thereafter it would be absurd to deny the strong element of calculation in the support which successive regimes elicited, when the business of ruling came close to being seen as the management of a political market.[5] None of the governments looked at in these essays was particularly successful in this respect. Nor was it perhaps surprising that the appeal which successive leaders tried to exert had a diminishing effect. The resources ran out, and the support ran out. Yet despite the gap between the promise and the fulfilment the Ghanaian voter still retained a belief that future rulers might be more rewarding (and, perhaps, less predatory) than their predecessors. It must have been so. For how else can one explain the massive response not only to the material promises but the moral appeal which Busia's Progress Party held out in 1969 ? Only by the time of the second *coup*, perhaps, had hope begun to grow grey hairs, as the writer noted in January 1972, in the somewhat tempered welcome given to Colonel Acheampong and in the spread of a more wary, more dispirited attitude towards politics among many Ghanaians.

Other aspects of the country's politics between 1945 and 1972 may readily be thought to extend, and by extension correct, what is set down in these essays; but within the narrow range of what is presented here the reader may observe that there appears from time to time a second dominant theme, that of the interplay of communal loyalties and elite rivalries. Throughout these years it was impossible not to be impressed by the strength of an intense local patriotism. If it is right to see political society in Ghana as a broad pyramid of power levelled off at the top on which there stands uneasily poised the ruling military and administrative elite while below them stretch the gradations of education and wealth—from the senior civil servants, lawyers and judges to the local contractor, trader, teacher, skilled artisans and wealthier cocoa farmers, down to the migrant labourers and the urban poor—it is also true that the main slopes of the pyramid are the ethnic solidarities—Ga, Ewe, Dagomba, Gonja, Tallensi, Akan (whether Fanti, Ashanti, Brong or Akwapim) and other local peoples—of which Ghanaian society is composed. A cross-section through the pyramid at a particular echelon could often be defined by wealth and occupation and, their usual concomitant, the level of education; but it was also necessary to see an educated market trader as belonging not only hierarchically but terri-torially to a particular point on the pyramid, and it was useful to remember (when talking politics) that a police officer who had risen through the pro-fessional ranks of the force, or a member of the Bar Association of wealth and social distinction, was likely still to retain something of his birth as a Ga or Fanti or Mamprusi.

There were, it is true, difficulties about applying such images too closely. The horizontal gradations of the pyramid, for example, though measured by economic standing and educational attainment, often varied according to location. A scarcely educated clerk of council-of no more than moderate means in, say, the Kassena-Nankani area in the far north, of which the local politics are described in some detail later,[6] had a much greater political say than his southern counterpart. Nor was it easy to place hierarchically the army officer whose authority was his occupation, or the

holder of a traditional office, at village level, whose influence was not yet
eroded. Similarly, as the writer has tried to argue in respect of each of the
elections of that time, there were problems in talking about the 'politics of
ethnic solidarity', for although at first sight there appeared to be a distinct
territorial base to the 1954 or 1956 contests or the 1969 election the detailed
pattern of constituency voting was not at all commensurate with 'tribalism'.
The principal source of conflict lay always in rivalry between neighbouring
towns or chiefdoms, or between migrant strangers and local subjects, or
among would-be party leaders, of the same ethnic origin, who tried to bind
their followers to their cause by a delicate network of group interests and
individual patronage.

Still, that is not to decry an interpretation of political behaviour at
popular level as being as much 'communal' as it was anything else, and if
it is asked how long the intensity of that local patriotism and the grouping
of power on a personal base will last, the most convincing reply is surely
that while 'tradition as chieftaincy' is likely to diminish (and there is clear
evidence throughout the essays of *that*) 'tradition as locality' seems likely
to continue as long as Ghana remains a predominantly peasant and small-
town society. Communal and personal relationships are bound to persist as
the stuff of village politics for a long time to come, and re-reading the
account of the 1956-58 election contests in Kumasi makes it clear that,
despite sharp inequalities of income and status, Ghana has a long way to go
towards the concept of class as a major source of conflict. There were, to
be sure, notions of class distinction put about by the party leaders in the
1950s and '60s. There was a good deal of loose talk in the party newspapers
at the time of the 1969 election from which it might be thought that there
were substantial social differences in membership between Gbedemah's
National Alliance of Liberals and Busia's Progress Party. But such dis-
tinctions were more easily claimed than substantiated, and although there
was every sign at constituency level of a political class on the make its
members were obliged to cast about on all sides for some foothold of power
by appealing to local loyalties or personal obligations.

Such were the two most memorable features of those years—a new elite
busily laying hold of the colonially fashioned State and (by way of contrast)
the splintered nature of political authority at local level. Of the two, the
most striking characteristic—certainly the one that stands out most clearly
for the writer in retrospect—is not the persistence of these territorial or
personal rivalries (the exact configuration of which were very much subject
to change) but the remarkable increase in number of an educated and semi-
educated elite on the higher slopes of the pyramid. They could, rather
remotely, be compared perhaps with other seekers after power and office,
such as the 'inevitable Parliament men, the Country Gentlemen, the Politicians, the Social Climbers, Placemen and Purveyors of Favours, Professional Advancement, the Services and the Law, the Merchants and Bankers,
Robbers, Muddlers, Bastards and Bankrupts' of Sir Lewis Namier's
eighteenth-century Parliament,[7] or the new ruling class in Professor
Plumb's account of *Political Stability in England*.[8]

But why, it may then be asked, did the *Ghanaian* parliamentarians fail to
retain control in 1966 and again in 1972? In a much quoted phrase, formerly
inscribed on the base of his statue, which, toga-clad and arm upraised in
party salute, stood outside the National Assembly until the soldiers allowed
the crowd to pull it down, Nkrumah had told his followers to 'Seek Ye First
The Political Kingdom'; but from the evidence adduced in these essays it
could easily be shown that neither he nor his successors ever found it.

Perhaps, however, some did ? In a sense, failure describes only the casual-
ties of the political warfare which, admittedly, were widespread among the
higher echelons of the party leaders. But for many of middle rank in political life, who gave time and effort after 1947 to politics at national and local
level, the bringing of the State under African rule and the transfer of large
sectors of the economy from expatriate to local interests were substantial
accomplishments. And if one adds to that the enlargement under Ghanaian
control of the public sector and the former colonial service, together with a
corresponding expansion of the professions, it would be perverse to deny
the extent of a remarkable transformation. The once narrow professional
elite of educated leaders, and the traditional spokesmen of an antiquated
indirect-rule system of administration, have given place to a broad administrative and managerial class entrenched within the newly independent
State. The fact remains, however, that the two military *coups* of 1966 and
1972 brought to the ground the parliamentary structure built up since 1950.
Was it simply that the CPP and the Progress Party lacked sufficient resources to regulate the social conflicts engendered by the transfer of power
to local hands, or did the former colonial State always lack the legitimacy
and the necessary coercion (once British power had been withdrawn) to
command respect for its authority ? In a sense the questions answer themselves. There was not only the failure of civilian rule in 1966 but the
second fracture six years later. Nor is it very difficult to put together an
explanation of what occurred, although whether such explanations are quite
satisfactory is another matter.

A lack of material resources ? That was true of both the CPP and the
Progress Party on the eve of their downfall, in sharp contrast with the good
fortune of the soldiers in their early years of office. A simple table can be
constructed:

Foreign trade (cedis, million)

	1965 (Nkrumah)	1968 (First military)	1971 (Busia)	1972 (Second military)
Exports	226·9	342·0	380·2	570·1
Imports	320·1	314·0	445·3	396·2
Balance of trade	—93·2	+28·0	—65·1	+173·9

Source: *Quarterly Economic Review, E.I.U., 1965-72*

Not the least of the CPP's misfortunes was to have suffered a sudden boom
in the 1950s and an abrupt halt to the economy a decade later. Similarly,
Busia's Progress government also moved (over a much shorter time) from
surplus to deficit to the horrendous devaluation of more than 40 per cent at
the end of 1971.

A lack of consent and attachment to the authority and institutions of
government ? That is much harder to assess. The volatility of the electorate
was described earlier, although it might also be said (and the evidence is
examined later) that both Nkrumah and Busia provided ample ground for
disenchantment with their policies.[9] It is also the case that the pull of
'alternative loyalties', narrower in scope than the State, and locally focused,
was often very strong. There are, of course, no Ghanaians in history except
to the extent—an inadequate extent ?—that colonial rule made them so. On

the other hand, it was astonishing, and strongly indicative of the ability of the members of that broad elite which we described earlier to see themselves as a 'political nation', to observe how quickly a country-wide following was put together north and south in 1968-69 behind *both* parties to the election. After all, the Progress vote of 876,378 was more than double that for the CPP during the comparable election of 1956, the party actually being given a higher proportion of the poll from a much enlarged electorate. Even the loser—K. A. Gbedemah and his National Alliance of Liberals—picked up more votes than the CPP had secured prior to independence.

In respect, therefore, of two of the main pillars of support needed—loyalty and jobs—the latter was very likely the more frail. None of the governments looked at in these essays was unequivocally sure that it could sustain a sense of national response to its authority; but none, certainly, was ever able to find adequate resources (assuming that such resources ever *are* adequate) for the political market. But is there not a third need in such precarious situations—political skills ? The party leaders would have been helped greatly had they possessed a more stable command of the resources of the State, and a more copious supply of such resources; if, that is, they had been able to meet a basic Ghanaian requirement for good government—larger rewards and more jobs within a settled framework of consent. It would also have been very useful if Ghana had been less diverse, and without a sharp edge of distrust between local communities. Yet it has also to be said that other newly independent States, more inveterately divided than in Ghana, and poorer, have been able to sustain a broader base of representative institutions than the military seem likely to be able to provide. Perhaps, therefore, the critical factor, or at least a strongly *contributory* factor, was that of political skill—of a steady balance and calm nerves—there having been, during both periods of party government, as much a failure of skills as of circumstance. Why should that have been so ? Very possibly for the reason half suggested earlier, namely the inexperience and, derivatively, the uncertainty with which a new elite faced the problem of having, quite suddenly, acquired power. However rapturously these newly elected leaders were acclaimed, they appeared very uneasy in office. The uneasiness came (the writer firmly believed) not only from the conditional nature of the support they were given but from the sheer novelty of their actually being in office, heightened by the certain knowledge that the loss of that office would carry, inescapably, great personal misfortune. To that general alarm there needed to be added, certainly in respect of Nkrumah and his colleagues, and very likely for Busia too, a marked distaste for any manifestation of opposition—a dislike carried to a pathological extent by Nkrumah towards the end of his rule, when politics as the practice of give and take, or even as the art of the possible, had clearly become an unattractive proposition.

Might it not be argued, however, that the breakdown of parliamentary institutions in 1966 and 1972 was as much because they were deliberately broken as because they were fragile or under strain ? Do *coups* in Africa need to be explained in terms other than their own provenance ? At one level of interpretation the two military interventions in Ghana had much in common. Both sets of conspirators were 'malcontents in uniform'[10] who were exasperated by the treatment they had received at the hands of the party government and reasonably sure that the regime had run out of the resources needed to keep intact their network of alliances. Looking back from 1972, the two armed incursions seemed to connect together, spanning a period of transition in the sense that the downfall of Nkrumah, followed by the failure of Busia, put an end to the struggle between party leaders whose original strengths and weaknesses owed a good deal to their rivalry as successors to the colonial government. The location of power today is much less certain, particularly since 1972, when Colonel Acheampong's NRC began to 'colonise' the former party-dominated State by appointing army officers to positions of authority at both national and local level. One may reasonably assume, therefore, that Ghana is now one of a number of States in which the army has taken its place either in the council chamber or sufficiently close to its doors to be able to impose its will on whoever rules by its favour.

Yet at the time of the first *coup,* as the writer has tried to describe when looking at the overthrow of Nkrumah, the problem was not seen like that at all. It was the confident assumption of many of the soldiers themselves that what was needed was simply a return to the past, or rather to a reformed past. There sprang up that endearing belief, which the writer was very willing to share, that democratic ways and a representative system of government could be restarted in the wake of the army once it had carried out its remedial task. In the early months of the NLC's rule it was agreeable to entertain such hopes and to share the jubilation of the crowds which, without need of curfew, celebrated Nkrumah's downfall. The former People's Party had been brushed aside with such ease that the memory of its heroic days was almost blotted out, and the quick success of the military seemed a direct measure of Nkrumah's failure. The army and police officers, too, were able to justify their intervention as being in response to a popular but suppressed demand, and it was demonstrably true that many Ghanaians welcomed the arrival of the soldiers and gave massive support three years later to Busia and his party as the clearest alternative to the CPP. Moreover the soldiers kept their promise. They quickly established a Constitutional Commission, summoned a Constituent Assembly, agreed to the formation of parties, held an election, promulgated a constitution and transferred power (a little hesitantly at the last) to the Progress Party. Yet there was no direct correspondence between the intentions of the soldiers and the particular success of the politicians. It could scarcely be argued that 1966 was 'Busia's *coup'* even in the sense of *qui facit per alia facit per se*. Nevertheless, it was confidently assumed by the army leaders of that time that there were acceptable alternatives to the CPP. It was as if they believed that what had gone wrong could be put right, like a clock which had stopped working, with a firm shake and new timekeepers.

The re-entry of the army in January 1972 was much more awkward to explain. It was, of course, different from the first *coup* if only by reason of being second, but it must also have been different too in its assumptions, since there was clearly no discernible alternative to its rule. In reaching his decision to intervene Colonel Acheampong seemed to confirm the suspicion that when the army withdrew in 1969 it simply remained at the frontiers of politics and could not be prevented from crossing them at will. But one may still draw the distinction between the two *coups* that, whereas the first did lead to a free election and a renewed attempt at parliamentary rule, the second intervention—a little over two years after the Progress Party took office—offers no such hope for the forseeable future. If, therefore, the 1966 *coup* was an attempt by the army to break the enforced monopoly of single-party government, and to restore competitive politics to a disfranchised electorate, the second may pessimistically be held to have signalled the permanent arrival of the military as a political force.

Does it matter ? The change has not so far been dramatic, a negative quality reflected in the absence of any great sense of destiny among the

military. In 1966 the army moved against a regime commonly held to be
on the left; in 1972 it overthrew a government thought to be on the right.
The pleasant fact of the matter is that political life in Ghana does not run to
extremes. There is no major class of extortionate landowners or landless
peasants, no spectre of famine and much less of the desperate poverty of the
urban dispossessed of Asia and Latin America. One might add, too, that differences of religion and language, though they exist, do not enter directly
and fanatically into political life. There was, to be sure, an unpleasant
Bonarpartist flavour to Nkrumah's government in its corruption of nationalist hopes, and single-party rule was harshly improved towards the end of
the first Republic. But there has been mercifully absent from Ghana, to
date, the organised brutality of many single-party or military-dominated
States: no forced confessions, people's courts, and the execution of political
prisoners. The twentieth century has not reached that far in Accra. And
yet—and yet—one may still regret the destruction of those high hopes of the
early nationalist years, and of the closing down of a political debate which
once gave life to parliament and an electorate which, never failing to respond
on each occasion it was able to record its choice, placed an endearing trust
in the exercise of its right to vote. That certainly is gone, and what little is
gained by the continuity of army rule has been lost—who can say now for how
long ?—in the denial of that trust.

For the details of much of the argument presented here the reader
must turn to the essays themselves. They stand as separate but linked
commentaries on the politics of those years, linked by their sequence and
by the persistence of a particular view of those politics which the writer
noted at the outset. Only in the last, long survey of the university is there
an attempt to move away from parties and elections, parliaments and the
army, and only in the closing pages of that account does the writer come at
all close to describing, with some degree of intimacy, the 'poorly-educated-
commoner elite' to whom he once owed, inexpressibly, a lasting debt. The
substance of the essay concerns the university at Legon and the difficulties
encountered in its relations with the nationalist parties and the present
military government. The final paragraphs are a brief remembrance of life
as an extra-mural tutor in Nkrumah's Ghana, although the author would ask
the reader to believe that such impressions as may be mirrored in that
account are only a pale reflection of the bright reality of those years.

Notes

1   The effect of the riots on the transfer of power in Nigeria has been
     recorded by Lord Foot. 'I arrived in Nigeria as Chief Secretary late
     in 1947. Sir John Macpherson came to take up his post as Governor in
     1948 ... The Richards Constitution had then been in full effect for
     little more than a year, and it had been stipulated that it must remain
     in force unchanged for nine years. We reviewed the whole political
     situation; we took into account the disorder and changes which had
     recently taken place in what was then the Gold Coast. We came to the
     conclusion that we must at once take a new initiative.' (*A Start in
     Freedom*, London, 1964, pp. 103-4.)
2   'The transfer of power in the Gold Coast, 1945-57', unpublished thesis,
     London, 1968.
3   See particularly John Dunn, 'Politics in Asunafo', in D. Austin and
     R. Luckham (eds.) *Politicians and Soldiers in Ghana, 1966-72*, ch. VII,

London, 1975, and J. Dunn and A. R. Robertson, *Dependence and Opportunity: Political Change in Ahafo,* Cambridge, 1974.

4 Chinuah Achebe, *A Man of the People,* London, 1966; and from the same novel a passage which might well have been written about 1966 or 1972 in Ghana: 'Overnight everyone began to shake their heads at the excesses of the last regime, at its graft, oppression and corrupt government: newspapers, the radio, the hitherto silent intellectuals and civil servants—everybody said what a terrible lot; and it became public opinion the next morning. And these were the same people that only the other day had owned a thousand names of adulation, whom praise singers followed with song and talking-drum wherever they went. Chief Koko in particular became a thief and a murderer, while the people who had led him on—in my opinion the real culprits—took the legendary bath of the Hornbill and donned innocence.'

5 The burden of Maxwell Owusu's very intelligent thesis in *Uses and Abuses of Political Power,* Chicago, 1971.

6 Chapters V and XI.

7 *The Structure of Politics at the Accession of George III,* London 1961.

8 *Political Stability in England, 1697-1725,* London, 1967.

9 Chapter XII.

10 Valerie Bennett's phrase in Austin and Luckham, *op. cit.,* Epilogue.

I

The Working Committee of the United Gold Coast Convention, 1947–49

When I was in Ghana last year, Dr Danquah very kindly allowed me to read and make notes on an early minute book belonging to the Working Committee of the United Gold Coast Convention. I thought it was very interesting, for it covered the years 1947-51, when discontent with colonial rule came to a head and produced first the UGCC—as it is easier to call it—and then its radical offspring, the Convention People's Party. The minute book was carefully, clearly written; it runs parallel to the early part of Nkrumah's *Autobiography* (chs. 5-12)—itself a valuable source of information—and it confirms, adds to and occasionally corrects the account given by Nkrumah of these interesting years when the colonial administration was beginning to retreat and the nationalists to advance. Moreover in its beginning lay its end: the two chief protagonists in 1947 were Dr J. B. Danquah and Dr Kwame Nkrumah; and, thirteen years later, they were still opposed, as rival candidates for the presidency of the new republic.

Brought together in August 1947, the UGCC can be seen as the first of the post-war political organisations, but it was also the confluence of earlier associations—tributaries of discontent which fed the torrent of nationalist agitation after 1945. This was the period when few of the leaders knew precisely what they wanted, but the mass of the people were becoming clear about what they disliked. Prices were rising, jobs difficult to get, cocoa incomes falling off as swollen shoot spread through the Akwapim and Akim areas; the more-than-barely-literate now included many from the middle schools, some with two or three years' secondary education, who disliked the alliance between the chiefs and the officials, who read of events in Burma and India and listened to those who had served abroad with the West African Frontier Force. Altogether there were four or five sections of Gold Coast society interested in nationalist politics, often closely related through family ties but sufficiently distinguishable to be looked at separately as they appear in the pages of the minute book.

There were the leaders of the UGCC—lawyers, merchants, graduate teachers. In 1947 this small independent professional and trading class could look back over more than fifty years of political effort, sometimes with, more often against the colonial administration. Educated at Mfantsipim or Adisadel College, later at Achimota, taking their degrees at English universities, they ran the newspapers, sat on the Legislative Council, and criticised the government through political associations like the Aborigines' Rights Protection Society, the National Congress of British West Africa, and local ratepayers' associations; they moved easily in English society without losing the awareness of their own African traditions: indeed, they were among the first to defend them; but they had a liberal view of society—a

---

* Reproduced from the *Journal of African History,* II, 2, 1961.

lawyer's view perhaps; they were never quite able to understand the appeal
or techniques of mass organisation; and they had a lawyer's caution, too,
against rash, precipitate action.

Their early rivals had been the chiefs—rivals, not enemies, for many
of the leading members of the 'intelligentsia' were related, by temperament
and some by blood, to the wealthy *amanhene* who also sat on the legislative
council and in the provincial councils of chiefs. Danquah was a younger
brother of the great Nana Ofori Atta I; his nephew, William Ofori Atta, was
the chief's son; J. W. de Graft-Johnson, the first (part-time) general secretary of the UGCC, had acted as secretary to the Western Provincial Council
of Chiefs. In the early years of the century the Cape Coast lawyers had
defended the Colony chiefs against attempts by the administration to limit
their powers, but in 1911 Nene Mate Kole, in 1916 Nana Ofori Atta, had been
appointed to the legislative council, the theory of indirect rule began to hold
pride of place, and native authorities were introduced in 1927 and
strengthened in 1944. The intelligentsia felt that they had been passed over,
denied their proper place as heirs of the British whose institutions they
knew and, for the most part, admired. And though the early quarrel between
J. E. Casely Hayford, the distinguished Cape Coast lawyer, and Nana Ofori
Atta I had been healed it was not forgotten. An uneasy relationship existed
throughout the 1930s and '40s between the chiefs and the intelligentsia; they
were able to co-operate together and often did so; but still the relationship
was not always an easy one. And by the end of the second world war the
wealthy 'merchant princes' of Accra and Cape Coast and Sekondi had further
reason to be discontented: they felt that they were being unfairly displaced
by the overseas firms. This was an old story, but it was given extra point
by the survival of war-time restrictions and a licensing system which
seemed to them to favour the European companies. Their case was stated
in homely terms by 'Pa Grant', the elderly wealthy timber merchant—the
founder-president of the UGCC—in his evidence before the (Watson) Commission of Enquiry in 1948.[1]

> ... we were not being treated right, we were not getting licences for
> import of goods, also we were not pleased with the way our leg. co.
> handled matters, because we had not the right people there.

Mr Dingle Foot, counsel for the UGCC, asked him:

> Your experience goes back a long way, Mr Grant; can you say generally
> what effect the activities of UAC have had upon the position of the
> African traders?

And Mr Grant replied:

> The African traders in general—we had several women—who at one
> time ... imported ...; today all these things are gone ... all died away
> because they have not sufficient capital to compete with UAC.
> At one time [Pa Grant continued] we had the Aborigines' Rights
> Protection Society, who were people who were taking care of the country.
> Later on, they were pushed out and there was a Provincial Council of
> Chiefs. The chiefs go to the council and approve loans without sub-
> mitting them to the merchant men and the tradesmen in the country.
> Thereby we keep on losing.

Some of the more active members of the 'intelligentsia' in the 1930s
had begun to find allies in the number of educated young men who had some-

thing more than primary, something less than university education, the
emphasis being on 'youth'—youth conferences, youth leagues, literate young
men's associations. The expression 'the young men' had a special connota-
tion in local history. In former times they were often the 'malcontents',
the commoners who held no stool office, who criticised and opposed the
established hierarchies of power. The tradition continued in old and new
forms. The illiterate young men, often led by those with some education,
voiced their grievances by using traditional positions—like that of
nkwankwahene and *asofoatse*—the 'spokesmen of the young men';[2] the
'clerks' and 'scholars' formed debating clubs, literary circles, improvement
societies, and looked for support from the older generation of educated
leaders. Danquah was busy among them, calling the first Youth Conference
in 1930, helping to stage the second at Mfantsipim School in 1938,[3] a third
conference the following year at Kumasi (where a decision was taken to set
up a permanent organisation in control of the local 'chapters'), a fourth at
Akropong in 1940 on 'The problems of our social and economic reconstruction in war and peace'. By 1941 the Youth Conference was presenting a
memorandum calling for a new constitution to the Joint Provincial Council
of Chiefs (it had already submitted one to Lord Hailey during his visit in
1940); later that year the 'Achimota Discussion Group'[4] and the Youth Conference came together in a joint conference; they met again at Wesley
College, Kumasi, in 1944.[5] Danquah in particular exercised his agile, fertile
mind devising schemes of constitutional reform,[6] trying to move along a
broad front of the chiefs, the 'intelligentsia' and the educated 'young men'.
A pace or two behind him came the newly appointed Governor, Sir Alan
Burns, who arrived in 1942 and instituted a number of reforms, culminating
in the 'unofficial majority' constitution of 1946: a constitution universally
applauded in its first few months.

   We are almost at the point now of the formation of the UGCC. But there
is another section of Gold Coast society to note: the cocoa farmers and all
those associated with the fortunes of the cocoa producer. The importance
of cocoa is generally stressed, and rightly so: it injected money into a slow-
moving economy and stratified Akan society, bringing a great mobility of
labour and capital and leading the farmer into nationalist politics. The
pattern of development is a fairly regular one from the time of the first
world war; a cocoa boom, followed by a fall in the price paid to the farmers,
who began to join together in a sellers' 'hold-up' and to frame schemes for
marketing and shipping the crop themselves;[7] then a second wave of prosperity, depressed prices again, more hold-ups and more schemes. This was
the pre-1939 pattern, and farmers slowly learned the value, and some of the
techniques, of organisation. The head farmers in each district met together
and turned for help both to the chiefs and to the educated minority. The
Youth Conferences and the local literary and improvement societies were
therefore paralleled by the farmers' unions—like the early Nsawam-Aburi
Cocoa Growers' Association and similar bodies—which tried to rival the
amalgamations among the European buying firms.[8] Many of the chiefs, as
wealthy cocoa farmers, were naturally sympathetic. The Central Provincial
Council resolved in 1930 that each state 'should form Cocoa Farmers'
Associations ... as against the manipulations of the Combined Cocoa
Pools'; and the large cocoa hold-up of that year saw the inauguration of the
short-lived Gold Coast and Ashanti Cocoa Federation. Then discontent sub-
sided, rose again in the even greater hold-up of 1937, was held in check by
the outbreak of war, and grew again after 1945. The chiefs were warned by
the government not to lend native authority support to the protest[9] but the

uneasy alliance of farmers, chiefs and the educated leaders continued. A
Kumasi merchant, Mr B. D. Addai, was elected president and chief farmer
of the Ashanti Farmers' Union, formed in 1937; Nana Ofori Atta gave his
support to the Sika Mpoano Akuafo Fekuw Ltd (Gold Coast Farmers'
Association) in the same year; John Ayew and Ashie Nikoe began their
Farmers' Committee of British West Africa Ltd in 1939. The contrast
between the confused state of the Colony chiefdoms and the established
unity of Ashanti was reflected in the relative coherence of the Ashanti
Farmers' Union and the multiplicity of farmers' groups in the south, but
Danquah did his best to form a Colony union and succeeded—on paper—in
May 1947. In pre-war years the government had tried to play the neutral
role of 'honest broker' between the farmers and the buying firms—an almost
impossible task in Gold Coast terminology; after 1939, it took more positive
steps. But, just as the 1946 constitution failed to satisfy the educated
classes, so the Cocoa Marketing Board established in April 1947 failed to
satisfy the farmers.[10] And it is doubtful whether any measure taken by the
colonial government in the 1940s could have assuaged the anxiety, fear and
anger among cocoa farmers as 'swollen shoot' devastated whole areas of
the eastern province, infecting—it was calculated[11]—50 million trees, a
quarter of the total crop, by 1948. The government moved from persuasion
to compulsion and finally to direct action: from January 1947 diseased trees
were cut down by labour gangs whether the farmer agreed or not, until by
the end of the year two and a half million trees had been destroyed.[12]
    One last general point. Prices rocketed in 1939-40, and continued to
rise throughout the early war years; and the rise affected most seriously
the unskilled labourer and artisan class, ill organised in frail trade union
associations in the towns. When the war ended, rice, flour, tinned meat and
fish, kerosene and cotton goods of all kinds were still hard to get, and very
dear when available; local staple food prices were 'probably about two and a
half times the pre-war level'.[13] Wages fell far behind. The strike of railway employees in November 1941 had started a series of stoppages and 'the
unrest was not to be wondered at, for the real wage index (for unskilled
labour in Accra) had fallen from 100 in 1939 to 66 by November 1941 and
even after the increase in wages (in December 1941) the real wage index
was still only 81'.[14] A second award in July 1947 raised the index to 91, but
this gain was eroded by a further period of inflation, when the purchasing
power of the labourer's wage, now at $2s\ 9d$ a day, dropped to 86 by November
1947, and 75 by August 1958. One particularly hard hit group of 'artisans'
were the drivers, many of them ex-servicemen, who found it difficult to get
petrol except at black market prices under an inefficient system of ration-
ing, and difficult too to escape the unpitying embrace of the Syrian trading
community which controlled the hire purchase of lorries and motor spare
parts. And drivers are quick messengers of discontent, good couriers for
political action.[15]
    It was under these conditions that Nii Kwabena Bonne, a Ga sub-chief
in Accra, began to organise his Anti-inflation Campaign Committee prior to
launching—in January and February 1948—a boycott campaign of imported
goods.[16] Rumour ran swift. It was generally accepted that the much disliked
Association of West African Merchants—formed during the war and not disbanded until April 1948—was hand-in-glove with the government to defraud
the African trader and consumer alike—perhaps even to keep the Gold Coast
in subjection while cocoa plantations were started in East Africa and European families encouraged to settle on the west coast.[17]
    This is the background, roughly sketched, to the formation of the UGCC,

a situation in which disaffection—and action—among one section of the community in one part of the country was likely to spread to other groups and
other parts, a very good situation for the growth of a political organisation
outwards from the towns into the rural areas and, especially, into the cocoa
belt. Only the north lay lapped in tribal quiet, the main concern of the first
session of the Northern Territories Territorial Council in December 1946
being the spread of cerebral spinal meningitis, and whether whipping was
the best way—and most members thought it was—to deal with children. The
rest of the country was stirring, and needed some form of national organisation to keep it stirred.

The idea of a new political movement was almost certainly Danquah's.
He was associated with several quasi-political bodies—representative on the
Cocoa Marketing Board for the Colony Farmers' Union, legal adviser
(February 1947) for the Ex-servicemen's Union, secretary of the Youth
Conference movement as well as the Joint Provincial Council's representa-
tive on the 1946-50 Legislative Council. Something was wanted to tie these
different bodies together, to replace the antiquated Aborigines' Rights
Protection Society,[18] and redirect the enthusiasm of the now moribund
youth movement. The idea of a new 'Convention' was explored in private
conversations as early as January 1947 in A. G. Grant's 'old offices at
Poassie Road, Sekondi, in conference with three friends—Williams, Blay and
Danquah'.[19] By April the idea 'had germinated in a special conference held
at Canaan Lodge, Saltpond, of about 40 representative leaders'; and 'after
months of preparation and propaganda' the United Gold Coast Convention
was launched at Saltpond on 4 August, Grant giving the inaugural address.
It was said to be a nation-wide movement which would draw chiefs and
people together, restore leadership to the right hands, knit together existing
organisations, and prepare for the time when the country would be self-
governing. There is a great liking in Ghana for 'national fronts', and the
UGCC was no different in this respect from earlier movements before the
war. But it was the first major political association to talk of self-government as necessary within its own time. It proclaimed its policy in phrases
that subsequently became famous, and the object of great controversy, as
being 'to ensure that by all legitimate and constitutional means the direction
and control of government should pass into the hands of the people and their
chiefs in the shortest possible time'.

Following its inauguration, the Convention set up a Working Committee
on 20 September 1947. And it is at this point that the minute book opens.

The committee[20] decided to meet once a month, to start a weekly
paper—to be called the *Star* (later the *Statesman*)—and, a fateful decision, to
employ a full-time, paid secretary. They were busy lawyers and businessmen. They were serious about the Convention, but although ready to hold the
reins they wanted a willing horse to pull the cart. Danquah had already
approached a young lawyer recently returned from England, Mr Ako Adjei,
who suggested, instead, the name of a friend, Kwame Nkrumah, whom he had
known since January 1939, first in America, where they were students
together at Lincoln College, Pennsylvania, later again in London with the
West African National Secretariat. Ako Adjei then wrote to Nkrumah, who
hesitated; Danquah told the Working Committee, and, when Nkrumah finally
agreed to come, they sent him £100 for his passage money out of a donation
fund of £175 10s.[21] This first meeting then concluded with a resolution:
'(*a*) that the Convention is of the opinion that the contact of chiefs and
Government is unconstitutional, and (*b*) that in consequence their position on
the Legislative Council is anomalous'.

There was a second meeting on 18 October, a third on 6 December, when decisions were taken to admit members at the age of sixteen, and to make local branches (as they came into being) financially self-supporting. On 12 December, the committee met the steering committee of the Joint Provincial Council and discussed a joint programme of action: the Convention and the chiefs were to collaborate to achieve self-government, and the latter would relinquish their seats on the Legislative Council. The JPC donated £5 5s to the Convention, and welcomed its approach to the chiefs, although some of these at least had second thoughts about it. Then on 28 December Kwame Nkrumah was introduced to the committee. He had travelled as a deck passenger, *incognito,* from Monrovia to Takoradi, spent a fortnight at Tarkwa and then came down to Saltpond.

'I am very happy to be here with you at last,' he told the committee; 'at the moment I cannot say anything more than to affirm that if you need me I am at your service.'

The question of salary then arose: £250 per annum was mentioned but, says the minute book, Nkrumah asked for permission to consult the chairman privately, explaining that he had been away from the country for twelve years and had 'no idea as to whether £250 p.a. would meet his present standard of living under local conditions'. The chairman pleaded for him and the amount was fixed at £25 a month, plus free accommodation and a car: a substantial amount at the time and worth a great deal more then than now; and the committee never quite made up its mind whether a full-time, paid secretary was merely an executive officer of the movement or a full member of the Working Committee. So far, however, all seemed well. Mr Blay 'expressed the faith of the Working Committee in the newly appointed secretary' and said that he 'hoped that Mr Nkrumah would use the Convention as if it were his own organisation'.

But it was clear that some members of the Committee were uneasy:

... led by Dr Danquah, the Working Committee tested the personal attitude and reaction of the General Secretary to the conflict of world political ideologies so far as it affected the aims and objects of the Convention ... [and] ... how Mr Nkrumah could reconcile his active interest in West African unity (through the West African National Secretariat) with the rather parochial aims of the United Gold Coast Convention.

Nkrumah replied that:

He believed in TERRITORIAL BEFORE inter-territorial solidarity. [Then there was a] further catechism in the use of certain catch phrases—especially during public speeches—which might invite the suspicion of the public as well as of officialdom regarding the political connections of the Convention with some unpopular foreign forms of government.

But some at least thought that they had picked the right man, and the entry concludes with the comment that 'the general Secretary was considered a capital asset for the Convention'. Nkrumah took office on 1 January 'with effect from 10 January 1948'.

This is unfortunately the last entry in the minute book before the riots in Accra on 28 February. But it is possible to trace the story through until the minute book resumes in June. Throughout January Nkrumah and Danquah addressed a number of meetings in towns in the Colony, including

a mass rally at the Palladium Cinema in Accra on 20 February arranged
by the Ex-servicemen's Union. Danquah took the chair at this meeting.[22]
He, Nkrumah, Ako Adjei, Ben Tamakloe and F. E. Laryea (secretary and
executive member of the Ex-servicemen's Union) spoke to the mass
audience of 9,000, which included many more than ex-servicemen. (It also
included a European communist, an employee of BOAC.) The ex-servicemen
were to march in procession and present their petition to the government
on Monday, the 23rd. The following day it was postponed to the 28th. In the
meantime Danquah travelled to Kibi, his home town in Akim Abuakwa, where
farmers were in an excitable mood,[23] and attended a meeting of the Akim
Abuakwa Farmers' Union. On Friday the 27th a second mass rally was held
at the Palladium in Accra, where Danquah, Akufo Addo, William Ofori Atta,
Obetsibi Lamptey—all Convention members—addressed the meeting; and the
ex-servicemen assembled the following day at 1 p.m. on the old polo ground.
Danquah, Quist-Therson, Ofori Atta left Accra at 7.30 a.m. that same
Saturday, 28 February, for Saltpond. By four o'clock in the afternoon the
procession of ex-servicemen in Accra had left its authorised route, moved
along Christiansborg Road to the castle crossroads, clashed with the police,
and two members of the crowd were killed when the European superintendent
of police opened fire. The same afternoon looting began in the commercial
quarter of Accra: Kingsway Chemists were broken into; someone found a
way into W. Bartholomew & Co. with a piece of scantling; then the Kingsway
Liquor Store was broached, drink was passed over the wall into Ussher Fort
prison, and the crowd battered down the gate to let the prisoners out. Looting went on late into the night, despite a heavy fall of rain at eleven o'clock,
and started again early on Sunday morning, and the news was carried on
Monday by lorry drivers and passengers to a number of near-by towns, and
to Kumasi (by train), where rioting broke out that evening—1 March—and was
not finally ended until 16 March.

The riots were obviously an extension of the boycott of imported goods
already organised by Nii Bonne. This had begun on 26 January in the Colony
and Ashanti, peacefully at first, then with threats and reprisals against those
ignoring the boycott, and the crowd demonstrated outside the magistrate's
court in Accra on 17 February during the trial of a chief charged with
imposing fines on non-boycotters. Then on 20 February—the day of the
ex-servicemen's rally at the Palladium—agreement was reached, at a meeting in the Chief Secretary's office, between representatives of Nii Bonne's
boycott committee, the Joint Provincial Council and the chambers of commerce: the boycott was to be called off on 28 February, and the firms agreed
to reduce their gross overall profit margin (of non-controlled commodities)
from 75 to 50 per cent for a three-month trial period. This was popularly,
and quite erroneously, interpreted as meaning a 50 per cent reduction in
price. And when goods appeared in the shops on the 28th only slightly
reduced, the crowd reacted as one might expect. It was probably this, coin-
ciding with the ex-servicemen's march, that touched off the riots.

It is difficult to believe now that the Convention leaders actually
promoted these upsets. More likely, as George Padmore thought, 'the
leaders merely fished in troubled waters'.[24] And unfortunately the minute
book is silent on how they fished, for it was confiscated by the police and the
next entry is not until 6 June. The most interesting point turns on what
happened at (probably) two meetings of the Working Committee immediately
before and during the riots. It is not easy to fix a date for the earlier meeting, for memories are now uncertain. It is clear that at one time Nkrumah
drew up a memorandum urging the formation of a shadow Cabinet 'to fore-

stall any unpreparedness on our part in the exigency of Self-Government
being thrust upon us', and setting out a three-phased programme of organisation: co-ordination of existing associations under the Convention and the
opening of branches and weekend schools; 'constant demonstrations throughout the country to test our organisational strength, making use of political
crises; and—the "third period"—(a) the convening of a Constituent Assembly
of the Gold Coast people to draw up a Constitution for Self-Government...
(b) Organised demonstration, boycott and strike—our only weapons to support
our pressure for self-government'. In his *Autobiography* the memorandum
is said to have been submitted on 20 January. George Grant and Awooner-
Williams, in their evidence before the Watson Commission, said that it was
produced at a meeting on 14 February but that Nkrumah was told to 'put it
by' and have it typed and circulated; this is repeated by Bankole Timothy
in his biography of Nkrumah, who says that the memorandum was put in 'a
circular letter to the members of the Working Committee dated
20 February'.[25] Either way, the memorandum was obviously too close to the
outbreak of rioting in Accra for it to have been anything more than a per-
ceptive appraisal of what was likely to happen. But—as we shall see—it
became a main ground of difference between Nkrumah and the rest of the
committee.

We move now to the actual day of the riots, 28 February, when the committee met at Saltpond. A Convention member—Mr Akufo Addo—telephoned
from Accra at about 5. 30 p.m. (*via* Mr Mends in Saltpond) to say that
serious disturbances had broken out in Accra, and it was decided that
Danquah, Quist-Therson, Nkrumah and others should leave immediately for
Accra to find out what was happening. Leaving Saltpond at 6 p.m. they
arrived around 8. 30 p.m., where, says Danquah:

> I saw a horrible sight. All about the central part of the town I saw big
> cars—the first that struck me was a big car near the Insurance Office—
> turned upside down and burnt. Another car near Chellaram I saw, and
> other cars too. I went through to the High Street and saw the whole of
> Kingsway Stores looted, glass broken. It was a terrible sight. I went
> through Station Road and found looting still going on in some parts.
> [The people] were excited and rushing into the street and taking the
> goods out. I saw policemen standing by doing nothing and some of them,
> in fact, taking part in the looting.[26]

Late that night Danquah, Nkrumah and Ofori Atta met the other officers of
the Convention in Accra; Danquah then telephoned Sekondi and got through to
the president. ' "Look here, Mr Grant, only this afternoon you said that we
should go slowly. Do you agree [that] the Governor should be recalled?"
He said, "Yes I agree. Go on." The same night I drafted the cablegram [to
the Secretary of State] but when I recalled him to read it to him he had gone
away, so I read it to Mr Williams and he said, "I agree with everything. I
give you my authority to go ahead. I will tell him." ' This is the account
Danquah gave the Watson Commission of what happened that night. The
cablegram was sent in the name of the president, eight thousand words long,
starting with 'Civil Government Gold Coast broken down' and stating that
the 'Working Committee United Gold Coast Convention declare they are prepared and ready to take over interim government'. Nkrumah also sent one,
much shorter but in the same vein, and with copies to—among others—the
United Nations, *Pan Africa,* the *New York Times* on one side of the world,
and the *New Times,* Moscow, on the other. Within a fortnight the six active

leading members of the Convention—Akufo Addo, Ako Adjei, Ofori Atta, Danquah, Nkrumah and Obetsibi Lamptey—were held in detention.

In retrospect the February riots can be seen as leading direct to the breach between Nkrumah and the Convention. Nkrumah welcomed the Watson Commission's findings that the Working Committee were directly connected with the disturbances. The rest did not. Grant, Awooner-Williams and Danquah protested strongly to the commission that they did not accept Nkrumah's plan of organisation: they had not read it fully, and now that they had, they certainly did not approve it: all the differences—of temperament, experience, status—came out into the open before the commissioners. When Grant was read the last section of Nkrumah's memorandum the old man became indignant: 'He never read that to our meeting.' 'If,' Grant was asked, 'if he had read it would he have approved?' 'We would have stamped on it,' Grant replied. 'We would not do anything he [Nkrumah] likes. We old men, like myself, permitting a young man here to do things without our consent that are not palatable to us? No.' But Grant still believed that 'from the way [Nkrumah] planned out his things, if we hold his tail I think he will work all right'. Danquah said that he hadn't read it and would have 'strongly disapproved and asked it to be deleted from our records'. De Graft-Johnson thought Danquah's telegram calling for an interim Convention government was 'premature'. But it is fairly clear that the Working Committee was on one side, its general secretary on the other.

The odd thing is, that this was not clear for some months to come. The minute book picks up the story after the release of the 'Big Six' to show how Nkrumah and the Working Committee of the Convention clung together for the rest of the year and until the middle of 1949, Nkrumah racing ahead but not wanting to break, the Convention suspicious—not quite knowing what to do with him, and alarmed to think what he might do without them.

The first serious crisis came late in August 1948, after a preliminary squabble between Nkrumah and Danquah over the committee's agreement that Danquah should accept an invitation to attend the London African Conference arranged by the Colonial Office for the autumn of that year: Nkrumah criticised the decision at a rally in Kibi at the end of July, and was made to write a letter of apology. The main quarrel came over the report by a committee of inquiry of two members of the committee—Obetsibi Lamptey and Ofori Atta—set up 'to enquire into the headquarters organisation'. The Convention was growing; branches flourishing in a number of towns in the Colony and Ashanti—two hundred and nine according to the minute book by August 1948; two members from Ashanti were added to the Working Committee—John Tsiboe (a Fanti, but managing proprietor of the *Ashanti Pioneer* in Kumasi) and lawyer Cobina Kessie. A strengthening of the headquarters organisation at Saltpond was obviously needed. But the main concern of the committee was the conduct of the general secretary, who was asked to withdraw from the meeting on 21 August while the others discussed what he was about. Nkrumah was active. This much the Working Committee knew. But they did not like the evidence that came out before the Watson Commission—evidence, for example, of the extraordinary 'document called the Circle' outlining an esoteric organisation which asked members to support the leadership of Kwame Nkrumah and to work for a Union of African Socialistic Republics;[27] they did not like the communist label hung round Nkrumah's neck by the Commissioners, nor rumours of a newspaper to be started by Nkrumah, nor his sponsoring of a Ghana National College for the expelled students at Cape Coast who had gone on sympathy strike when the six were arrested.[28] Moreover the 'fact emerged', Obetsibi

Lamptey reported, 'that the General Secretary had been carrying on a certain correspondence inimical to the interests of the Convention' especially
with pan-African associations overseas. So Nkrumah was called in and
questioned by Akufo Addo:

> Why do you persist in using the word Comrade as a term of address?
> Why do you still continue connections with the West African National
> Secretariat?
> Why do you welcome the Watson Commission's laying the blame for the
> disturbances on the Convention?

The committee was not satisfied with whatever reply Nkrumah gave; he was
told that he was 'interdicted from duty as from today's date [21 August]',
and would be 'informed of the charges against him upon which he would be
requested to stand his trial'. During the interdiction he would receive his
salary. De Graft-Johnson would act as full-time secretary.

The next meeting—held at Nana Ofori Atta's house in Accra on
3 September—brought further recriminations, for it coincided with the first
issue of Nkrumah's own venture, the *Accra Evening News:* a remarkable
instance of Nkrumah's half-in, half-out position in the UGCC. The chairman
now demanded Nkrumah's total removal from office, and indeed he was found
'guilty' of going against the Convention. Then Blay and Dr Ansah Koi suggested he might be made a vice-president. Akufo Addo and Danquah amended
this to honorary treasurer, and a majority agreed.

Here was a real Frankenstein situation: 'the humble and obedient
servant of the Convention', as Nkrumah professed himself to be to the
Watson Commission, was now very much of a mixed blessing to the Working
Committee; they would have liked to dispense with him, only they feared what
he might then do—and there was evidence enough that he had done a great
deal already in the name of the Convention that they disliked. Moreover
there were wild undercurrents of unrest still. We can turn the metaphor and
say that the Working Committee, like the sorcerer's apprentice, had called
up a force stronger than it liked, which might well engulf them. For this was
the flood tide of nationalism when youth clubs and associations were formed
in the towns and there were angry clashes between farmers and the agricultural department with its gangs of labourers. The *Accra Evening News* kept
up a steady stream of invective and exhortation. But there was no clear
pattern of discontent: it was as yet impossible to say whether the local youth
associations and improvement societies were part of, auxiliary to, or in
opposition to the Convention; even in Accra there were fourteen 'Convention
Clubs' which the Working Committee knew little about. Only on one point
was it becoming clear where the Working Committee was at variance with
the mass of popular agitation. A young Conventionist, Sacki Scheck, was busy
in Sekondi demanding a 'target date' for independence—1 April 1949—and
claiming (according to the minute book) that if by then 'we haven't got self-
government we shall begin to free ourselves according to our own proclaimed programme of action'. To many the Convention's policy of 'self-
government within the shortest possible time' meant 'within a few months',
and it was soon to be shortened to 'self-government now' as excitement
mounted during the latter half of 1948 and 1949; now, for the first time, large
numbers of ordinary people, some literate, many illiterate, were drawn into
political argument.

> The most indubitable feature of a revolution [says Trotsky], is the
> direct interference of the masses in historic events; ... at these

crucial moments when the old order becomes no longer endurable to
the masses, they break over the barriers excluding them from the
political arena, sweep aside their traditional representatives, and
create by their own interference the initial groundwork of a new
régime. . . .

The Gold Coast in 1948-49 was a very long way from Russia in 1917. Still,
the situation was disturbed enough to place the Convention leaders in a
recognisably familiar quandary: how to promote a revolution by constitutional means; and the relationship between Nkrumah and the Working Committee now reached a second turning point. The riots were the first dividing line between them. There was now to be a second.

During the September session of the Legislative Council the Governor,
Sir Gerald Creasy, announced that a representative committee would be set
up to examine the constitutional proposals suggested by the Watson Commission. The Working Committee decided to accept membership.[29]
Although this was useful in the drawing up of the first national constitution
for the country, it was a fateful decision, for it linked the members of the
Working Committee publicly with a constitutional (moderate) path of reform;
it diminished the enormous prestige won by their detention earlier in the
year. It also tied them to committee meetings. Nkrumah—who was not
asked to join the Coussey Committee—was uncommitted, and free to help
organise the radical 'Committee on Youth Organisation', with K. A.
Gbedemah as chairman and Kojo Botsio as secretary. From that time forward the Convention and its former secretary were never able to come
fully together again, and the CYO was the direct progenitor of Nkrumah's
Convention People's Party.

But still a final break was postponed. At its meeting on 23 October the
Working Committee was told that Nkrumah had acknowledged receipt of the
letter terminating his appointment, but that he had declined the offer of the
treasurership. The following month he changed his mind and accepted the
post. And early in December the committee agreed to invite K. A. Gbedemah
to become the new general secretary, 'especially as he could speak so many
of our vernacular languages'. It shows the Convention still hoping to live up
to its all-national character, trying to provide a link between the youth
movements and the chiefs, although even the latter proved refractory. For
the Working Committee had met the Joint Provincial Council early in
September at Dodowa in full conference—twenty-two Convention members
and a large gathering of chiefs; and a complete 'reconciliation' had been
effected—so it was believed—between the intelligentsia and the chiefs. This,
too, was as illusory as the stormy alliance between them and the 'youth'.
Danquah said (minutes, 4 December 1948) that 'the chiefs had broken faith
with the Convention by their action in proceeding to make nominations [to
the Coussey Committee] without first consulting the political organisations
in the country'; it was in breach of the 4 September agreement, and a 'strong
formal protest' was agreed on. At its next meeting, however, on 8 January,
the Convention was rebuffed on a different front when a letter was read from
Gbedemah declining the offer of secretaryship. At that same meeting protests were read from Kumasi against Danquah's attendance at the London
African conference, and against the decision to form part of the 'Coussey
Committee'. From a great height of popularity in March 1948 Danquah and
his fellow lawyers were now brought to the defensive. But it would be wrong
to regard the Convention as powerless. It still had an honoured name. It
was still the only political organisation which could claim country-wide

support, even if the multifarious nature of its membership made discipline impossible. It was still capable, for example, of Calling Sacki Scheck before it (20 February 1949), rebuking him and suspending his membership. One of its leading figures, Obetsibi Lamptey—'Liberty Lamptey'—was still sufficiently popular to have the backing of the Accra youth organisations to be returned unopposed in a by-election to the Legislative Council.

And Nkrumah was still unable to decide whether to force the break. At the meeting on 8 January Danquah asked Nkrumah about the Youth Organisation and the Ghana Colleges. Nkrumah—who was still treasurer—replied that the Ghana Colleges were his own affair and refused to discuss it; the youth movement, he said, was an 'ally' of the Convention. The Working Committee then 'expressed its appreciation of the motive behind Mr Nkrumah's connection with these organisations and demanded that he should 'produce the Constitution of these organisations for examination'. This ambivalence was to continue for a further six months.

A month later, at a meeting in Danquah's house in Accra, the committee set forth its *apologia*; it had decided in January, it said in a statement for the press, to

> accept the Coussey Committee on Constitutional Reform and to try and work it despite its shortcomings. The country's hope for the design of a self-governing constitution is at present centred on the Coussey Committee and no one can tell how long it will take to come to the end of its report.... It is within the knowledge of those actively abreast with the making of Constitutions that it is an arduous task. In our present situation until the Coussey Committee's Report is issued to the Legislative Council, is debated by that body and receives the approval or disapproval of the general public, there is nothing gained to fix a target date for the coming of the new Constitution.... Our policy is that it should be at the earliest possible time and we counsel all patriots of the country to work steadfastly for the coming of the great event.

This was not the sort of truth that did the Convention any good, and it conflicted directly with the demand for immediate self-government in the constitution already put out by the Committee on Youth Organisation, meeting in secret session at Kumasi during the Christmas holiday—a constitution clearly the handiwork of Nkrumah, and published in his newspaper on 29 December. There was a preliminary showdown between them at a meeting in Saltpond on 20 February—exactly a twelvemonth after the triumphant Convention ex-servicemen's rally at the Palladium cinema:

> Since August last year [the minute book gives Nkrumah as saying] things had not gone on well between himself and the Working Committee. What pained him most was a letter he alleged to have been written by an Accra member of the Working Committee to a high official recommending his deportation ... the masses appreciated his contribution to the aims of the Convention [but] he had not been understood by the Working Committee as a body. [He assured the committee that] he promoted the youth organisation to rally all sections of the youth of the country under the banner of the Convention [and] the Ghana Colleges were started to 'save the face of the Convention'.

This did not go down too well. He was asked to retire, while the committee agreed to condemn the formation of the CYO and to issue a statement for the press disassociating the Convention from the Ghana Colleges—in which, said Danquah, 'Mr Nkrumah rather stole a march on the Convention.'

Nkrumah was called back but—astonishingly—he and they agreed that the CYO should be reconstituted and brought under a sub-committee of the Convention. Nkrumah was also to state publicly that the Ghana Colleges were his own affair. These and other matters were then left to be sorted out by an Easter delegates' conference to be held at Saltpond on 16 April.

Even that solved nothing—precipitated nothing. The CYO held its own meeting two days before the delegates' conference and decided that:

> the Committee on Youth Organisation ... is prepared to accept the proposed terms of the Working Committee to reconstitute the CYO on only one consideration, that Kwame Nkrumah is reinstated now as the General Secretary of the UGCC, otherwise it gives notice here and now that the organisation still continues to function until such times as he is reinstated.

The statement was signed by Gbedemah as chairman, Kojo Botsio as secretary, and by an executive of six—Dzenkle Dzewu, Eben Adam (from Tamale), K. W. Asaam, Bart Plange, Hannah Cudjoe, Sapa Williams—and 'fourteen others representing Youth Organisations in the Colony, Ashanti NTs and Transvolta'.

The delegates' conference two days later added to the confusion. The Working Committee managed to get the CYO 'disestablished'—or so it thought—and brought within the Convention. But Nkrumah was not reinstated. And the committee was obviously divided among itself: the older, more conservative members—Awooner-Williams and de Graft-Johnson—were angry and contemptuous, the others more moderate. At its next meeting, on 14 May, John Tsiboe asked 'whether the Convention stood for unity or dissension?'. 'Although we are for unity,' Awooner-Williams replied, 'we should not allow ourselves to be dictated to by the masses.' He thought the CYO should be 'banned', although how this might be done was another matter. The CYO was not a good organisation, and 'although in matters religious he was personally cosmopolitan in outlook and belief he felt that all the anti-Christian writings of the local press was inspired by the CYO and other communist agents in the country'. Nkrumah protested strongly at this, and the others supported him. Danquah thought the position was confused: the CYO was 'disestablished' and yet it had been given representation on a new sub-committee on youth organisation. Ako Adjei said that this was all right because he believed 'that there was no fundamental difference between the CYO and the Convention'.

How long the CYO and the Convention might have gone on in hostile alliance one cannot say: certainly not beyond the nomination period for the first general elections. But they were a long way off. Then a third issue arose—third in sequence to the riots and the appointment of the Coussey Committee: a ludicrous issue on the surface, but it helped to drive the CYO and the Convention beyond reconciliation. This was the visit of Sir Sydney Abrahams, a former Gold Coast Attorney General and chairman of the Gold Coast Athletics Association. While attending the Africa conference in October 1948 Danquah had met Abrahams at a tea party in Lancaster House, and Abrahams expressed his willingness to visit the Gold Coast again to advise on sport. The Colonial Office agreed, Sir Sydney arrived, and was given a bad press. Nkrumah exploited it to the full:

> ... The people of the Gold Coast [said an editorial in the *Accra Evening News*], are now politically wide awake and cannot be lulled any longer by any unbecoming tactics of the Imperialists to divert our

attention from the goal of full Self-Government this year... first things first, Sir Sydney! Please go back and tell Britain that we are ready for full Self-Government now; anything short of that will be unacceptable to us. We are in earnest; our 'eyes are red', and we shall not rest until we have obtained full Self-Government for the people of this country, this year.... [30]

The Working Committee had to discuss the problem, since Abrahams had suggested that he might speak on Convention party platforms. After some argument, it was agreed that he might. Then the rumour spread that a sinister motive lay behind the sports mission; namely, that the UGCC leaders had accepted large sums of money from the United Kingdom government with which they were supposed to deflect peoples' interests from politics to sport. [31] The accusation was as groundless as it was preposterous, but it did a great deal to poison the atmosphere—already bad—between Nkrumah and the Working Committee.

In the end, the demand for a complete break between the Convention and the 'youth' of the CYO—although 'youth' now included Gbedemah, who was thirty-seven, Botsio, thirity-three, Nkrumah, forty—came from Accra. The regional council of the Convention on 6 June called on the Working Committee to dissociate itself publicly from the *Accra Evening News*, the Ghana Schools and Colleges, and the CYO. At long last, too, the full report of the Committee of Enquiry into Headquarters Organisation, appointed in August 1948, was now ready: twenty-five typed pages of recommendations for strengthening the Convention under a new general secretary and a hierarchy of nine assistants. The UGCC was trying to stir itself once more for action.

It was now too late. The final break was less than a week away. The Committee met on 11 June and tried to sort itself out: it passed two clear resolutions:

(1) that the CYO is incompatible with membership of the Convention, since 'it is clear that the CYO is working against the Convention and is determined to break the united front of the country';

(2) that Kwame Nkrumah should be served with charges on the grounds that the CYO 'having been disestablished by the Delegates' Conference [he had] continued to associate himself with the activities of the CYO'; moreover, he had 'disregarded the obligations of collective responsibility and party discipline ... having publicised ... in the *Accra Evening News* opinions, views and criticisms assailing the decisions and questioning the integrity of the Working Committee'; he had undermined the Convention, abused its leaders, and stolen their ideas.

But the CYO had already decided to leave the Convention. It had met at Tarkwa, the mining centre in the western province, early in June, where 'the discussions that took place lasted for about three nights and proceeded into the early hours of the morning'. [32] The brief account given by Nkrumah is a little puzzling: the CYO, he says, decided to 'resist' his removal by the Working Committee from the general secretaryship of the Convention, but also to take the CYO out of the movement in order to make it the groundwork of a new political party. [33] The latter policy carried the day and—on Sunday, 12 June

before an audience of about sixty thousand people—on behalf of the CYO, in the name of the chiefs and the people, the rank and file of the Convention, the Labour Movement, our valiant ex-servicemen, the youth movement throughout the country, the man in the street, our children and those yet unborn, the new Ghana that is to be, Sergeant Adjety and his comrades who died at the cross-roads of Christiansborg during the riots of 1948, and in the name of God Almighty and humanity[34]

Nkrumah declared the birth of his Convention People's Party.

Once again, then, the Working Committee had been outmanoeuvred. The same Sunday—12 June—its members moved from Saltpond to continue their meeting at Sekondi, where Grant lay ill. Grant is recorded as saying that he considered the new party an 'insult and a challenge which we should not condone'. Ofori Atta warned members that if they 'meant to save the country from the rot to come we must take strong measures', while Obetsibi Lamptey tried to cheer the meeting up by saying 'Britain would never give power to any group of irresponsible people anywhere in the Colonial Empire'. And on this note of doubt the affair should have ended. The common front was now divided. A new organisation had been formed. But Ghana politics are rarely clear-cut. There is a postscript to add, for two attempts were made at a last-minute reconciliation by calling in outside 'arbitrators'.

When the Working Committee met again on 26 June at Grant's house in Sekondi it discussed a telegram from Kojo Botsio:

Accra 13/6/49 Secretary U.G.C.C. Saltpond.
Convention People's Party under leadership and chairmanship of Kwame Nkrumah inaugurated in Accra Sunday 12 June 1949 aims at Self-Government Now for Chiefs and People of the Gold Coast, a democratic government and a higher standard of living for the people. Kojo Botsio Secretary.

The committee replied to this in similar terms:

Saltpond 15/6/49. All members of the United Gold Coast Convention are warned that the Convention has no connection with the newly formed Convention People's Party under the chairmanship of Kwame Nkrumah STOP Pa Grant expects loyalty of all Conventionists STOP Formation new party at this juncture inimical to interests of country STOP Acting Secretary.

Argument then broke out during the meeting over the *Ashanti Pioneer,* which had come forward in support of Mr Krobo Edusei, the Ashanti Youth Association and the Ashanti Ex-servicemen's Union—known supporters of the new party. John Tsiboe protested that the paper was an independent journal and that its views were his own concern. Heated words must have been used, for, says the minute book, 'at this point at Dr Ansah Koi's suggestion Mr Sam Duncan led the meeting in prayer...'. Then at 1 p.m. Nkrumah arrived, saying that he had not read the charges and was not prepared to answer them except at 'a General Assembly of the rank and file of the United Gold Coast Convention, at a Delegates' Conference'. Danquah agreed. Others did not, and Nkrumah withdrew. It was then that Grant suggested that arbitrators should be called: ministers of the Church and trade union representatives in Sekondi. Shortly after two o'clock Nkrumah re-entered, saying that he had read the charges now, he was sorry if he had said that he did not trust the Working Committee to give him a fair hearing, and he was prepared to answer the charges against him. Then from 2.15 p.m. until 8.10 p.m. the arbitrators sat on the case. Unfortunately there is no record in the minute book of what happened during those six hours. The Working Committee were in a dilemma, for it was clear what would happen if the issue went to a delegates' conference. However, it is recorded that following the arbitrators' 'award' the committee agreed, after some dispute, to resign. A press statement was drawn up:

> At a meeting of the Working Committee held at Sekondi on the 26th June 1949 members of the Working Committee by a resolution agreed to resign their membership of the Working Committee and accordingly placed their resignations in the hands of the president.

Three reasons were given: (*a*) certain decisions of the Working Committee had been challenged by branches, (*b*) there had been a 'whispering campaign' of lies and abuse against them, and (*c*) the award suggested by the arbitrators contained

> decisions and recommendations which in the unanimous view of the Working Committee are impractical and unworkable within the framework of the Constitution of the UGCC, in particular the decision that although it was wrong for the Convention People's Party to have been formed it should nevertheless be retained as an additional party within the Convention with its own Chairman.

Although formally dissolved, the Committee was now reconstituted as an executive council to carry through the arrangements for an emergency delegates' conference at the end of July. For example, they met in Danquah's house in Accra on the 21st, when Grant said that he too would resign if the arbitrators' award were accepted, and Nkrumah telegraphed 'categorically refusing to attend'. Ten days later the delegates, who, says Nkrumah, numbered 'between forty and fifty thousand people',[35] assembled at Saltpond. (There is no record in the minute book of what happened.) Nkrumah says that 'the delegates' conference endorsed the recommendations of the Sekondi arbitrators'; then dispute arose over whether a new Working Committee should be elected, and two more arbiters were called in—this time two chiefs—who recommended that Nkrumah should be reinstated as general secretary of the Convention, and that the CPP should be disbanded. And, says Nkrumah, 'in spite of what this would mean to me and the fact that it would certainly antagonise my supporters who were not prepared to accept any compromise, I agreed to accept their decision'—provided that a new executive committee was elected to work with him.[36] Argument broke out again and the delegates passed a vote of no confidence in both the president and members of the ex-Working Committee. But it was the crowd outside the conference room which decided the issue by prevailing on Nkrumah to resign from both the executive and the membership of the Convention. The CPP was to stay and the break was final.

The remainder of the minute book carries the story down to the beginning of 1952—through the rapid decline of the UGCC after the publication of the Coussey report in October 1949, the joint 'self-government now' resolution passed by the Ghana Representative Assembly on 20 November, and Nkrumah's campaign of 'Positive action' in January 1950, telling how its leaders tried to make something of a united front again with the chiefs in the Joint Territorial Councils' meeting in August 1950, how it lost the 1951 elections, accepted its position as a parliamentary opposition, and—at the close of 1951—issued a 'seven point scheme for Gold Coast liberation', holding its last meeting in Mr Cobina Kessie's house in Kumasi on 19 January 1952. The critical months were June-August 1949, and I have thought it best to stop at that point and look back at the nature of the conflict between the Working Committee and Nkrumah, between the UGCC and CPP.

In fairness to the UGCC, which does not make a very good showing, it should be said that the apparently trivial, verbal difference in policy between

it and the CPP was in fact quite genuine. Both sides wanted self-government. But the lawyer leaders of the Convention could not follow Nkrumah or
the CYO into absolutist demands. Hence the cautious phrase 'self-government in the shortest possible time'. They allowed their heads to rule their
hearts; the CYO followed its heart. Whether this made much difference in
the long run is doubtful. The 1951 election would have been held whether
the CPP existed or not, and the constitution which replaced the 1950
'Coussey constitution' in 1954—introduced following Nkrumah's 'motion of
destiny' as prime minister—was much like the minority report drawn up by
the Convention leaders on the Coussey Committee.[37] Where the difference
lies is in the nature and quality of the party machine shaped by Nkrumah.
The CPP drew people together along a broad popular front, enabling the new
State to enter independence within a party framework of unity. Whether this
could have been done at a slower pace by the Working Committee is doubtful. True, there was a strong undertow of radicalism in the towns and the
southern rural areas pulling the Working Committee along with it, and if
Danquah or Ofori Atta had not kept up with its demands no doubt someone
else would have done—Kwesi Lamptey, perhaps, or Gbedemah, or Botsio.[38]
But the great need was not so much of a leader as of an organisation.
Nationalism was gathering strength, but it was not yet focused. A disciplined
party organisation was necessary to steady it, and to enable it to focus on
the still very artificial Gold Coast State. Instinctively perhaps, but by an
instinct drawn out of experience, Nkrumah recognised this need: 'mass
movements are well and good', as he says, 'but they cannot act with purpose
unless they are led and guided by a vanguard political party'.[39] And it was
the peculiar misfortune of the Convention leaders to engage a general
secretary who was so much better at running a political party than they
were that there was no good reason, in the end, why he should not run it
without them.

Looking back from 1949 over the preceding two years, it is easy to see
how unlikely it was that Nkrumah and the Working Committee would tolerate
each other. Nkrumah's first thought in London on receiving Ako Adjei's
letter was that it would be 'quite useless to associate myself with a movement backed almost entirely by reactionaries, middle-class lawyers and
merchants, for my revolutionary background and ideas would make it
impossible for me to work with them'.[40] His second was that he would
accept Danquah's invitation, but 'I was very sure of the policy that I would
pursue and fully prepared to come to loggerheads with the Executive of the
UGCC if I found that they were following a reactionary course'. True, this
was written *ex post facto,* at the end of 1956, and in practice, as we have
seen, Nkrumah followed a much more hesitant, wayward path. But, although
unknown in the Gold Coast in 1949, Nkrumah was better equipped than the
other members of the Working Committee to understand the business of
political organisation. It was, as he says, 'rather like the dawn of action at
the end of a long and intensive training'—in America and London, pan-
African meetings, committee work, party organisation, and a great variety
of political activity of one kind and another. Yet there is another impression, too: of his caution. Dislike of a break with the Working Committee
runs side by side with the fact that he was committing its members to a
more extreme course than they were prepared to follow. The probability
is—as later during the days of 'Positive action'—that Nkrumah himself was
being pushed from behind by his less cautious followers.[41] If that is so, the
minute book is a good early example of one aspect of Nkrumah's leadership,
of his ability to carry a very mixed following along an empirical course.

The insistent slogans and 'leftist' phraseology of the *Accra Evening News* and the CYO covered a useful streak of caution, although there was also a readiness to act radically when it looked dangerous to seem too timid.

From the Working Committee's point of view, a precedent was established that its members never forgot. To them the CPP was a treacherous break-away movement, and what was sauce for the UGCC goose would be a good sauce for the CPP gander if every occasion arose—a thought which must have disturbed the peace of mind of CPP leaders in subsequent years.

By June 1949, Dr Kwame Nkrumah, expatriated by the Convention in 1947 to take up the secretaryship, had for reasons that are now obvious to all, so sabotaged the effort of the principal leaders of the Convention and so discredited me and all my principal colleagues that he was able to mislead the masses to follow him ... He filched our name, our 'S.G.' policy, our branches, and even our colours—to establish a separatist group—the Convention People's Party—which, as he falsely claimed at the time, was formed 'within the Convention in the name of George Grant, of Ghana and of God'.[42]

That is how it looked to the Working Committee, and there is some truth in the allegation: when the CPP was first mooted, says Nkrumah, 'much discussion took place on the name to be given to the party. The most popular suggestion that was made was "the Ghana People's Party"... [but] in order to carry the masses with us, we all agreed that at all costs "Convention" must appear as a part of the name'.[43] It is easy therefore in retrospect to sympathise with the Working Committee; less easy to do so at the time, in 1948-49, when it looked as if it was trying, in a hapless Canute-like way, to stem the high tide of a radical nationalism. This was never really the case. The broad nationalist front started under UGCC leadership fractured quickly along moderate versus radical lines—it is probably fair to add 'along lines of economic and social interest' too.[44] But the strength of the political struggle in the Gold Coast at this time was the general agreement which existed between all sections of local society—the lawyers, the 'youngmen', the farmers, even many of the chiefs (at least south of the Volta)—on the desirability of self-government.[45] There were differences over methods and between leaders but not on ends, not even—in 1949-50—on the form of self-government that the end should bring.

Postscript.

One legacy of this early period is almost certainly Danquah's: the invention and popularisation of the name 'Ghana'. 'I conceive', he wrote to the Watson Commission on 15 April 1948, 'that the first act of the constitution-making body will be to make a clean break away from the memories of the old days of exploitation and imperialism, and the colonial adjective Gold Coast will give way to the substantive name of the people and country, Ghana and Ghanaland'.

Notes

1   Col. No. 231, and the record of evidence submitted to the commission.
2   These were titles which the Ashanti Confederacy Council abolished in 1936, when it was unanimously agreed 'that the positions of *nkwan-kwahene* and *asafoakye* and also *Asafo* should be abolished from the whole of Ashanti in view of the fact that they are the cause of political

troubles throughout Ashanti'. But as late as 1944 four subjects of the Nkoranza Stool in north-west Ashanti were charged with undermining the authority of the chief, brought before the local court, found guilty and removed from the district by order of the Ashanti Confederacy Council because 'they were the cause of political unrest and disorder in the Nkoranza Division'. One of them was said to be 'though not officially recognised ... the acknowledged leader of the "young men" [and] this would appear to have been the cause of much misfortune, for organised leadership of the *nkwankwa* or the common people, called *nkwankwahene*, is abolished in Nkoranza'. Their crime was to question the collection of the levy; they were illiterate, and wrote their petition through a letter writer, who used 'unhappy and misguided words'. See appendix U, *ACC Minutes*, 1945. The Chief Commissioner, of course, supported the chiefs. Sir Alan Burns paid tribute to 'the chiefs and other public men' who helped in 'the setting up of Native Authorities ... who are proving themselves the true leaders of their people. Their conduct is in marked contrast to that of those disturbers of the peace who, for their interests, endeavour to sow discord in the states and to stir up stool disputes' (*Debates*, 18 March 1947). Within five years the 'disturbers of the peace' were in office; within seven the chiefs were stirring up trouble in their districts.

3   It was this conference that published *First Steps towards a National Fund*; its members consisted of representatives from the Aborigines' Rights Protection Society, the Provincial Councils, municipal parties and local youth and literary societies—the Sekondi Optimists' Literary Society, the Accra Young People's Club, the Moonlight Literary and Social Club, the Anum Improvement Society, the Ewe League, the Asante Kotoko Society, and similar groups.

4   Started in 1938-39 by members of the Achimota School staff, who held their first study conference in January 1939, publishing its discussions under the title Quo Vadimus? or Gold Coast Future

5   See *Pointers to Progress ... The Gold Coast in the next Five Years* (1942), and *Towards National Development: Post-war Gold Coast* (1945). The 1944 conference called for the solution of problems by 'united and positive action'—a phrase taken up again later by the CPP with great effect.

6   See especially Danquah's scheme for constitutional reform, approved by the JPC, the Ashanti Confederacy Council and the municipal members on the legislative council, submitted to the Secretary of State during his visit to the Gold Coast in 1943.

7   An early report on cocoa—W. S. D. Tudhope, *Enquiry into the Gold Coast Cocoa Industry*, 1919—said, 'an extraordinary feeling of pessimism had taken possession of the majority of people everywhere'. Farmers 'complained of the high prices they have to pay for European articles or goods they want to buy whereas everything they have to sell is at a discount'. A 9d or 1s 6d cutlass had gone up to 3s 6d or 4s 6d; cocoa in Kumasi was 5s a load: it had been 25s to 30s a load at the end of 1915, but by 1917-18 'very large quantities of cocoa had to be destroyed ... in the remoter districts because it could not be sold for anything in their own villages and to transport it to the nearest market would have cost more in carriage fees than they could have obtained for it'. There was a 'strong feeling that of recent years they have been unmercifully exploited by the local buyers and shippers'. Therefore the 'formation of Associations of Cocoa Growers is being very much thought of

especially among the older growers ... their one ambition ... appears
to be to enable them to ship their own cocoa'. These are the conditions
described again by the better known (Nowell) *Commission on the
Marketing of West African Cocoa,* Cmd. 5845 of 1938.

8   1919 the formation of the African and Eastern Trading Company out of
F. A. Swanzy, Miller Bros. and others; 1929, formation of the United
Africa Company.

9   See the case of Inspector of Police *v.* Asare Panyin, 1931, when judgement was given that a chief had no power to stop the sale of cocoa, and
that an oath sworn to prevent such a sale would be a criminal offence.

10 Notwithstanding Danquah's membership of the Board.

11 Watson Commission report, s. 263. The price paid per load of 60 lb
went up from 40s in 1947-48 to 65s in 1948-49, but this did not help the
farmer whose trees were being cut down because of swollen shoot.

12 'An official observer had this to say about the atmosphere prevailing
immediately after the war in a swollen shoot area: "It is a widespread
economic depression which has affected the social and moral life of the
community.... it has created a sensation. The disaster is felt
appallingly." ' (P. Hill, *The Gold Coast Cocoa Farmer,* 1956, 67.)

13 Watson Commission report, s. 192.

14 'An Index of Real Wages of the Unskilled Labourer in Accra', W. B.
Birmingham, *Economic Bulletin* (Ghana), IV, 2, No. 3, 1960.

15 Most of the 'Syrians' are from the Lebanon. The near-monopoly that
these hard-working, family businessmen had over the hire-purchase of
lorries and of motor cars for taxi use was greatly modified early in the
1950s, when the big commercial companies began to offer hire-purchase
terms.

16 See the statement made to the Watson Commission by representatives
of the Anti-inflation Campaign Committee, who said people had no
objection to restrictions during the war; 'they understood that and were
glad to help win the war. [But] the war had been over three years'.
A good account of the boycott campaign can be found in Nii Kwabena
Bonne's *Milestones in the History of the Gold Coast,* 1953, chapter IX.

17 See the representation by the TUC before the Watson Commission.
'Putting it plainly,' said Mr Wood, 'years ago they were not accustomed
to seeing European children with their mothers ... in the streets of
the Gold Coast; ... every mail boat, one or two hundred [Europeans]
landed, and some came by air.' He thought this followed a deliberate
policy of 'population dispersal' by the United Kingdom government.
The belief that UAC were starting cocoa plantations in East Africa
probably owed something to the groundnut scheme, something to the
argument after the first world war between Leverhulme and the
Nigerian and Gold Coast governments over palm-oil plantations.

18 And yet it was the president of the Aborigines' Society who sent £50
through Mr Ashie Nikoe to the fifth Pan-African Congress at Manchester
in October 1945. Formed in 1897, the ARPS slowly faded out of
existence in the 1940s.

19 See the Foreword by George Grant to *The 'P' Plan,* issued by the UGCC,
January 1952. Williams=Mr F. A. Awooner-Williams; Blay=Mr R. S.
Blay—both lawyers.

20 G. A. Grant, chairman; R. S. Blay, vice-president; J. B. Danquah, vice-
president; F. A. Awooner-Williams, treasurer; W. E. A. Ofori Atta;
J. Quist-Therson; E. Akufo Addo; J. W. de Graft-Johnson; W. O. Essuman,
assistant secretary; A. Mends, financial secretary. A third vice-

president—K. Bentsi Enchill—was sick, died shortly afterwards, and his place was filled by S. W. Duncan.

21 Made up of donations by Grant, £100, Awooner-Williams, £25, Blay, £50.

22 Danquah's son had volunteered for service with the army in 1943 and was in Burma until the end of the war; two queen mothers of Accra spoke at the rally, recounting people's sufferings during the war. Ako Adjei quoted from a copy of the Burmese Independence Bill then before the United Kingdom parliament. Events in Asia were very much in people's minds.

23 '... on my way from Tafo as I was going to Kibi I was tackled by a large number of farmers with their drums, and with their faces marked with red ochre. They said they had come to meet me and asked the reason why I had signed the Beeton report [on the cutting out of swollen shoot-infected trees] agreeing with the cocoa trees being cut down. It took a considerable explanation to make them understand that I did not sign the Beeton report ... but that my name appeared in the report as the first witness ...' (Danquah's evidence given before the Watson Commission.)

24 G. Padmore, *The Gold Coast Revolution,* 62. The Gold Coast government saw clear evidence of a communist bid for power, planned terrorism and assassination. Danquah published an article saying, 'The hour of liberation has struck', in which he wrote that 'in this crusade the Working Committee is acting constitutionally but it will not be afraid to act'. Nkrumah had a communist party membership card; and, said the government public relations office, the 'release of convicts [from Ussher Fort] is of a pattern familiar in communist disorders when the communists are seeking power' ... But then the government, like the ex-servicemen and the farmers, were in an uneasy state.

25 Bankole Timothy, *Kwame Nkrumah,* 47.

26 This and subsequent quotations are taken from the record of evidence given before the Watson Commission.

27 Nkrumah told the Watson Commission that this 'was "a dream" which he had carried round with him for some years'. It was used by a student group (says Nkrumah) within the West African National Secretariat. *Autobiography,* 60.

28 The idea of a 'National College to serve the needs of the students' who had gone on strike in Cape Coast, and were expelled in May 1948, was agreed on by the Working Committee on 6 June, but it was Nkrumah who carried the idea through.

29 This was the 'Coussey' Committee on Constitutional Reform, appointed in December 1948, which produced its *Report* in August 1949. There were six UGCC members on the committee—B. D. Addai, E. Akufo Addo, J. B. Danquah, George Grant, E. O. Obetsibi Lamptey, W. W. Taylor, and many of the forty members (thirty-one 'commoners' and nine chiefs) were, like Nana Ofori Atta II, sympathetic towards the Convention.

30 Quoted in B. Timothy, *Kwame Nkrumah,* 62-3.

31 The amount usually mentioned was £25,000, because this was the amount asked for by Kojo Thompson, a member of the former legislative council, from the representative of the Chamber of Commerce as the price of withholding criticism of the Association of West African Merchants. See Martin Wight, *Gold Coast Legislative Council,* 173.

32 *Autobiography,* 100.

33 'The younger elements among the youth, led by Kofi Baako and Saki Scheck, were opposed to the formation of a political party as they

insisted that by remaining within the UGCC the CYO would eventually
capture the initiative. The other section, headed by Kojo Botsio, Komla
Gbedemah and Dzenkle Dzewu ... maintained that under the circumstances the CYO should immediately capture the political initiative of
the rank and file from the UGCC by completely breaking away from the
movement and forming itself into a separate political organisation.'
(*Autobiography*, 100.)

34 *Autobiography*, 105. The 'six-point programme' of the new party is
    given on p. 101.
35 *Autobiography*, 106.
36 *Ibid.*, 106-7.
37 See the 'Coussey report' (col. No. 248), sections 443-64. The minority
    report also wanted the abolition of the Governor's power of veto. Signa-
    tories were B. D. Addai, W. G. Essien, Nana Ofori Atta II, E. Akufo Addo,
    George A. Grant, Cobina Kessie, Dr J. B. Danquah, E. O. Obetsibi
    Lamptey.
38 What would have happened had, say, Mr Gbedemah become the Working
    Committee's first general secretary? He refused early in 1949, but by
    that time the dispute had already arisen between Nkrumah and the
    committee.
39 *Autobiography*, preface, ix.
40 *Ibid.*, 62.
41 See the brief account by Sir Charles Arden-Clarke of 'positive action':
    'I have good reason to believe that some at least of the party leaders
    would have preferred not to resort to "positive action" but to await the
    results of the general election, of the outcome of which they were fairly
    confident. But they found themselves enmeshed in the toils of their own
    propaganda. The tail wagged the dog ...' (*African Affairs*, January
    1958.)
42 George Grant in his foreword to *The 'P' Plan*, 1952.
43 *Autobiography*, 100-1.
44 See the early pamphlet *Freedom for the Gold Coast?* by Thomas
    Hodgkin, who thought that 'the CPP interprets democracy in its more
    traditional radical sense—the rule of the common people, the poor, the
    illiterate. The UGCC interprets democracy in its modern Tory sense,
    the rule of the enlightened and prosperous minority.'
45 By the officials, too, *ex post facto* the *Annual Report* for 1947 said that
    'the Gold Coast is still the peace-loving country which it has so often
    been described to be'; the UGCC was not welcomed: 'a new movement,
    the United Gold Coast Convention ... sprang up during 1947 and
    declared as one of its main objectives the attainment of full self-
    government in the shortest possible time. The movement has not so
    far contributed to the solution of the practical and urgent problems
    facing the country but has confined itself to an appeal to nationalistic
    feelings'. By the end of 1948, on the eve of being displaced by the CPP,
    the UGCC had become respectable. But then, so had the CPP by the end
    of 1951. The administration had great powers of adaptation.

II

The Convention People's Party in 1958

I   Origins

The CPP originated as a break-away movement—led by Nkrumah, K. A. Gbedemah, Kojo Botsio, Krobo Edusei and others—from the (1947) United Gold Coast Convention, which was quickly eclipsed by the new party at a time of discontent with colonial rule. The CPP was also the outgrowth—and the drawing together at national level—of local youth movements, improvement societies, debating clubs and sports associations among those who were increasingly dissatisfied with the native authority councils of chiefs and elders. A further ingredient was the vague, ill informed interest among the educated minority in the post-war nationalist governments of 'Commonwealth Asia', an interest quickened by the recent memory of overseas service among the small number of ex-servicemen. But there were also local grievances. Two in particular helped the CPP to muster a mass support in Ashanti and the south. One was the high cost of imported articles (including cotton piece goods and cutlasses) for which the blame was placed on the expatriate, mainly British, firms. Secondly, there was dismay turning to anger among cocoa farmers in the Akim and Ashanti cocoa-growing areas over the methods adopted by the colonial government to try and control the spread of the virus disease 'swollen shoot': the infected trees were cut out compulsorily (or, through bribery, passed over) by gangs employed by the Department of Agriculture. It was this combination of particular grievances and the weakened appeal of colonial rule which produced first the UGCC and then the CPP.

We should note the social origins of the CPP as a self-proclaimed 'people's party' led by those who were impatient with the lawyer-like caution of the UGCC. Why were they impatient? Partly, no doubt, because they were of a radical disposition, but the disposition had its origins in their determination to seize control of the mechanisms of power and wealth. There took place, therefore, a displacement of power not only from the colonial alliance of officials and chiefs to nationalists but from the lawyers and businessmen to the larger number of teachers, traders and clerks in the towns and villages of Ashanti and the south. Of course, that is a distortion, since to try and explain Ghanian politics in class terms is to leave out not only the majority of the population of peasant smallholders but primary loyalties to family, Stool, village, district and even 'region'. None the less, it is right to recognise the social difference in origin between the UGCC and CPP leaders, and the use made of it by the latter in their appeal to the 'common man'. Of more direct consequence, no doubt, in 1949 was the fact

---

Seminar paper given at the Institute of Commonwealth Studies, University of London, October 1958.

that so egotistical a leader as Nkrumah was unlikely to accept second place
to Danquah and the rather lordly members of the UGCC Working Committee.
So Nkrumah resigned from the post of general secretary of the UGCC and
proclaimed the birth of the CPP on 12 June 1949 in Accra with the simple
programme of 'Self-government now'. The demand carried the party
through to independence (particularly after 1951, when its leaders were in
office), since they could then appeal to interests as well as to ideals.

The CPP was also the child of colonial times, of that peculiar twilight
period of rule when the British not only gave up the imperial ghost but
ceased to whimper on the grave thereof. By 1950 the colonial administration in Accra, under a new Governor, Sir Charles Arden Clarke, had respon-
ded to the need to move towards its dissolution, and it turned to the ballot
box for help. The CPP owed much of its early success to the franchise
provisions of the 1950 constitution, drawn up on the basis of two sets of
recommendations: those of the Watson Commission (invited from London
to inquire into the 1948 riots) and the Coussey Committee on Constitutional
Reform (appointed by the Governor locally). The CPP hardly hesitated about
deciding to contest the first general election in 1951, and it constructed an
electoral machine for the task which was moderately efficient. So it
acquired a double legitimacy, in the starry eyes of the people and in the
watchful eye of the colonial officials. Even Nkrumah saw the point. 'When
the time comes for a ruling to accord self-government it will do so more
willingly if it can hand over to a properly constituted political party with a
majority backing than to a revolutionary nationalist movement' *(Autobiography,* page ix). Later the party was attacked with its own weapons—by
majority parties in the north, in Transvolta and in Ashanti. The colonial
scapegoat was finally slaughtered against the darkening sky of the CPP's
own difficulties, but the point is worth stressing here that the goat was very
willing to be slaughtered. One round of rioting in 1948, another in 1950, and
the sacrifice was almost complete. Indeed, by the mid-1950s it was the
colonial government which pushed Nkrumah and the party into its third
election victory, and then reconciled the victors and the losers in order to
be able to transfer power to the CPP on 6 March 1957.

Worth stressing, too, was the newness and rawness of the party: hardly
born in 1949, yet in office early in 1951. Its members were without experience of power or government, none of its leaders having sat on the early
Colony legislative councils and few of them having any knowledge even of
the limited apprenticeship afforded by a Native Authority system of control.[1] Prior to 1951 the British had been busy training the wrong people for
political power—the intelligentsia and the chiefs, who were now pushed
aside by these new leaders. It is worth asking, therefore, how strong was
the party at independence in 1957?

II   *The dominance of the CPP*

It was less strong than one might suppose at first reckoning, much of its
strength in 1949 being the reflection of the incompetence of those who
opposed it. Consider three interesting sets of statistics:

1   Over 70 per cent of the electorate does not vote: They—the missing
     voters—may one day vote for the CPP; but they may not. (Table 1.)

Table 1

	(a) Eligible electorate	(b) Registered electorate	Voters*	
1954	2,451,000	1,225,603 = 50%	706,720 = 58% of (b):	29% of (a):
1956	2,451,000	1,459,743 = 60%	697,237 = 50% of (b):	29% of (a):

*Taking into account three uncontested seats in 1954; five uncontested in 1956.

2   The CPP has never won more than 60 per cent of the votes. (Table 2.)

Table 2

	Constituency seats	CPP votes	Seats	Non-CPP votes (including independents)	Seats
1954	104	391,817 (55%)	71 (68%)	314,903 (45%)	33 (32%)
1956	104	398,141 (57%)	71 (68%)	299,116 (43%)	33 (32%)

Notes
There were three uncontested CPP seats on 1954, and five in 1956.

The high proportion of seats gained reflects the usual exaggerated result of the British electoral system. The non-CPP vote includes many who voted for 'independent CPP' (i.e. would-be CPP) candidates, especially in 1954. Even so, the party's victories have not been automatic. In the 1956 Togoland plebiscite CPP policy was outvoted in the southern half of the region.

3   The CPP is unevenly distributed in strength throughout the country. (Table 3.)

Table 3. The 1956 election

	CPP Votes	Seats	Opposition Votes	Seats	Independents Votes	Seats
Accra	27,076	3	4,764	0	—	—
Akim-Abuakwa	19,932	5	13,419	0	374	0
Rest of the South	132,016	36	14,883	0	9,162	0
TVT	55,508	8	25,969	3	20,107	2
Ashanti	96,968	8	127,098	13	503	0
North	66,641	11	74,172	15	8,665	0
	398,141	71	260,305	31	38,811	2

Nevertheless power attracts, and the fear of losing of power tends to attract absolutely—particularly among traditional leaders, e.g. the Na Yiri (the Mamprusi paramount) and the Asantehene, who ended their opposition to the CPP shortly after independence and declared their support for the government of the day. The rising fortunes of the CPP can be seen in the figures for the national assembly:

	CPP	Opposition
March 1957	72	32
August 1958	79	25

A similar swing was noticeable in the municipal elections. And yet the opposition survives, despite a pretty clear indication by Nkrumah that he now has no wish for it. It is true that there are social relationships and locality ties between CPP and opposition members; there is a working 'camaraderie' in parliament; but how long the present tolerance can continue is another matter. It is reasonable, however, to argue—given the plurality of Ghanaian society—that opposition will always be there, and that opposition members of parliament will be removed only by legislation. They are unlikely to be eliminated through the ballot box.

III Organisation and structure

Using M. Duverger's terms, the CPP is to some extent a 'mass party', organised through branches on the basis of an open membership and an individual subscription (which is certainly erratic), and a number of ancilliary associations closely linked to the parent body. Selective discipline is said to increase at higher levels in the party. When, for example, Mumuni Bawumia (United Party) crossed the floor in parliament in June 1958, Kofi Baako (Minister of Information) said:

> If Members of the Opposition want to cross to this side, all we need is sufficient benches and we shall receive them; ... But membership of the CPP is not the same as crossing the carpet... I should stress that their acceptance into membership of the party will have to be considered by the Central Committee of the Party, and the Parliamentary Committee of the party in consultation with the constituencies concerned. Much also depends upon their own activities henceforth. [Hansard, 7 June 1958]

That was theory. In practice the party makes full use of those useful to it, from whatever quarter they come.

Formal structure

According to the party's constitution, 'The branch is the basic organisation of the party'. Branches are based on villages and towns (or town wards). They deal 'direct with their respective constituency headquarters', whose function it is to carry out the 'basic policy and Programme' laid down by the national annual conference, guided by its national executive. This in turn has an inner controlling body—the central committee, described as the 'Directorate' of the national executive. The central committee normally consists of the leader and eight members selected by him and approved by the national executive. Nkrumah says that it 'takes two full years for a co-opted member to qualify for full membership', but it is difficult to see what

meaning can be attached to such statements. There are regional organisations, drawn from the constituencies and assembly members of the region,
which are larely advisory. There is a national secretariat in Accra under
the supervision of the central committee and managed by the party's general secretary.

Where does power lie within this ramshackle structure? In practice
it is divided between the central committee, the constituency headquarters
and the branches, with a very strong bias towards the centre. The linchpins
are the secretaries, who in rural constituencies are usually the only full-
time officials, appointed by the general secretary with the approval of the
central committee. The central committee dominates the party; Nkrumah
dominates the central committee. But the CPP is not yet a power-centred
monolith, and as long as it retains its popular base it is always likely to be
subject to internal movements of dissent.

The party and parliament

The party constitution is quite clear on the relationship it wants between
the party and its MPs:

> The central committee shall work in closest collaboration with all
> members of the party in the National Legislative Assembly.
> The Parliamentary Committee shall be under the direct super-
> vision and control of the Party Leader, who will report to the National
> Executive and Central Committee on the work, activities, and general
> behaviour of all members of the party in the Assembly.

But if, in theory, parliament plays a subordinate part in the whole life of the
party, in practice the difference between the CPP in parliament and the CPP
regarded as a national body is slight. There are non-parliamentary members on the central committee (e.g. the general secretary of the TUC), but
since 1949 the key members have been Nkrumah, Gbedemah, Botsio, Welbeck,
Baako and Edusei, all of whom are Ministers. The 'Directorate' of the
national executive thus forms an inner Cabinet council, as well as being
an inner party group. Parliament has been an extremely useful instrument
of party policy, although it is probably not regarded by the party as anything
more than that. After all, to most of its members the party ante-dates
parliament in the sense that a national Assembly came into being only in
1950. In short, both party and parliament are novelties.

Finance

The party's general funds, according to the constitution, are derived from
'membership dues and other sources approved by the Party'. There is an
admission fee of 2s and membership dues of 3d a month. But such sums
are very small beer compared with the inflow from party-dominated State
organisations like the Cocoa Purchasing Company. The opposition National
Liberation Movement, according to Baffour Akoto during the recent Kumasi
inquiry, spent 'about £70,000' on building the movement's organisation and
preparing for what became the July 1956 election. Much of this came from
favourably disposed native authorities and chiefs, and the CPP is certainly
no worse off in its access to public and private funds.

Ancillary organisations

The party is suspicious of loosely affiliated organisations, which, says its
constitution, 'are apt to cause divided loyalties; so, as much as possible,

only individual membership should be encouraged...'. Despite this, and particularly now that the party has become a government, the CPP likes to work through 'front organisations'. These are either party movements set up to rival existing associations (e.g. the Ghana Moslem Council *v.* the Moslem Association Party) or organisations 'captured' by the party (e.g. the Ghana Ex-servicemen's Union) or specially designed by the party (e.g. the Ghana Workers' Brigade).

There are also the party's own subsidiary organisations—notably the CPP Women's League (which is given a special section in the party's constitution), the National Association of Socialist Students' Organisations (NASSO) and the CPP Youth League. Each has its special function. The Women's League *is* the party, but with exclusively women's activities, interests and officers. NASSO is the party's training school where lectures on African socialism are held and courses of party instruction planned. The Youth League is a young members' organisation (the actual age limits are from fifteen to thirty) which acts as a recruiting agency for the main body of the party.

IV   Party tactics and appeal

Tactics

(a) *The cult of the leader.* Nkrumah is the life chairman of the party and is in undisputed control. There is a deliberate exaggeration of his position. He is 'Africa's Man of Destiny', the 'Star of Ghana', 'Osagyefo', 'Founder of the Nation'. His head appears on the coins, his statue (dressed in a northern farmer's smock) stands outside the parliament house, his birthday is a public holiday. No criticism of him personally is ever heard at the party's conferences or in its newspapers. He is, as a new party leader, something like a former chief writ large, and loyalty to his name can reach surprising limits—although, like the loyalty to a chief, it is dependent on the fact of power, and unlike the Stool of which the chief is custodian there is clearly no 'primordial attachment' to the actual office of President.

(b) *The mass popularisation of the party and government policy,* e.g. the carnival atmosphere of party rallies, newspapers which look like a tropical hybrid of *Titbits* or *Answers* in their early days. There is a colourful joyousness about the party as a nationalist movement, with its 'prison graduate caps', cloths overprinted with Nkrumah's picture, headkerchiefs, belts and handbags stamped with the CPP's colours.

(c) *The use of local traditional issues.* The party has to weave its support from local threads as well as from its general appeal, and it makes good use of ancient rivalries, e.g. the (Ashanti) Brong CPP vote in 1956. If Ashanti sentiment is turned against the CPP, the party opposes this by appealing to a wider Ghanaian nationalism, but also by encouraging a narrower interest ('Brongland') against Ashanti and the Asentehene. Many parallel examples can be found, and it forms part of what the CPP describes as 'tactical action'—a mode of conduct not easily distinguishable from the political skill of good opportunists.

The party's appeal

(a) *The 'doctrine of the common man'* goes back to Nkrumah's early pronouncement in 1949: 'in ourselves we are nothing; it is the people who give us strength'. The CPP knows how to speak the language of the market place and it can still appeal to the disinherited, the 'verandah boys'. Party constituency officers and assembly members in Ashanti and the south, with exceptions, are 'commoners': they do not belong to the established families of chiefs, nor are they from the lawyer-merchant group—the 'intelligentsia'. But the CPP does not have a monopoly of such talent. The rank and file of the (Ashanti) NLM is much the same in age, education, occupation and 'commoner status', being drawn from the same political class—indeed, many were CPP members prior to September 1954.

(b) *The promise of material benefits*. 'Knife and fork' questions form the substance of its election promises, viz. 'Materialise your dreams through operation 104'. Its party 'litany' is often recited as 'Blessed are they who took part in Positive Action, for they shall have their better reward', a necessary precondition of loyalty among its members, who quite plainly see the party as an instrument of private profit as well as of national unity.

(c) *Nationalism, socialism and an 'African personality'*. All three have been emphasised from the beginning. The party's *Aims and Objects* include 'Working with a view to abolish imperialism, colonialism, racialism and tribalism', and supporting 'the demand for a West African federation and of Pan-Africanism by promoting unity of action among the people of Africa and of African descent'. In both the 1954 and the 1956 elections the slogans were used: 'Vote CPP and save Africa'; 'A vote for the CPP is a vote for black Africa'. The stress on 'socialism' is readily explained. The party is socialist primarily in the sense that the leaders believe that they can use State controls to manage the economy (in which they are likely to be unsuccessful) and the resources of the public sector to consolidate the party (for which there is ample evidence of success). There is little that is egalitarian about the party's members. 'In order to establish equality one must first establish inequality.' Had the leaders encountered Marx's dictum they would certainly have given it full endorsement.

The party's appeal has usually been couched in these general terms. It has avoided the particular in favour of the general, e.g. 'Blessed are they who reject the Coussey report, for they shall know freedom'. But it also draws support from particular sections of the population. An example of party propaganda making a direct appeal to cocoa farmers is printed in the appendix, although the CPP cannot be seen in any sense as a 'smallholders' party'. Cocoa farmers are intensely interested in the politics of cocoa, but between 1954 and 1957 they were divided politically by traditional, regional, and individual loyalties.

V   Stresses and strains

Although successful in three general, and a number of municipal, elections, the party is very nervous. And this alone accounts for a good deal of its clumsy authoritarianism since independence. Where does this sensitivity come from? I suggest:

1   The party came to power too quickly, and had to make the change from a nationalist movement in opposition to a party government in power, with much of its machinery of organisation (and members) untested by any long period of trial.

2   The national framework of parliamentary government is also very new. It was born, more or less, with the CPP, i.e. in 1950. Its roots are

shallow, as the 1954-57 constitutional controversy over federalism
showed.

3   Since 1951 the party has been seriously challenged by what it fears
     most—dissenting movements based on strong regional—traditional—
     confessional emotions, e.g. the Moslem Association Party, the Togo-
     land Congress, the Northern People's Party, the National Liberation
     Movement and, immediately after independence, the Ga Shifimo Kpee.
     The last three came suddenly and unexpectedly, and gained rapidly in
     strength.

Internal strains

Behind the enormous personal authority of Nkrumah, divisions are discernible:

1   *The Gbedemah—Edusei—Baako contrasts.* Gbedemah, the Minister of
     Finance, conscious of Ghana's need of help from abroad and (as the
     party's national organiser) conscious of the fickleness of the Ghana
     electorate. Krobo Edusei, advocate of a 'get tough' policy, leading an
     Ashanti CPP wing in 1954-56, urging republican status, Nkrumah as
     President, and the elimination by 'preventive detention' of the opposi-
     tion. Kofi Baako, the would-be ideologist, eager to bolster policy with
     socialist theory.

2   *The constituency officials.* In 1954 the authoritarian centre overreached
     itself when it tried to impose its candidates on the constituencies.
     Local party officials and members protested; many were expelled; many
     more deserted to the NLM, which at one time had eighteen former CPP
     members out of its executive of twenty-one. The tug and pull between
     the national executive of the CPP and the constituency organisation
     have been there since it started.

3   *The rank and file,* loyal to Nkrumah but with strong local ties, e.g. the
     party finds it difficult, outside the municipalities, to put up non-local
     candidates. The mass of ordinary members are not (yet) worried about
     corruption or deportations, but they are prepared to resist too much
     pressure from any government which pushes a policy of centralisation
     too fast. And still 70 per cent of them have yet to cast their vote.

Patronage and corruption

These are not denied. Both are needed as an additional cement of party
unity. CPP candidates who lost the 1956 election were given diplomatic
appointments abroad, directorships on the public corporations, jobs in the
Workers' Brigade or in regional commissioners' offices, or scholarships
to study law. Politics in Ghana are the politics of clientelism, but, since
independence,

>   Unnumber'd suppliants crowd Preferment's gate,
>   Athirst for wealth and burning to be great,

and it may come to pass, in the post-independence world of distributory
politics which the CPP struggles to control, that there will not be enough
benefits to distribute. Ideology is no substitute for patronage. But if the
party leaders, led by Nkrumah and aped by his followers, use 'African
socialism' and its attendant cluster of beliefs to justify not only single-
party rule but the dearth of material rewards, the effect might be very un-

pleasant. Poor dictators tend to be even nastier than those of abundance.
In so far as ideology was ever part of the CPP programme of action, as
distinct from its platform of appeal, it lay in the demand for self-government at the expense of the British. The victims of single-party rule, in the
name of Nkrumaism and the misty notions of pan-Africanism, could come
only from among local opponents of the party.

VI   The party in power

Since the CPP took office in 1951 certain broad tendencies have made themselves apparent. Party control has been extended over most aspects of
public life, although not as yet over the judiciary or public service. The
power of the CCP is likely to increase until the party is dominant throughout
the country. And from being a dominant party, it may bully its way to an
absolute monopoly. Yet the constitution, and the way parliament works, are
based on a two-party system. Hence the intention of the government to alter
the constitution.

The CPP is also likely to go on centralising power at the expense of
traditional institutions. The three strongest centres of chieftaincy are
Mamprusi, Akim Abuakwa and Kumasi. Each has been subjected to government enquiry and pressure; each was an opposition stronghold; each has been
forced to declare its support for 'the government of the day'. Yet it is
worth noting that there is no sign of any attack on chieftaincy itself, which
is one more structure of local power to be brought into subordination by the
replacing of awkward Stool holders with compliant chiefs, a policy picked up
from colonial practice.

The accretion of power is also justified by the need to hurry the pace
of economic advance, but how that is to be done remains unsure. Despite
the socialist language, there is little evidence as yet of any major move
against private capital, whether at home or from abroad, and the Volta
River project is very dependent on outside help. Nor is there likely to be
any attempt to collectivise agriculture: like the chief, the peasant smallholder has a very permanent look about him.

The CPP's anti-colonial stance *is* emphasised strongly. 'Independence
for the Gold Coast will be incomplete,' says Nkrumah, 'unless it is linked
up with the liberation of other territories in Africa.' 'Pan-Africanism' is
a major national theme of policy because of Nkrumah's personal insistence
on its importance: in the constituencies, however, it is less than froth on the
strong brew of local politics.

VII   The leader

Nkrumah is perhaps the least 'Ghanaian-looking' of all the CPP leaders,
coming in from outside after many years abroad. His authority is very
great, but I would put more weight on his skill as a manipulator of party
(and State) power, in relation to the various interest groups which jostle for
a share of government patronage, than on the bestowal of a charismatic
authority from on high. It is true that Nkrumah has an immense appeal for
many ordinary Ghanaians, who have little difficulty in attaching magical
qualities to his rise to power. But one must be careful. Supernatural
powers are attributed to all the heroes of Ghanaian folk lore, but such
attitudes are also accompanied (in a traditional setting) by a very prosaic
assessment of the actual exercise of power. Obeisance to authority does not
exclude criticism of it, and chiefs are praised in extravagant terms until

the final hour of their destoolment, when the charges brought against them
usually go back to the first day of their rule.

Whether Nkrumah's response to this public adulation is simply a hard-
headed appraisal of its advantages I do not know. That he has a taste for
praise is surely undeniable. And I end this paper with two quotations—the
second a quotation within a quotation—which seem to me very ominous.
Both are from Nkrumah's *Autobiography:*

> Capitalism is too complicated a system for a newly independent nation.
> Hence the need for a socialistic society. But even a system based on
> social justice and a democratic constitution may need backing up,
> during the period following independence, by emergency measures of a
> totalitarian kind. Without discipline true freedom can not survive.
> [Page x]

> Who is he that would become my follower?
> Who would sign himself a candidate for my affections?
> The way is suspicious, the result uncertain, perhaps destructive.
> You would have to give up all else. I alone would expect to be your sole
>   and exclusive standard.
> Your novitiate would even then be long and exhausting.

> > [Preface, quoting Walt Whitman]

Appendix A

Extracts from the party's newspapers, the *Evening News* and the *Guinea
Times.*

1   EVEN THE COCOA FARMERS WILL YIELD 104 FREEDOM

         All Ghana farmers declare faith in Nkrumah

Every cocoa farmer in this country knows that his destiny and the
future of his great industry hinge on '104 Freedom' completely won
under the banner of the common man's own CPP. Ask any farmer at
all in this country and he will tell you. Our eyes have seen for the
first time in history the Cocoa Marketing Board's 4,000 ton ship
charted for carting our cocoa. The farmers' own organisation, CPC,
will have 250 tons loading space allocated to it on this new ship. Not
only that. Here is a resolution just passed by the United Ghana Farmers' Council to Nkrumah: 'That we assure you, that once your government has been the first to give loans to farmers to extend and reclaim
their pledged farms, we are going to register in our thousands and vote
you and your men into power again, for we believe that with you as
Prime Minister the needs of the Gold Coast farmers shall be fulfilled'.
And so say all of us.

Accra Evening News, June 1954

2   *Election Special*

         BEFORE VOTING THIS MORNING READ THIS

         by The Editor

Today, the eyes of the whole country—and, in fact, the outside world, to
a certain extent—are focused on Accra because of the municipal election which is taking place.

Accra being the capital of Ghana is one of the reasons for which a desperate effort is being made by the C.P.P. and the United Party to capture the seats in the municipality.

Each Party puts forward its programme and policy during the campaign period with vim. That is as it should be, since the electorate should be made fully aware of the policy of each party to enable them to decide which programme and policy to support.

THIS IS DEMOCRACY AT WORK EVEN THOUGH THE OPPOSITION SHOUTS LIKE MAD DOGS THAT THE GOVERNMENT IS DICTATORIAL.

We should like, at this juncture, to re-iterate what we had cause to say sometime ago, to wit, that there is excess of democracy in Ghana. If that were not so the people should not have been plagued now and again with acts of violence by the Opposition necessitating the imposition of curfew et. al.

Yet the very instigators and organisers of violence are the ones who chatter about dictatorship and intimidation.

Guinea Times, June 1958

3   *Satudi Zongo Nomba Wan Gossip*

Goodibning mah gutfrenshs! Yesteday mah big fren broddah Dokita Ankurumah lef dis we Ghana heya for go besit for Amirika ko Kanada. Ah go for de Earpot but ah not get de chansh for see am bifor in go for de allopilane way i tikkam go.

Dokita Ankurumah was compiny by Mister Kofi Abrako an Mister Kojo Boshow. But today a hrat annuder powertri lek dem wan way a hrat for yelcam Dokita Ankurumah won i can bak from de Ait Mimipendence Yaprikan Sitates. De powertri ebe dis:

Gutbar, gutbar for Ankurumah
Gutbar for Amirika
Go see you gutfren Harsenhar,
An, Deefeebikar him.
Worl Kanada piplos go gilad
For see you for dem pilace
Becus long tiem dem heya de nim
Dem callam Ankurumah
Ah sorri dat you neber hreed
Dis powertri bifor
Ah dirin too mush pito las' nite
For Beekend Banana.
De tiem ah hreesh for de Earpot
You piplos go long tiem
Ah look up see de allopilane
Ah wabe gutbar for wup.
All Yankees piplos go be gilad
For see you in dem town
For see you an' Kofi Brako
And Kojo Boshow worl
Jes now dem day for Kanada,
Nes tiem for Amirika
Dis moon go die bifor dem cam
Meet we for Ghana heya.

Gutbar, gutbar, Ankurumah
Worl Ghana day wit you,
Birin happi nuus for Ghana heya
And hrat for *Yiblin Nuus*.

Professor Yaro
Evening News, July 1958

Extract (3) is a humorous daily item in the paper, which now includes
M. Camara Laye's lessons in French, and news items in English, Hausa, Ga,
Fanti, Twi, Ewe and, occasionally, Arabic. Rough translation:

Saturday Zongo No. 1 gossip

Good evening, my good friends. Yesterday, my big brother and friend
Dr Nkrumah left Ghana to visit America and Canada. I go to the airport
but I did not get the chance to see him before the aeroplane took him
away.

Dr Nkrumah was accompanied by Mr Kofi Baako and Mr Kojo
Botsio, But today I wrote another poetry like the one I wrote to welcome
Dr Nkrumah when he came back from the Eighth Independent African
States. The poetry is this:

Goodbye, goodbye for Nkrumah,
Goodbye for America.
Go and see your good friend Eisenhower
And Diefenbaker.
All the Canadian people will be glad
To see you for their place
Because for a long time they hear the name
Which they call Ankrumah.
I'm sorry you did not hear
This poetry before;
I drank too much *pito* last night
In the Weekend in Havana [night club].
By the time I rushed to the airport
You people had gone a long time.
I looked up and saw the aeroplane
And waved goodbye for [them] up there.
All American people will be pleased
To see you in their town,
To see you and Kofi Baako
And Kojo Botsio all.
Just now they are for Canada
Next time for America.
This moon will die before they come
To meet us here in Ghana.
Goodbye, Goodbye, Nkrumah
All Ghana is with you.
Bring happy news for Ghana here
And write for *Evening News*.

Appendix B. A note on tradition

It is sometimes suggested that the CPP is tradition embodied in national,
party form. It is not surprising (it is argued) that the CPP should claim

control of all political groups and structures, or that it should insist on
their subordination to the party in power. The leaders are behaving traditionally, transferring Akan practice to the nationalist State—a pyramid of
power, with dissent at the top, where the Leader sits enthroned, but with
rivalry at intermediate levels between the different segments of the party
and its ancillary wings, as in the multiple structure of an Akan chiefdom.
For both party leader and traditional chief there is the ultimate sanction
of popular disapproval—the withdrawal of 'mass support', and the need to
reconstruct the pyramid with a different office holder.

So the thesis runs. And at first sight there is some point in arguing
the case for the rooting of present politics in the past. Ghanaian society *is*
deep-rooted. Despite all the arguments about modernisation and transition
there is much less discontinuity in Ghana than in the industrial societies
of the West: customs, beliefs and ceremonies are village-based and peasant-
based still for the majority of the people. But is that true of modern political life? Those who are most actively in search of power are the furthest
removed from traditional structures of control—and indeed have tried
to struggle out of them. They are a new elite, eager to use the power of the
State to become a new economic class, and they are uneasy in their seizure
of control because of the danger of competitors, many of whom—the NLM,
NPP, MAP—are much like the CPP though clothed in semi-traditional dress.
It is really necessary, therefore, to reach back into the locally horizoned,
custom-sanctified, territorial-kinship groups of an Akan chiefdom to explain
the desire for total control on the part of those who fear they might lose
what they have so recently acquired?

A similar problem arises over what we might call 'parallelism'. A
particular feature of contemporary politics may also be found strongly in
earlier times, but that does not necessarily mean there is a causal relationship. There are clear parallels between the traditional payments with
which chieftaincy issues were decided and the corrupt practices of party
politics. The account by Meyer Fortes of chieftaincy elections among the
Tallensi comes close to the present writer's own study of a northern
election. Busia, too, has described how the traditional Akan payment of
aseda was swollen to excessive proportions: to be elected to a Stool, he says,
some chiefs 'are known to have spent more than £100 and one informant
estimated that he had spent over £1,000'.[2] The Ashanti Confederacy Council
complained as early as 1938 that 'the practice of people offering and accept-
ing bribes to destool and enstool a chief has become common', and that it
'has been the source of political unrest'. It may be, then, that traditional
practices are a fertile soil for the growth of modern abuses: the 'thanksgiving fee' *(aseda)* prepares the way for the 'dash' and the bribe. But—and
it is a big 'but'—money and politics have gone together in most political
systems; it is not a peculiarity of 'African transitional society'. After all,
Eatanswill is a parody of British, not Ghanaian, elections.

A further difficulty: 'tradition' is itself a changing pattern. 'Very deep is
the well of the past', and a great deal can be extracted from it to suit whatever arguments one wishes to defend in relation to the present. The past not
only includes centuries of chieftaincy government, such as that described
by Bowdich and Dupuis in Ashanti in the early nineteenth century (descrip-
tions which may also be true only of that particular historical period), but
fifty years of colonial rule which tried, with varying success, to work through
traditional institutions; and, by working through the chiefs and their advisers
as 'native authorities', it inescapably distorted their position. There are
variations in area as well as in time. The Akan tradition is of an elected

chief chosen from a royal family or families, popularly acclaimed, and capable of being dismissed by a constitutional process of 'destoolment'. Northern chiefs are very different. They were either warrior rulers who among the Dagomba, Gonja, Wala and Mamprusi were imposed on conquered peoples, and not subject to dismissal: 'The holder of a Dagomba chieftainship cannot be deprived of his office except by death . . . . A chief who misruled his area in days gone by was made war against and slain.'[3] Or they were little more than the heads of ruling lineages until puffed up by the British, who insisted on finding 'natural rulers' where none existed.

It seems that all that one can safely argue is as follows.

1. That traditional institutions as they had become by 1949 were such as to provoke a reaction to their control among the educated class. Political associations existed already in the towns; but the UGCC and the CPP were new in the sense they spread into the rural areas, and they succeeded partly because of a growing discontent with native authority rule. There is early evidence of such discontent in the grievances of the educated minority over their exclusion from many NA courts and treasuries, in the number of destoolments during the inter-war period in Ashanti and the south, in the revival of local *asafo* companies of 'youngmen' among the Fanti, and in attempts by chiefs' councils (notably the Ashanti Confederacy) to suppress 'traditional offices' once held by commoners. One of the features of the *first* election, therefore, was the 'CPP versus tradition' battle, most vividly illustrated in the defeat of Nana Sir Tsibu Darku IX, Kt, Omanhene of Asin Attandasu (nominated by a fellow paramount chief, a Divisional Chief, and the Denkyira State Council secretary) by Mr Pobey Binee (CPP)—a locomotive driver—who was nominated by a petty trader, a fitter and a farmer.

2. By 1954 local loyalties were being stressed by politicians who turned for support to traditional authorities: the Northern People's Party and the Northern Territories Territorial Council, the NLM and the Asanteman Council, and more recent movements like the Ga Shifimo Kpee, which enlisted the Ga chiefs (and gods) against the CPP. In return the CPP found allies among chiefs and local movements which wanted governmental power for local ends, e.g. the Brong-Akyempim movement, anti-Omanhene chiefs on the Akim Abuakwa State Council, the Navropio in the north who used the CPP to raise his own little chiefdom above that of his neighbours. By becoming 'mass politics' nationalism was necessarily forced into a trading position which included bargains struck between the central government under party control and local centres of traditional authority.

3. If, therefore, by tradition is meant loyalty to family, lineage and Stool, or the local patriotism which determines the political affections of very many electors, then of course it is a living force, adding that pervasive element of 'localism' to the more recent phenomenon of social groups whose boundaries are the nation.

4. To draw precepts about the party State from traditional practices is at best bewildering. Equally unconvincing cases could be made for using 'tradition' to support CPP claims to a corporate monopoly of power on the ground that the party is the traditional council writ large, and United Party arguments for the legitimacy of opposition arising from the customary right of destoolment. You chose your tradition and you justify your party.

5. There is still an evolving and decaying pattern of traditional authority located in the former native authorities, which were subject to colonial structures of control. Indirect rule is far from being extinct, and the nationalist party has inherited the colonial world to make full use of its central powers of direction. A dominant fact of politics (as of a good deal

of Ghanaian life in general) over the past half century has been the intrusion of colonial rule, and of Western-based values of very great influence—Christianity, capitalism, education, bureacracy, nationalism. The nationalist reaction took the form not of a return to tradition but of a seizure of the intruded institutions by new leaders. There must be, inescapably, *some* transfer of beliefs, including beliefs about how men should behave politically, from the colonial-traditional past (whatever is meant by that) to the nationalist present (however impermanent it may be). But how can one be sure of the source of the transfer, or of its potency in relation to what is newly created by the novel circumstances of the nationalist period? David Apter has made a brave if, at times, muffled attempt to link the 'traditional past' with the 'nationalist present' in a truly pioneering volume, by arguing that 'chieftaincy as a sanctional source, a symbolic referent, an integrational integer, and for ethnic and sub-ethnic definition, represents the orientational base out of which the characteristic authority of Nkrumah ... has developed. Without an understanding of the functional requisites of Gold Coast chieftancy, the present role of Nkrumah in political institutional transfer cannot be fully comprehended' (*The Gold Coast in Transition,* p. 108). I am not sure that I fully grasp what is being said here, but I am inclined to wonder whether one could, in practice, be more precise. For how could one be sure of what was, in effect, being developed 'out of' rather than 'away from' the traditional authority represented by the chief? Has it been possible to recast the 'functional requisites' and the veneration of Ghanaian chieftaincy so as to bestow a comparable authority on the central government in Accra? Chieftaincy was prescriptive in its authority, honoured by time, sanctified and given meaning by kinship ties based on descent. Can one see Nkrumah and the CPP in comparable or transferable terms? As for the people at large, among whom it is certainly true that custom and ceremony are living forms, there is perhaps only one general proposition that one might hesitatingly advance: that, among the Akan at least, the electorate is unlikely to be shocked by the sudden fall from power of those in authority over them. But as to how a prime minister or party leader might be destooled, there's the rub.

6. At a general level, it is proper to recognise that Ghanaian society *is* profoundly conservative. To understand how much so one has only to move from the centre of the city to its outskirts or from the small urban centres to the countryside. Order and hierarchy are apparent in almost every aspect of social and political life. Nor do communal ties mitigate the authority of the old over the young or of the rich over the poor. Indeed, they enshrine such relationships, and the marked obeisance to social order has its political counterparts. One should add, however, that if traditional values are deep-rooted it is primarily because not much has happened to uproot them: there is as yet none of the desperate rural poverty of Latin America or the grim urban poverty of nineteenth-century Britain.

Notes

1   Except in the north, where the handful of educated clerks, schoolteachers and traders, some of whom turned to the CPP after 1954, were active in the native authorities and as advisers to chiefs.
2   K. A. Busia, *The Position of the Chief in the Modern Political System of Ashanti.* London, 1951.
3   *Enquiry into the Constitution and Organisation of the Dagbon Kingdom,* Accra, 1932. It is true, however, that under various external influences, attempts are being made to introduce the notion of 'destoolment' or—since the warrior chiefs of the north sit on royal Skins—'deskinment'.

III

The Ghana parliament's first year

The first year of independence brought no startling changes to the Ghana parliament. The 1957 Ghana (Constitution) Order in Council, and the Act of Independence, established a unicameral 'National Assembly of the Parliament of Ghana' on the basis of the 1954 Assembly, which was itself a reformed version of the first national Legislative Assembly of 1951. The practice of ministerial responsibility was introduced in 1954 (it is written into the 1957 constitution) and, because of the strong party character of the government, works well. The executive is over-large, having more than twenty Ministers and fifteen Ministerial Secretaries out of a total Assembly of 104, but with over two-thirds of the seats in the Assembly the government can afford to be generous and must make sure of support from a wide party following. Since independence parliamentary life has flowed surprisingly smoothly, the opposition taking its full part in debates and in committees of the House—including the Public Accounts Committee, which has eight government and four opposition members. It is true that a number of Bills have been fiercely opposed, clause by clause, in full debate and in committee—notably the Ghana Nationality and Citizenship Bill, the Emergency Powers Bill, the Deportation Bill and the Avoidance of Discrimination Bill. Sittings have occasionally had to be suspended and the Speaker has had to use a strong hand to curb the more spirited members, but these struggles have taken place in parliament, not in the streets. The language of debate is often unbridled, charges of fraud, dictatorship, violence and peculation being made freely across the floor; but Ghanaians are not mealy-mouthed, whether in English or their own tongue, and tempers lost in the chamber seem quickly to be recovered in the members' room.[1]

Perhaps one should add, too, that party struggles over citizenship, or deportation orders, or the appointment of Regional Commissioners have taken place alongside a good deal of parliamentary business of a non-contentious kind—amendments to the Prisons' Ordinance, the strengthening of the new Ghana Court of Appeal, an improvement to the Road Traffic Act, etc, etc. Private members' motions have a good hearing in Ghana and there is probably a greater opportunity for individual members to assert themselves than in the more disciplined House of Commons. Question time is fully used—more fully than necessary, according to the Speaker's Office—and members on both sides are learning to drag information out of a reluctant Minister, or make him uncomfortable if he does not answer to their satisfaction. On both sides, too, there has been a constant echo of constituency needs in the stress on 'development'.

There are several reasons for this better atmosphere. The grant of independence itself, following the July 1956 elections, did much to clear the air. So long as there was still a third party—the colonial power—to the

Parliamentary Affairs, **XI**, 1957-58.

dispute between the CPP and the opposition the latter was tempted to appeal to Britain for help and to establish its claim, at all costs, to a share of power. Such an attitude exasperated the CPP, which in its turn resolved to demonstrate, at all costs, its greater strength. But once power had been handed over, both sides began to recognise the necessity of having to live together. Secondly, there has been an accumulating experience of the handling of parliamentary ways, and of getting things done in debate, committee and legislative measures. Thirdly, the Assembly had been fortunate in its officers: Emmanuel (now Sir Emmanuel) Quist was Speaker of the House from 1951 to November 1957 and president of the Legislative Council before that. K. B. Ayensu has been an extremely capable Clerk since 1953 (Deputy Clerk, 1953-55; Clerk from 1955). A history of seven years is not much, but it is something, and there are several members on both sides of the chamber who are good at being parliamentarians and who seem to have the feel of the House

How important is parliament? Or, who rules Ghana? There is no doubt as to the answer to the second question: it is the party. For nearly ten years now the Convention People's Party has combined the material advantage of a mutual benefit society with the fervour of a nationalist movement. The segment of Ghana which is political and modern took shape on 12 June 1949 with the CPP; what happened in 1951 was that the party agreed to work within the new constitutional framework. It is the party which dominates the political life of the country, which is extending its control over trade unions, farmers' groups, ex-servicemen and local government associations, and which sees itself as having to capture the parliamentary machine. It tries to play a Tudor role—organising, consolidating, laicising the nation—and its parliamentary role is very much a subordinate part of its general movement and life.

Parliament might occupy a more prominent place if there were other rooted institutions for which it might become a focus of interest. But, except for political parties, there are few nationally organised societies capable of informing or persuading or moving the general public for or against a particular act of government policy. The trade unions are divided, the Farmers' Council and the co-operative movement are under party control, the Chamber of Commerce is uncertain of its role, and the most widely circulating newspaper—the *Daily Graphic*—is prevented by its expatriate origins from having any definite national or political standpoint. The result is that the ordinary member of parliament, unable to find any great measure of active support at a national level, stands defenceless (and usually penniless) before the party's central executive. Over most major issues of policy he must exercise his own judgement, supported by whatever facts he can discover for himself. Admirable as this may sound in theory, in practice it places a very heavy burden on the ordinary back-bencher, and especially on the small group of opposition members.

Interest might also be greater if parliament were seen as a critical battleground between the two rival parties. But the most marked feature of the past twelve months has been the decline of the opposition. Despite the energies of its twenty to twenty-five members in parliament, there are few (outside the loyalist ranks of the United Party) who believe that the CPP will be seriously challenged for a long time to come, in or out of parliament. The remarkable thing is that the United Party exists as much as it does. It has to struggle not merely against the better organised, better financed government party but against a number of intangibles. There is the immense prestige which the CPP enjoys as the principal author of independence—of being so clearly on the winning side, and the opposition equally clearly on the other: power attracts and near-absolute power attracts absolutely. There is the belief that the government, as the powers that be, are right and that 'they that resist shall receive to themselves damnation'.[2] And there is the persistent argument that continual opposition is unnecessary,

> *Mr. Salifu Yakubu.*[3] I do not intend to say very much about the activities of the Opposition now. I have been in their camp ever since the last general election. I have been one of the most important members of the Opposition, and I am not prepared just yet to say much about their secrets. At no time have the Opposition supported a motion by the Government. But if there is to be democracy, why should the Opposition continue to reject all motions and Bills which will be in the best interest of the country? (Uproar.)[4]

What is surprising, then, is the vitality of the small opposition group. The government party has so much to offer—a ministerial secretaryship, membership of numerous government missions abroad, appointments to public corporations: all the advantages of power. The opposition has very little, least of all the hope of an early assumption of office.

Just as it would help parliament if the opposition were stronger, so it would help the opposition if it could find a more definite standpoint from which to attack. During 1955-56 the strong regional traditional loyalties evoked by the National Liberation Movement and the Northern People's Party produced something approaching a mass opposition movement. But much of this emotion has been emptied out of the NLM and NPP by their merger into a 'United Party' which, the attraction of federation gone and the main lines of the constitution having been settled, finds it difficult to attract more than minority support. One can indicate certain lines of direction that each party distinctly follows. The CPP believes that a centralisation of authority is necessary to knit the country together and to carry out development on a national scale: the opposition would like to see a greater regionalisation of powers and a greater local control of development schemes. The CPP is a radical, vaguely socialistic party; the United Party has a more tender regard for traditional institutions. But these are shadowy differences, and it is difficult to see what is left to the opposition other than to act as a reservoir for those dissatisfied with the ruling party.

What the effect will be on parliament, should the opposition continue to dwindle to the point where criticism ceases to have a buoyant support to sustain it, remains to be seen. There are two possibilities. One is that a great deal of the present vitality of debate will disappear and, with it, something of the life of parliament itself. Parliament may then become little more than a formal recording machine of party decisions—a reduction in function that very likely no one wishes it to suffer. The other possibility is that the CPP back-benchers, confronted with only a handful of opposition members, may feel more free to act independently. If the CPP is to remain unchallenged in power for a long time to come there is certainly everything to be said for having party disagreements argued out in parliment. There was a greater swing of opinion among the CPP rank and file during 1952-53 than after the growth of the NPP and NLM; and should the opposition again decline in strength the same back-benchers might win back their former courage. Even some of the excitement of the secret party executive meeting might then be transferred to the open debate of parliament.[5]

Were such changes to occur, much else might have to alter. A single-party Assembly, or a heavily dominant-party parliament would need as much care to safeguard its autonomy—and very likely greater care—than the more

familiar Westminster-style legislature. The party would have to face demo-
cratically in on itself. Is the will to keep debate alive present in the CPP
leadership? At the highest level there is little evidence of a liking for dissent and a good deal to indicate a taste for autocracy. Left to itself, therefore, the ruling party might possibly restrict its network of interests and
stifle dissent, although since its formation it has been a very loosely
arranged movement, and it is not easy to believe that it can be straight-
jacketed into total submission. Of greater importance, perhaps, is the fact
that despite the obstacles (often deliberately placed) in the way of the opposition and despite its now much diminished state, the United Party can still
command support at local level. For it still remains the case that since the
nationalist party came to office it has been quite incapable of meeting every
claimant to its favours. Viewed, as it increasingly needs to be, as a distributory party of benefits, the CPP has to act as best it can on a 'trickle down'
principle; but for many the benefits which trickle down through the party
are either non-available or derisory. It seems unlikely, therefore, that the
United Party, or whatever takes its place, will be finally extinguished, or
even fall below a minimum level of attraction in many areas. There will
always be those who, individually or communally, turn for an alternative
to the CPP either in the hope of future reward or simply out of a profound
distrust of those who *are* benefited. For the past twelve months the National
Assembly has above all reflected this dominant-majority/aggrieved-mino-
rity debate: hence its focus on practical demands for 'development' of a
very local nature which come 'trickling up' from the constituencies.

What are the prospects of parliamentary government in Ghana? On the
whole they are good. It is easy to forget that since 1951 the Assembly has
continued to carry out its main task of providing a government, enabling it
to work and subjecting it to criticism. It is probably true that the general
mass of the people would not view very seriously the reduction of parliament to an occasional formal appearance, but there is no sign that its members have any intention of letting that happen. On the contrary, during 1957
the Assembly met in ten months out of the twelve. And the main complaint
of the opposition has been not that the government ignores parliament but
that it has been over-quick to use its power to secure legislation of a radical
kind. There is no shortage of candidates at election time, and an MP is
known in his constituency to be an important person. Once elected, he takes
his parliamentary duties seriously,[6] and most MPs visit their constituencies
regularly not only to maintain their networks of support but to try and explain new legislation and their own part in it. Debates are well reported in
the local papers, and the *Official Report* is printed and published within
twenty-four hours of debate.

Note

The optimism shown here, which did credit to the writer's heart, if not
his head, was founded on a belief that Ghana could follow, no doubt in its
own way, the path stumbled along by other Commonwealth States in Asia,
East Africa and the Caribbean. That road was blocked in 1966, although on
the eve of the first military intervention part of the CPP in parliament was
still struggling to keep debate alive. From the time of the single-party
republic, however, members of parliament were under sustained attack
from stronger rival sections within the CPP. Early in 1965, for example,
the party newspaper, *The Spark*, called for reform of the Assembly in order

to put an end to the 'capitalist formula' of 'career parliamentarians'.
Under such a system (it was said),

> Members could be withdrawn from Parliament at any time on the dis-
> cretion of the Central Committee of the Party... it is proper that the
> Central Committee, the collective leadership of the Revolution, should
> exercise this power.... The selection of new members should be guided
> by a few rules... foremost amongst such rules is ideological orienta-
> tion. We have reached a stage where only such persons who are ideo-
> logically sound—the test to be made by the General Secretary himself—
> should be considered as MPs.[7]

In June that year the charade of the 1965 election took place: 198 members
of a new parliament were returned unopposed for the single party after approval by the Central Committee. Parliament limped on, and a few MPs
continued cautiously to speak out, despite the Detention Act. Then, in February 1966, it was all over, and the soldiers put an end to President, party and
parliament alike. Debate re-started (in quasi-Westminster form) during the
Constituent Assembly of 1968-69, and in the Progress-dominated parliament
of the second Republic, but that too ended in the second military *coup*.

Notes

1   There can be a common appreciation of material benefits:

GV Cars (Allocation)

> *Mr E. I. Preko* asked the Minister of Finance how many of the GV cars
> were sold to Members of Parliament; and how many were sold to
> Government Members and how many were sold to Members of the
> Opposition.
> *Mr Bensah.* Of the cars purchased by the Government for use by
> official visitors to the Independence celebrations, seventy-six have
> been allocated to Members of Parliament on application; forty-
> seven to Government supporters, twenty-eight to members of the
> Opposition, and one to an Independent member.
> *Mr Preko.* How many cars were allocated to Members of the Opposi-
> tion?
> *Mr Bensah.* The cars available for distribution included Jaguars,
> Chevrolets, Wolseleys but the majority of the Jaguars went to the
> Opposition.
> (*Ghana Parliamentary Debates, 2 May 1957.*)

2   A number of prominent chiefs and their state councils recently declared
their intention to support 'the government of the day'; it was this decision that led three prominent members of the opposition, Mumuni
Bawumia, MP, Mahama Tampuri, MP, and T. K. Yentu to state that they
were resigning from the United Party.
3   Elected as a NPP candidate in 1956 and crossed over to the government side in March 1958.
4   *Debates,* 14 March 1958.
5   The fact that there is less difference in Ghana than in many other parliamentary systems between membership of the Central Committee of
the party and membership of the Cabinet may help to give party decisions a constitutional setting. There are non-parliamentary members
on the Central Committee of the CPP (e.g. the General Secretary of the

Ghana TUC) but since June 1949 it has included, among others, Nkrumah, Botsio, Gbedemah, Welbeck, Baako, Edusei—all of whom today are Ministers.

6   And can be quick to defend his privileges. When the *Daily Graphic* misreported action taken by the Deputy Speaker in the course of debate (12 June 1957), Mr Kofi Baako, supported by Mr B. F. Kusi for the opposition, strongly requested the Speaker to demand an apology, and the Clerk was then 'directed to call upon the Editor of the *Daily Graphic* to explain'.

7   *The Spark,* 28 May 1965. Quoted in Trevor Jones's study of the CPP (London, forthcoming).

IV

Voting in an African town

Several studies of the origins and growth of nationalist movements in Africa
have appeared in recent years; but still very little is known in detail of
party divisions among the new African electorates. We know *how* the voter
casts his ballot, but not *why* he chooses to support a particular candidate or
party.[1] Ghana is a case in point. In the 1956 general election 398,141 voters
turned out for the Convention People's Party; 299,116 voted for one or other
of the opposition parties. By breaking down the vote on a regional basis we
can see that the main weight of support for the opposition lay outside the
large southern region—the former Colony area.[2] Nevertheless, the CPP won
eight of the twenty-one seats, and 96,968 out of 224,569 votes, in the strongest area of opposition, Ashanti. We can carry the breakdown of voting one
stage further and say that, within the former Ashanti region, the CPP vote
was particularly heavy in the western Brong constituencies: 38,373 against
25,633. These abstracts are useful in plotting the general division of voting
in the country at that time, but they leave a great deal unexplained. Even
within the traditional heartland of Ashanti, in the cluster of states grouped
around Kumasi, the CPP was given a substantial vote. The opposition, including independents, picked up *some* votes (ranging from less than 1 per
cent in eastern Nzima to over 70 per cent in Agona Kwabre) in ninety-nine
out of the total of 104 constituencies. What was the basis of this division between voters? Was it the same in the previous elections of 1951 and 1954?
Has it changed significantly during the three years of independence since
March 1957? The following account tries to answer these questions in
respect of one area only, a relatively sophisticated part of the country,
where wealth and tradition have combined to produce a highly politically
conscious body of voters—the municipality of Kumasi. The focus is narrow,
but for that reason perhaps the picture which emerges is clearer than a
general survey would be of voting patterns in the country as a whole.

'Wealth and tradition': both these characteristics of the town bear
directly on its politics: 'tradition' because the long period of Ashanti power,
from the early eighteenth century until 1874, when Sir Garnet Wolseley
destroyed the old town by setting fire to it, is not forgotten either by the
present generation of Ashanti or by the stranger communities who have
made their home there today: memories stretch back a long way and play
an important part in deciding party allegiance among the 60,000 (in 1959)
registered voters. Southerners especially remember tales, handed down
from generation to generation, of Ashanti arrogance and power.[3] Most
Ashanti are very conscious of their history. The 'young men' can tell their
story, in recent times particularly, of the harsh rule of some chiefs; but they
too, on occasions, lament with their more conservative elders the present

Written in conjunction with Professor William Tordoff, and reproduced
from *Political Studies,* VIII, 2, 1960, with permission of the editor.

reversal of Ashanti fortunes. For it is the south now which dominates the
rest of the country by reason of its greater weight of population and the
operation of a 'one man, one vote' electoral system. Out of the total of 104
seats in the Ghana parliament the south has forty-four, the north twenty-six,
the Volta region thirteen, the remaining twenty-one seats being divided
between Ashanti and (since 1958) the Brong-Ahafo region.

The wealth of Kumasi, like its military prowess, is well attested in
history. The destruction of the town by Wolseley and the period of intermittent civil war which followed must have brought trade almost to a stand-
still; but from 1901 onwards, as a British colony, Ashanti prospered. The
population of Kumasi doubled in twenty years, and more than doubled again
in the next two decades.[4] By the early 1920s the town had recovered its former position as a great inland commercial metropolis for the coastal hinterland trade, for cocoa particularly but as an entrepot for an enormous
variety of goods. The story in its early stages can be traced quite easily
through the annual *Colonial Reports* for Ashanti: the extension of the railway
to Kumasi in 1903, which linked the town with the old sea port at Sekondi;
the 'building craze' led by the chiefs be fore the first world war, when many
of the old thatch-covered houses were replaced by solid brick buildings with
iron or shingle roofs; the formation of a Public Works Department, and the
draining of the swamps in the centre of the town. The second stage came in
the 'reconstruction period' in the early 1920s, with the demolition of dilapi-
dated, insanitary areas like Old Asafo to make way for a new network of
roads and commercial premises leading to the great central market, which
opened in 1925 with an estimated 2,000 vendors; by 1957 it covered an area
of more than twenty-five acres, with over 8,000 traders, 'not counting the
traders' relatives and assistants'.[5] More recently Kumasi has fed fat on
high cocoa prices. Prices rose from (in local terms) an average of 7s 6d a
load of 60 lb in the decade before 1939 to the Marketing Board's controlled
price of over £3 a load after 1945. Farmers, storekeepers, petty traders,
taxi drivers, the overseas firms, and local Ghanaian businessmen prospered
on cocoa and its sales.

The picture is not, of course, an uncommon one in West Africa, except
perhaps in one important particular: the rate of growth of a private trading
wealth in local African hands. It is this which impresses the visitor to
Kumasi as he drives through New Asafo or Mbrom or Ashanti New Town,
through street after street of huge two- and three-storeyed concrete houses,
many of them well established, others newly begun or awaiting the next cocoa
season for the roof to be completed or a third storey to be added to the
existing building. Kumasi has the look of a private enterprise town, and this
is borne out by the findings of the government *Survey of Population and
Household Budgets* carried out between 1953 and 1955 in the three municipalities: Accra, Sekondi-Takoradi and Kumasi. It found that 'Kumasi, with
only 34 per cent of all families having wage incomes, was by far the least
dependent of the three principal urban areas on employment', its 'non-wage
incomes' were derived mainly from local trading and crafts, and were the
'principal source of livelihood in the city'. By contrast, in Accra 57 per
cent of all families depended on 'wage incomes', and in Sekondi-Takoradi
the proportion was as high as 69 per cent. This means a much greater dependence by Kumasi on the fluctuations of trade and its local determinant—
the main-season cocoa harvest and the price fixed by the Cocoa Marketing
Board; but with it has gone a greater freedom of political activity.

As wealth poured into the town it attracted more than Ashanti traders.
Southerners were no longer afraid to live and work there. And as communi-

cations became easier by rail and road, and amenities were provided by
way of a hospital, schools, electricity, a pipe-borne water supply, and housing
estates, whole new districts were settled by Fanti, Gā and Ewe families
from the south. To the north-east of the town the Zongo settlements of
Hausas, Zabermas, Gaos and migrants from the Gold Coast north spread
their crumbling tenements and compounds. Their interests were watched
over by a Muslim Zerikin Zongo and the various tribal heads, all of whom
paid allegiance to the Asantehene. These stranger communities tended to
keep their identity, following the ancient Ashanti practice of dividing their
own compounds from those of the Muslim and other immigrant groups.
Thus it is possible today to describe many of the electoral wards in the
town as having a preponderance of Ashanti or Northern or Fanti voters;
others are distinguishable by religion rather than by origin: the suburbs of
Suame and Aboabo, the one to the north-west, the other to the north-east of
the town, are both Muslim wards and tend to vote the same way, although the
former is inhabited mainly by Ashanti converts to Islam—the *asante
nkramo*—and the latter by Hausa and Zaberma traders. By the middle of the
present century the Ashanti were outnumbered in their own capital, the
overall tribal distribution listed by the 1955 *Population Survey* showing:

Origin of families	%
Ashanti	45
Fanti	16
Ewe	6
Gā	3
Northern Ghana	24
Nigerian and other non-Ghanaian	6

There is one other facet of Kumasi political life to be noted. Despite the
bustling wealth of the town, living conditions are wretched for large sections
of the populace. The *Population Survey* found that 'over 60 per cent of all
persons enumerated' were living more than three to a single room. The
rich live very well indeed, but the poor are very poor. No precise statistics
are available of the relative wealth of each ward, but, from experience and
observation, the poorest sections of the town are to be found in the Muslim
and northern immigrant wards. The housing estates of southern clerical
workers and artisans form a relative prosperous middle stratum. The
Ashanti wards range from the wealthy merchant- and professional-class
district of Mbrom to the squalid alleyways and crowded compounds in
Adum and Ashanti New Town where the so-called 'verandah boys', city-born
and bred, manage a tough, cheerful existence by a little burglary, a little
pimping, a little honest work, as the occasion or opportunity arises. More
will be said of these differences later in an analysis of the ward-to-ward
vote.

Finally one should add that superimposed on these differences of origin
or religion or wealth is the familiar conflict between the old traditional
order, characterised by respect for chiefs, and the newer 'detribalised' life
in which associations are formed of a modern 'Western' kind: improvement
societies, trade unions, parties. Such conflicts did not arise overnight. As
early as 1909 the annual *Report on Ashanti* observed that 'the Ashanti
organisation, so powerful in olden days, still maintains many elements of
cohesion, but with the spread of Western civilisation and more liberal ideas,
the inevitable conflict between youth and authority has already commenced'.
In the inter-war years the discontented 'young men' used the weapon of
destoolment in an attempt to reassert what were held to be the traditional

rights of the commoners; after the second world war unrest of this kind was
given a new political direction by Krobo Edusei, Atta Mensah and others
through the Ashanti Youth Association and, from 1949 onwards, the CPP.
Kumasi became a centre of nationalist agitation, much of it directed against
the chiefs.[6] But one must be careful not to over-simplify: tension between
the chiefs and the young men undoubtedly influenced the pattern of voting in
Kumasi from 1949-50 onwards, but it existed often enough within the individual voter: the young Ashanti storekeeper might be drawn to the new
comradeship of the CPP but at the same time still be capable of being
moved by a deep emotional loyalty to the Golden Stool. Moreover the often
violent disputes which took place between the traditional state councils and
the radical CPP rank and file from 1949 onwards merely emphasised what
was already notorious—the turbulent, unruly nature of Kumasi society.
Kumasi apparently like its politics rough. At the height of Ashanti power
Bowdich complained that the 'lower order of the people were ungrateful, in-
solent and licentious. The King repeatedly said that he believed them to be
the worst people existing, except the Fantee'.[7] A half-century later Kumasi
was divided to the point of civil war over the succession to the Golden Stool.
Today it is the Action Troopers (and their rivals, in 1956, the Action
Groupers) or the Builders' Brigade who keep the political cauldron bubbling.
        We turn now to the record of voting since 1950. This is a convenient
starting point because of the change brought about by the growth of nationalist organisations in the country. There were earlier elections in Kumasi,
on the basis of adult suffrage of both sexes, from the time when the Kumasi
Public Health Board was replaced by a town council in 1943, but the number
of voters was extremely small, and parties were not much more than *ad hoc*
electoral organisations grouped about individual candidates: in 1943 voters
numbered 821 out of a total registration of 3, 805; in 1947 registration rose
to 7, 042, the number of voters (in four out of the six wards) to 1, 014. But
from 1949 onwards the CPP carried everyone before it. Muslims, Ashanti,
southerners, traditional elements, rich and poor—all but a handful of misguided individuals were, it seemed, united along a broad anti-colonial front
which demanded 'immediate self-government now'. In Kumasi the municipal
elections (in five wards) in November 1950 brought the remarkable result:
CPP, 6, 210; People's Democratic Party, 37; independents, 13. A similar
landslide took place the following February, in the first general elections
for the new Legislative Assembly. Archie Casely-Hayford, a Fanti, defeated
his Ashanti opponent, B. D. Addai, with 8, 358 votes against 570. In the same
election the party captured every one of the eighteen rural Electoral
College seats in Ashanti. Nationalism had won its first major victory.
        Within three years, almost to the day, it experienced its first check. As
the wave of nationalist emotion receded, local interests began to stir.
Throughout Ashanti and the south during 1952-53 tax riots occurred over
the raising of the levy by a number of the newly elected CPP local councils.
In Kumasi the first break in the party's hold on the town came from the
Muslim community. The immediate ground of complaint lay in an endless
dispute over the allocation by the CPP-controlled municipal council of
market stalls. But in general the Muslim saw themselves as a minority
group whose rights were in danger of being trampled on. Their position in
the town had indeed changed drastically. From being a superior group in
traditional times—literate, able to keep accounts, religious, skilful in trade,
good warriors, with a knowledge of trade born of their contacts with the
larger Muslim world, and greatly respected on that account—they had been
gradually overtaken by the modern world, displaced by European trade,

religion and power, and were now despised by the southern immigrant as
belonging to the backward, remote northern hinterland. They felt that they
must make their voice heard and their strength known through their own
efforts. 'True Muslims can never be friends with the CPP,' Alhaji Alfa
Larden[8] wrote to the *Ashanti Pioneer;* 'the Muslim Association is prepared
to hold the devil by the throat until everybody is free in the country.' Their
opportunity came in February 1954, with the second round of municipal
elections, now divided between twenty-four wards. The Muslim Association
put up seven candidates, four of whom were elected—three in the northern
Zongo area and one in Suame, the *asante nkramo* ward. The total Muslim
vote came to 3, 000, out of just under 20, 000. It was the most serious setback
so far to the party, not merely in Kumasi, but in the country as a whole.
    Thereafter troubles multiplied. The Muslim opposition could be con-
tained: it could win wards but not a constituency. More serious was the
sudden surge of discontent within the party itself over the question of
regional representation under the proposed new constitution. The CPP
Ashanti members joined forces in the Assembly with representatives of the
Asanteman Council to demand thirty seats for Ashanti instead of the twenty-
one proposed by the Van Lare committee on representational and electoral
reform. Following a protracted and bitter debate, the committee's recommendations were accepted by the Assembly, but discontent continued in
Ashanti. The Ashanti Youth Association suspended two of its leading members. Amoo-Gottfried and Atta Mensah, the former for signing the Van Lare
report, the latter for voting in favour of the government's Proposals in the
Assembly. A statement was issued saying that the AYA 'holds the view that
in all things affecting the national interest it shall hold itself independent.
It further holds the paramount view that in the recent issue of electoral
representation it shall support a national united front of the Ashanti nation.'
This was one of the earliest reappearances of a phrase—'the Ashanti nation'—
taken up later by the National Liberation Movement and used to rally a mass
opposition to the CPP.[9]
    When the date of the second general election was announced the CPP
found itself in further difficulties. A torrent of applications for the party's
nomination poured into the national headquarters. The Central Committee
laid down the rule that, where possible, the existing Assembly member
should be re-nominated; elsewhere the local constituency organisations were
asked to send a short list of names to Accra for the final decision. But the
party could not hope to avoid division on this basis of selection, with over
seventy vacancies to be filled and a long list of party members in the constituencies who considered that they had at least as good a claim as anyone
else to draw £960 in the new Assembly. As soon as the headquarters
issued its approved list, in April 1954, 'rebel candidates' appeared. Ashanti
was the centre of disaffection, with twenty official candidates and twenty-
seven rebels, in addition to candidates of the opposition Ghana Congress and
Muslim Association parties. The rebels were advised in as strong a
language as the party's leaders could command to withdraw their nomination. Some did—although only two in Ashanti—and were accepted back into the
party as 'prodigal sons'. The rest were publicly expelled from the party by
Nkrumah early in May at a mass Whitsuntide rally in Kumasi.
    By mid-1954 a perceptive observer within the CPP of the political
scene in Ashanti should have been able to advise caution: the Muslim vote in
Kumasi, the outcry over the Van Lare report, and the rank-and-file revolt
in the constituencies were dark shadows cast on the eve of the 1954 election.
But if such advice was given it was ignored. The results of the election,

which gave the party seventy-one seats out of the 104, brushed any criticism aside. In Kumasi the combined opposition/rebel vote in the two constituencies totalled 5, 246 against 17, 355, a sizable minority but hardly a threat; the party also won sixteen of the nineteen rural seats, two going to CPP rebel candidates and one to Dr Busia, the only successful Ghana Congress Party candidate in the country. Few bothered to note the surprisingly high anti-CPP vote in Ashanti as a whole, which reached 41 per cent of the total poll,[10] or to draw a lesson from the north, where the Northern People's Party, formed hurriedly in May 1954, showed how strong the amalgam of local and traditional interests could be by winning sixteen of the region's twenty-six seats.

It is against this background that the sudden rise of the National Liberation Movement in Ashanti should be seen. Precipitated by the government's decision to peg the local cocoa price at 72s a load, despite local constituency promises during the election of £5 a load, the NLM spread rapidly out from Kumasi through the Ashanti states traditionally connected with the Golden Stool. Large numbers of dissident CPP members went over to the new movement. Farmers were drawn in through a sense of grievance over the cocoa price and a re-stirring of traditional loyalty. Chiefs, including the Asantehene, were brought to the forefront of the movement: to them it looked as if the long winter of discontent under the British and Nkrumah was drawing to a close. *Hiems transiit, imber abiit et recessit.* The appeal was as much to the heart as to the head, but the NLM went further than tradition. It not only aroused deep emotions: it had all the characteristics of a mass popular movement. By 1955 the assistant general secretary was quoting Mazzini, saying that the NLM had 'made the people's cause our own; we have taken spontaneously into our hearts the sorrows of a whole generation; a nation is incarnate in us'. This was the nationalism of the CPP taking fresh root, and finding a new growth in local soil.

While voicing its Ashanti appeal, the NLM attempted also to draw in comparable local groups against the CPP. It succeeded with the Muslim Association in Kumasi, which, while remaining a separate body, promised its full support under Alhaji Amadu Baba, Zerikin Zongo.[11] (A smaller group under Mallam Mutawakilu, who had a long-standing grudge against Amadu Baba over the question of funds for the new Kumasi mosque, sided with the CPP.) It failed with the group of Brong states in western Ashanti. But, taken by surprise, its local party organisation shattered; the CPP, for the first time since its formation, was forced on the defensive. Violence broke out in a number of districts of Ashanti as the NLM tried to halt the machinery of negotiation already set in motion by Nkrumah between the Gold Coast and British governments, until Kumasi became, by night especially, a city of policy patrols and armed party gangs. Finally the NLM got its way. The Secretary of State insisted that fresh elections should be held before the final grant of independence, and a date was fixed in July 1956. Voting was farily heavy in Kumasi, the combined North and South constituencies showing a total vote of:

NLM-MAP alliance   19, 447
CPP   11, 956

Such has been the record in Kumasi of the three general elections: a sweeping victory for the CPP in 1951, discontent mounting throughout 1954, and a sudden swing in 1956 to the NLM, which returned Cobina Kessie, an Ashanti standing for the Moslem Association Party, and the late Kurankye-Taylor, a Fanti standing for the NLM. A close analysis of the voting under

these conditions is not easy: too much is masked under the emotions evoked
first by one side and then by the other. But in 1958 municipal elections were
again held in the town; and in the following year the death of Kurankye-
Taylor brought a parliamentary by-election in the Kumasi South constituency.
These two elections were important as being the first major test of party
strengths in Ashanti since independence. The NLM had now merged with
other opposition groups to form the new United Party, but both sides—CPP
and UP—had their loyalist rank and file and a considerable body of supporter
voters in the town. It is to these two elections, against the background of
party developments since 1949-50, that we turn now for an answer to the
question originally proposed: what decides party allegiance and voting
divisions in a town such as Kumasi?

The overall vote in the 1958 municipal elections was: CPP, 22, 660; UP,
18, 586; independents, 209. The UP leaders were greatly dismayed, despite the
narrowness of the margin between them and the CPP: with fourteen seats
against seven, the latter regained control of the municipal council, which they
had lost when a majority of the former CPP councillors went over to the
NLM between 1954 and 1957. Fourteen months later (14 April 1959) the UP
was again defeated in the parliamentary by-election. This time the margin
between the two parties was extremely close, because of the split in the
Kumasi CPP executive between James Owusu and B. E. Dwira over the chairmanship of the municipal council. Dwira was defeated in the council election,
offered the parliamentary nomination, rejected it, changed his mind, found
that he was too late—the nomination having been decided in favour of someone else—and thoroughly annoyed, decided to stand as an independent 'rebel
CPP candidate'. The final voting figures, after a recount, were: CPP, 9, 032;
UP, 8, 653; independent, 1, 339.

We now reach the central questions. The UP lost both elections, but
in both it was successful in a number of wards. *Why did the UP win these
and fail in others? And where did the CPP win the greater part of its support and why?*

In the by-election the UP defeated the CPP in five of the thirteen wards
which make up the Kumasi South constituency; in the municipal elections,
in 1958, it won in three of those five. These three, with the voting figures,
are shown in table 4. Ward 5 starts at Mbrom, a 'superior residential area'
where most of the wealthy Ashanti lawyers and businessmen have their
extremely comfortable homes; it runs across the bottom of Ashanti New
Town and takes in part of Manhyia, to the immediate north of which lie the
Asantehene's palace and offices. *The ward is predominately Ashanti by
origin.* As the name 'Ashanti New Town' suggests, the district is comparatively recent, dating from the end of the post-war reconstruction period of
the 1920s. Most of its families are petty traders, barkeepers, fitters, taxi
drivers, sandal makers and carpenters. (It is a good area, for instance, in
which to buy an elaborately ornamented gold-studded coffin.) Mbrom is an
opposition stronghold. Ashanti New Town is divided almost evenly throughout the district between the two parties, and indeed includes both the UP
and CPP Ashanti regional headquarters. The size of the CPP vote in the
ward as a whole, representing roughly 40 per cent of the votes cast, shows
that the Ashanti vote here at least is divided, the greater part going to the
UP.

Ward 2 is much the same. It centres on Adum, which lies at the heart
of traditional Kumasi. The ward contains a number of very poor compounds
and shanty stores where goldsmiths and ivory carvers still carry on a limited trade; it is also a prostitute district, and most of the girls are sympa-

thetically inclined to the CPP. Adum Street itself and the narrow alleyways which lead off from it are a very tough area where CPP-NLM clashes were frequent and violent during 1955 and 1956. Again the vote is divided: a majority for the opposition, but with an impressive CPP minority vote.

Ward 16, Suame, is solidly UP. In both elections the party had an easy victory, with the CPP at the bottom of the poll in 1959. The ward lies to the north-west of the town, away from the main Zongo area, but it is predominantly Muslim; it is here that the *asante nkramo* live—the Ashanti who follow the Koran, converts to Islam over the past 150 years. Thus antipathy to the CPP stems from a combination of Muslim *and* Ashanti separatism. Local feeling is extremely bitter towards the CPP as the party which banned the Muslim Association Party (by the Avoidance of Discrimination Act in November 1957) and which deported a number of leading Kumasi Muslims after independence. The ward is probably below the average income level for Kumasi; junk yards and tumbledown motor repair shops lie scattered among crude, half-finished houses and shacks. It stands in sharp contrast to Mbrom, its near neighbour and political ally. But any appeal which the CPP might have as the party of the (once) disinherited, or as the party in power which can offer development, falls on deaf ears.

We turn now to the CPP. Gaining ten of the fifteen wards in 1959, like the UP it was overwhelmingly successful (in both elections) in three (table 5). What can one say about these wards? First, that all three are of comparatively recent origin; secondly, *all three are predominantly non-Ashanti*, with a large number of southerners. Ward 3, Bompata and part of Fanti New Town, and Ward 4, New town Ejisu Road, lie towards the centre of the town

Table 4

	1958*			1959*		
	UP	CPP	Ind.	UP	CPP	Ind.
Ward 5	3, 147	2, 257	27	2, 148	1, 264	208
Ward 2	504	487	—	404	359	32
Ward 16	967	535	—	889	161	168

*The uneven size of the wards (in 1958 Ward 5 had 8, 119 registered voters against 1, 385 in Ward 2) is the result of the uneven growth of the city. Neither party has yet sought to alter ward boundaries in its own interests.

Table 5

	1958			1959		
	CPP	UP	Ind	CPP	UP	Ind
Ward 3	1, 013	256	—	708	192	131
Ward 4	1, 011	486	—	668	414	121
Ward 17	579	218	—	298	95	81

and, despite their name, represent an early wave of southern settlement. Ward 17 consists of part of two new housing estates, Kwadaso and Suntreso, where the 1955 *Population Survey* found that out of 247 families enumerated only eighty-eight were of Ashanti origin. Most of these Fanti, Ewe and Gã people are either artisans (carpenters especially) or teachers and clerical workers. On the housing estates, with their neat rows of small two- and three-roomed bungalows rented from the government, the proportion of wage-earning families rises steeply: 79 per cent in the sample survey carried out at Suntresu, with the high average wage income of £17 13s a month. (This may be compared with the *Survey* figures for the Hausa Zongo area in Kumasi North, where the number of wage-earners (in 1955) was found to be 25 per cent of the total families, and the average wage was only £9 a month.) Many of these southern communities are very conscious of the fact that they are 'strangers' in the town, despite the polyglot nature of Kumasi's population. The belief that Ashanti would still dominate the south, if only it knew how, is still strongly held: one hears frequently the charge of NLM hostility towards southerners during the pre-independence time of troubles, and the general complaint that the Ashanti are 'too proud' and 'clannish'.

So we reach the general conclusion that in Kumasi, since independence; (1) the Ashanti vote has been divided between the two main parties roughly in the proportion of 40 per cent CPP and 60 per cent UP; (2) the southern immigrant communities have voted strongly for the CPP; and (3) the Muslims hardly less strongly for the UP. And if the wealthy Mbrom district and the poorer Adum Street compounds are typical, then one can add that the CPP—although the minority party in each area—probably picks up its greatest support from the more humble quarters within the Ashanti wards.[12]

One must be careful not to make too precise a picture out of the results of two elections, within a little over a year of each other, and in so politically volatile a town as Kumasi. There are individuals and smaller minority groups who do not run to rule. Thus Mr Joe Mainoo lives in the upper-class Mbrom district, is a wealthy trader and cocoa buyer, and comes from the royal chiefly house at Ejisu. But he supports the CPP and stood for the party (and lost) in Ashanti New Town ward in 1958. (he is now chairman of the Tema Development Corporation.) Mr J.W. Tsiboe, on the other hand, is a Fanti, long resident in Kumasi, founder and proprietor of the Abura Printing Works, which publishes the *Ashanti Pioneer*, a Kumasi daily broadly sympathetic to the UP. Some Muslims, drawn from several tribal groups, support Mallam Mutawakilu and the CPP—particularly now that Mutawakilu has been made Zerikin Zongo in place of the deported Amadu Baba. And there are other considerations, quite apart from differences between and within each community, which affect the vote, e.g. the fact that the UP leaders are handicapped by lack of funds, in contrast to NLM days, when Stool funds were put at their disposal. One should add, too, that the UP undoubtedly appeals to a small educated minority of both Ashanti and non-Ashanti voters who dislike the growing authoritarianism of CPP politics. The broadening base to the CPP from 1957 onwards can also be explained partly in terms of the attraction of power: there is a strong desire to be on the winning side. Lastly, we should stress that the Kumasi electorate, like that in Ghana as a whole, is an unpredictable one, and what happened between 1950 and 1956, or in 1958 and 1959, should not be taken as an easy guide to what may happen during the next decade.

Despite these cautionary provisions, however, we think that the ward results of 1958 and 1959, following the three general elections, do give a

Table 6

Ward	1958			1959		
	CPP	*UP*	*Ind.*	*CPP*	*UP*	*Ind.*
6A Booth I	164	161	1	169	259	11
6A Booth II	186	192	—	65	50	6
6B Booth I	146	176	—	106	162	8
6B Booth II	130	226	—	88	164	5
6C	129	62	1	87	35	10
6D Booth I	95	269	1	79	187	8
6D Booth II	95	276	1	85	194	5
6E Booth I	257	211	2	145	162	36
6E Booth II	194	203	3	143	166	12
6F	211	206	1	144	169	10
	(1,617)	(1,982)		(1,111)	(1,548)	
6G Booth I	539	79	4	320	66	48
6G Booth II	526	119	17	254	48	28
6H	246	16	—	146	34	9
	(1,311)	(214)		(720)	(148)	
Totals	2,928	2,196	31	1,831	1,696	196

reasonably clear picture of the present pattern of voting. And in further evidence, as a kind of final 'proof'—if the word is accepted subject to the general *caveat* entered above—we set out in table 6 the full details of one ward where the results puzzled us because they seemed to be at variance with the general rule, until we investigated further.

The ward is Asafo, a traditionalist Ashanti area. Yet the CPP won. Why this was so became clear, however, when the ward results were looked at polling booth by polling booth. In both elections the UP had a clear lead over the CPP until the boxes in the last three booths—6G, I and II, and 6H—were opened. Then the vote swung heavily the other way. This, we found, was because the Asafo ward boundaries include a large settlement at New Amakom of Northern, Fanti and Ewe carpenters and motor fitters, whose workshops and compounds stretch back along the Kumasi-Accra road. These *awuna* people, as they are known in Kumasi (a corruption of Anloga, in south-east Ghana, whence the main body of settlers migrated), were an isolated CPP stronghold throughout the period of NLM dominance. And it was this enclave of mainly southern residents within an Ashanti ward which tipped the scale against the UP both in 1958 and 1959.

Postscript

One fact at least stands out clearly from the foregoing: local communities in Kumasi tend to vote as a bloc when they are away from their home area or,

like the Muslim groups, when they feel themselves to be set apart from the
main body of the populace. But despite the rise of the NLM in 1954 Kumasi
is a long way from communal voting. The CPP succeeded there as elsewhere precisely because, from the very beginning of its career, it empha-
sized its national non-tribal character: its 1958-59 vote in the Ashanti
wards of Kumasi was surprisingly high. The same cannot be said with certainty of the UP. As a rough check of the breadth of appeal of each party
one can say that, in the three Ashanti wards examined, the CPP polled nearly
42 per cent of the vote in 1958 (the 1959 by-election is complicated by
Dwira's candidature), the UP just over 58 per cent. In the non-Ashanti
wards the UP percentage dropped to under 27 against 73 for the CPP. This
is something of a shot in the dark, for no one knows exactly how Ashanti
the 'Ashanti wards' are, or how many Ashanti there are in the 'southern
immigrant wards'. But in so far as the ward results are an approximate
guide, and listening to the UP propaganda in Kumasi, with its emphasis on
cocoa and regional rights, it seems reasonable to describe the UP as rest-
ing (in Kumasi at least) on a narrower basis than its opponents.

The accompanying tables show that in each of the elections dealt
with a fairly high percentage of the electorate has not voted; and a few
thousand more must be added to the non-voting figures to include those who
do not even get their names entered on the register. Why are there so
many non-voters? A complete explanation is not yet possible on the evidence available. But, within the limits of the present discussion, three facts
may be noted. First, the poll was higher in the 1958 municipal election
than in the parliamentary by-election a year later: 68 per cent against 49
per cent. Secondly, a comparison between the percentage poll in the CPP-
dominated wards and that in the UP wards in 1958 shows a higher vote
where the CPP is the stronger party:

	CPP majority			UP majority		
Wards	3	4	17	5	2	16
% poll	74	78	61	67	72	53

Thirdly, the drop in the number of voters in 1959 was heavier on the CPP
side (table 7).

What can one say about these three facts? The high vote in 1958 can be
attributed to a determination on the part of the CPP to recapture control of
the municipal council, at the heart of the NLM-UP stronghold. K. A.
Gbedemah, the party's most able organiser, was in charge of the campaign,
and every ward candidate made an extra effort to 'get out the vote'. The
UP was less energetic, and over-sure of its strength. So shaken were its
leaders after their defeat that some of them believed that the government
had printed and imported into the election additional false ballot papers.
We do not think this was so because of the impartial and open way in which
the papers are printed[13] and the need to reconcile the number issued, the
number cast and the number unused. (We would not, however, rule out the
possibility of some impersonation.) The diligent campaign conducted by the
CPP and its experience of electoral organisation (plus its greater financial
strength) probably accounted also for the second fact: that where the CPP
is strong, it is very strong.

Why did the number voting drop so heavily in 1959? The most likely
explanation, in view of the pronounced fall in the 'CCP wards', is the reluc-

Table 7

	Ward 3		Ward 4		Ward 17		Ward 5		Ward 2		Ward 16	
	UP	CPP	UP	CPP	UP	CPP	UP	CPP	UP	CPP	UP	CPP
1958	256	1,013	486	1,011	218	579	3,147	2,257	504	487	967	535
1959	192	708	414	668	95	298	2,148	1,264	404	359	889	161
	64	305	72	343	123	281	999	993	100	128	78	374

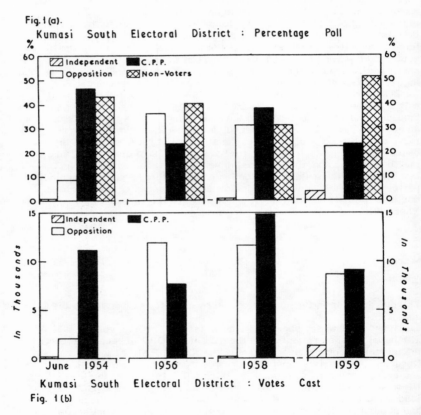

Fig. 1 (a).
Kumasi   South   Electoral   District : Percentage   Poll

Kumasi   South   Electoral   District : Votes   Cast
Fig. 1 (b)

Explanation. Fig. 1 shows the relative party strength in the Kumasi South
electoral district over the period 1954-59. It covers two general elections
(1954 and 1956), one municipal election (1958), and one by-election (1959).
Fig. 1 (*a*) gives the percentage poll, i.e. the votes cast for each party and for
independents expressed as a percentage of the registered electorate, and
fig. 1 (*b*) the votes cast for each party and independents. Before 1954
Kumasi formed a single electoral district, returning one member only to the
Legislative Assembly; from 1954 the town was divided into two electoral
districts, Kumasi North and South, each returning one member.

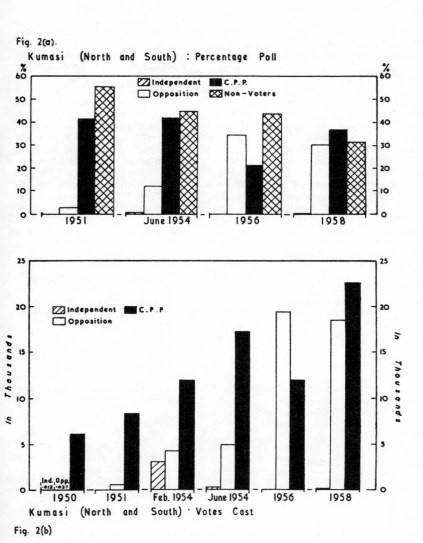

Fig. 2(a).

Kumasi (North and South) : Percentage Poll

Kumasi (North and South) · Votes Cast

Fig. 2(b)

Fig. 2, therefore, shows the relative position in Kumasi as a whole over the period of the three municipal elections (1950, February 1954, and 1958) and the general elections (1951, June 1954, and 1956). Fig. 2 (*a*) gives the percentage poll, and fig. 2 (*b*) the votes cast. We were unable to obtain reliable figures for the registered electorate in the 1950 and 1954 municipal elections; these elections have therefore been omitted from the analysis of the percentage poll.

A final point to note is that 'non-voters' includes a very small number of votes which were cast but not counted, i.e. spoiled papers.

tance of some CPP electors to decide between Dwira, a well known figure in Kumasi and a rebel CPP candidate, and Owusu-Afriyie, a little-known lawyer but the party's official choice. The size of Dwira's vote does not give a fair picture of his position. He was, after all, the most prominent CPP figure in Kumasi during the days of NLM ascendancy and, on that account, was very popular among some sections of the party. It is probable, therefore, that some—perhaps many—CPP supporters, not wishing to choose between Dwira and Owusu, refrained from voting. We were told repeatedly that, had Nkrumah not paid a sudden eve-of-poll visit to Kumasi in a vain attempt to persuade Dwira to stand down, the latter's vote would have been much higher. Nkrumah's intervention probably swung a large vote away from Dwira, but not all of it went to Owusu: some probably refused to vote at all. To support this view one can point to the heavy drop in the CPP vote in Ashanti New Town (Ward 5), and among the non-Muslim Ashanti compounds in the Suame-New Tafo district (Ward 16), where Dwira was particularly popular. If we are right, then, the large number of abstainers is further evidence both of the strength of local feeling in the city and of the remarkable hold that the CPP has on its supporters, who preferred to show their displeasure by withholding their vote rather than by open positive rebellion.[14]

The foregoing does not explain the bedrock of non-voters—those who register (or who are registered by zealous party agents and registration officers) but who are apathetic or busy or sick or away or who dislike the rowdiness of Kumasi politics.[15] Kumasi is very little different in this respect from the rest of the country, and it would be interesting to know who does and who does not vote in Ghanaian elections.

Notes

1   To cast his vote, a registered elector went behind a screen and placed his ballot paper in the box carrying the symbol of the party or independent candidate he wished to support.

2

	Opposition vote*	% of total vote in the area	Seats	Total seats
Southern Ghana	42,602	16	0	44
Rest of the country	256,514	55	33	60

*Opposition here includes independents; that is, all non-CPP votes.

3   There is good historical evidence for such tales. Dupuis, who was the British consul in Kumasi at the height of Ashanti power in 1820, found that along the southern approaches to the city 'every town and village were overawed by a dread of the vengeance of Ashantee, or in strict alliance with that powerful nation.... From the Pra southward, the progress of the sword down to the very margins of the sea may be traced by mouldering ruins, desolate plantations and osseous relics'. See *Journal of a Residence in Ashantee,* London, 1824.

4   1911 census: 18,853; 1921 census: 23,694; 1931 census: 35,839; 1948 census: 78,483; Ministry of Housing 1959 estimate: 101,000.

5   See P. C. Garlick, *African Traders in Kumasi,* 1959, published by the Research Division of the Economics Department, University College of Ghana.

6   Rumours and allegations of wrongdoing by traditional leaders sometimes ran to extraordinary proportions: in 1949, for example, it was believed by many nationalist-minded young men in Kumasi that the Asantehene had conspired with the government and the University College to sell Lake Bosumtwi; the Great Oath of Ashanti had to be sworn to try to convince the populace that a request by geologists to examine the floor of the lake did not amount to an acquisition order for the entire area.

7   T. E. Bowdich, *Mission from Cape Coast Castle to Ashantee,* London, 1819.

8   Deported in 1957.

9   The phrase had also been used at the end of the nineteenth century before the exile of Prempeh, and at the time of the restoration of the Confederacy in 1935.

10   Votes cast—163, 054. CPP, 95, 845; non-CPP, 67, 209, including 37, 582 for the 'rebels'. Six of the eighteen CPP seats were won on a minority vote.

11   Deported in 1957.

12   Voting in Mbrom: 1958, CPP, eighty-nine; UP, 194; independent, three. 1959: CPP, fifty-two; UP, 168; independent, fourteen. Voting in Adum (Ward 2), as quoted earlier, was extremely close.

13   'Impartial and open way' in the sense that party agents of both sides are present during the printing of each set of ballot papers, and take part in the strict security arrangements made for their safekeeping.

14   An additional and simpler explanation of the decreased poll may be that of weariness: it was, after all, the seventh time that the electorate had been asked to go to the polls since the end of 1950. The vote was high in 1958 because it was the first big struggle between the CPP and the opposition after independence. Perhaps the by-election, a little over a year later, over-taxed the readiness of the Kumasi electorate to turn out once again.

15   The CPP vote may possibly have been low in 1956 because of the fear of violence. This is the CPP explanation of its defeat in the two Kumasi constituencies. But support for the NLM came first—the violence afterwards.

V

Elections in an African rural area

What happens when an African tribal community is suddenly brought within a parliamentary system based on adult suffrage? On the surface the process is a familiar one: an election date is announced, parties begin to be active, candidates are chosen, a government information van goes round to explain the procedure of voting, polling day arrives, and the member for X constituency is declared returned. The electorate has made its choice and the new member takes his seat in parliament. But in substance, what happens? What are the issues on which the electorate divides—supposing there is a contest? How does a candidate put himself forward? What should he do, or have in his favour, in order to win? And—the most difficult question of all—how *real* are such contests in the local understanding of what an election is about? The following account is an attempt to answer these questions for the Kassena-Nankanni North and Bongo constituencies in northern Ghana during the 1954 and 1956 general elections.

Political development in the northern region was swift from 1954 onwards. The 1950 constitution enfranchised the north only indirectly: the region returned nineteen members through a central Electoral College in Tamale based on district councils. Then in 1953 the Van Lare commission on representational and electoral reform divided the area into twenty-six single-member constituencies; this was one-quarter of the proposed new Assembly, a rich electoral prize. Parties appeared: the CPP, which already had a regional office in Tamale, although little more than that, and the Northern People's Party. The latter, in its early stages, was hardly a party in the usual sense of the term—it had very little formal organisation outside the Northern Territories Council—and each candidate in the northern constituencies in 1954, whatever party label he adopted as his election symbol, fought his own battle on his own terms. After 1954, however, the scene changed rapidly. Branches of both parties began to be opened in the larger centres of population, and the extent to which parties won support among the educated minority in the north can be seen by a comparison (table 8) between the number of independent and party candidates who stood for election in 1954 and 1956.

The two constituencies which form the particular subject of this paper are in the extreme north of the northern savanna belt—in the poorest area

---

Reprinted from *Africa,* XXIX, 1961, 1-17, with the permission of the publisher. No authorities are cited in this article, the evidence being based on field work carried out during a number of visits to the area between 1954 and 1960. However, I should like to thank Professor Lucy Mair for enabling me to see more clearly the social anthropological situation of the societies whose problems I have tried to describe.

of the least developed region. The district was cruelly laid waste in the half century before the extension of British rule to the north, the local tribal peoples—Kassena, Nankanni, Frafra and kindred groups—being constantly raided by armed mounted adventurers under Songhai and Mandingo leaders. Today the district is thickly populated. One estimate places the population per square mile of farmable land in Bongo at over 450,[1] and the thin top-soil, over-cultivated and under-fertilised, yields barely sufficient millet and guinea corn to maintain even a subsistence economy: in recent years food has had to be imported from neighbouring settlements. A characteristic feature of the district is the spread of homesteads, each with its thirty to forty relatives, living inside a walled compound of neatly thatched huts of puddled mud, and tilling a small acreage of farmland. There are 'towns'—Paga, Chiana, Mirigu, Bongo and others—but with the exception perhaps of Navrongo and the near-by large trading town of Bolgatanga they hardly warrant the name; properly speaking they are market centres which have grown in the shadow of the chief's compound and the District Commissioner's office.

Table 8

	Independents				Party Nominations			
	Candiates			% of total vote	Candi-dates			% of total vote
	dates	Seats	Votes		dates	Seats	Votes	
1954	36	6	60,328	31.3	44	20	132,351	68.7
1956	10	0	8,665	5.8	52	26	140,994	94.2

Election campaiging in such an area calls for skilful understanding. Arguments must be couched in local terms; they must contain points that the elders can weigh carefully, since emotional appeals in the name of 'Self-government' or 'Africa' or 'Freedom' are likely to meet with a blank response. What is important is the support of influential groups, and a candidate will try to enlist on his side the chief, the *tendaana* (or *tigatu* among the Kassena), the clan elders, heads of compounds, the popular young men, and the few wealthy individuals who, because of their wealth, command respect. It means vigorous propaganda through a maze of sandy paths stretching from one homestead to another, sitting down patiently to drink and talk with the elders, gaining approval by coming if possible as the emissary of the chief, enlisting sympathies and arousing emotions along familiar lines of argument, and showing yourself to be a generous, open-handed person.

There is one particular group to win over: the handful of educated young men in each locality. In Bongo in 1954-56 there were only about twenty to twenty-five altogether who could claim to have had any schooling, but they were of enormous importance in the election campaign. In Kassena-Nankanni there were many more, thanks to the work (over nearly fifty years) of the White Fathers' mission. In both constituencies this educated minority acted as voluntary propaganda agents who were listened to by the illiterates as having the mystique of belonging to the outside literate world, and because they held position of key importance in local affairs—clerk to the local council, registrar of the native court, teachers, catechists, letter writers, and so forth. The more active among them had sniffed the national-

ist air from the south in the early 1950s although without knowing quite what
to do about it: a 'Frafra Youngsters' Organisation' was formed in 1951 which
met irregularly in the large market town of Bolgatanga and held debates on
'modern topics'—'the reform of native authorities,' 'parliamentary democracy,' 'monogamy, polygamy, and Christian teaching' and the like; but it was
not until the first party administration was formed under Nkrumah between
1951 and 1954 that parties began to stir in the district.

The Kassena-Nankanni District

As the name implies, we are dealing with two communities—the Kassena
and Nankanni peoples. The district was brought together in 1936 as a native
authority of ten confederated chiefdoms, of which five were predominantly
Nankanni—Navro, Kologo, Naga, Mirigu, Sirigu—and five predominantly Kassena—Paga, Chiana, Kayoro, Katiu and Nakon. The ten chiefs were co-equals
within the federation, a president being elected every three years from
among their number; none of the ten was officially accorded 'paramount'
status: that is, none was gazetted or received the salary of a paramount
chief.
     This was the official position of the federation, and the official status
of its member chiefs. However, the chief of Navrongo in the southern area
of the district gradually gained an ascendancy over the others. Navrongo
is a good market centre where the main road from the south divides west to
Tumu and Lawra along the northern boundary of Ghana, and north to Ouagadougou in Upper Volta. Partly for this reason the town became the administrative headquarters of the whole Kassena-Nankanni area, where the
British District Commissioner had his office and court house. Because of
the presence of the DC and the large market Navrongo was also the earliest
centre in northern Ghana of mission activity by the White Fathers, who
moved there from Ouagadougou in 1906. The Navropio (*pio* = chief) naturally
benefited. Chief since 1945, an astute, self-educated ex-government servant
(a PWD station foreman) of great strength of will, he did everything he
could to emphasise the *de facto* superiority of his state over the other nine
states of the confederacy. The difference between Navrongo and the other
'towns' became more and more marked. Strangers who arrived in the district believed it to be the local 'capital.' Litigants came to have their cases
heard at the District Commissioner's court. Christians bicycled in to hear
mass at the mission church. The market outgrew all other markets in the
neighbourhood, the lorry park was always crowded with vehicles making the
journey between Ougadougou, Tamale and Kumasi.
     Navropio's fellow chiefs watched this growth of Navrongo with a jealous
suspicion. And early in 1951 their fears were increased when L. R. Abavana,
a close associate of the Navropio, was one of the nineteen successful candidates from the Northern Electoral College to the new Legislative Assembly. After an initial period of 'neutral support' for the government,
Abavana joined the Convention People's Party. This was with the support of
the Navropio, who had very early learned the advantage of being a good
government man. To the other chiefs Abavana's election, his membership
of the party and his appointment in February 1954 as a Ministerial Secretary looked like a succession of major triumphs for the Navropio—further
evidence that the latter wished to raise himself about his nominally co-
equal chiefs.
     We must now look at the north constituency within the Kassena-Nankanni
district.

Kassena-Nankanni North

The Van Lare commission divided the Kassena-Nankanni into two constitu-
ences, the electoral sub-districts corresponding to local council areas. The
north constituency was delimited as follows:

	Population
Paga local council area	12, 077
Chiana local council area	9, 059
Kayoro, Katiu, Nakon area	7, 826
Mirigu, Sirigu area	18, 594
1948 census figures	47, 556

The constituency comprises the five Kassena chiefdoms—Paga, Chiana,
Kayoro, Katiu and Nakon—and two Nankanni chiefdoms, Mirigu and Sirigu. It
is the most densely populated of all the twenty-six northern constituencies
and one of the smallest in area: the distance from east to west is approximately fifteen miles, from north to south only six miles.

The announcement of a date (June 1954) for the second general election
saw the CPP and the newly formed Northern People's Party compete for
candidates in the north, although neither had any great knowledge even of its
own supporters in the region. The CPP National executive members, meeting
in Accra, decided that Abavana was the obvious candidate for Kassena-
Nankanni South; but they were less sure of what to do in the north constituency and had neither the time—with over a thousand applications to consider for Ashanti and the southern constituencies—nor the detailed knowledge
to assess the situation in so remote an area. Presumably they took
Abavana's advice, and they offered their support to J. E. Seyire, a local
storekeeper. Seyire had been one of the handful of early CPP supporters in
the Navrongo district who in 1951 felt that loyalty and service should now
have their reward. But the reward he wanted was the party's nomination
in his own area—Kassena-Nankanni *South,* in place of Abavana. The National
Executive continued to support Abavana and told Seyire that it would support
him only in Kassena-Nankanni North. He refused, being quite certain that
he would lose there, and like a great many other party members throughout
the country in 1954 he filed his nomination papers as an independent. The
result of the election in Kassena-Nankanni South was L. R. Abavana, CPP, 5,
796; J. E. Seyire, independent, 3, 344.[2]

This brief account of events in the south constituency has a direct bear-
ing on the election in Kassena-Nankanni North. Here the CPP was unlucky,
for early in 1954 C. K. Tedam, a young head teacher in Paga and one of
Seyire's friends, was also considering standing for the party in the north
constituency. (This was one reason why Seyire refused to stand there.)
Tedam had been attracted to the CPP, partly because of Seyire's own advocacy of the party, partly because he was beginning to be interested in
nationalist ideas. He had already made a name for himself as a member of
the local Kassena-Nankanni district council by bitter attacks on the Navropio, sucessfully resisting the chief's attempt to become both president
and chairman of the council—an attitude which would have earned him the
party's commendation in other parts of the country at this time. When he
heard that Seyire had been told to stand in Kassena-Nankanni North he was
understandably offended. And, like Seyire, he decided to stand as an independent. The CPP was thus left high and dry. But it was determined to have

a candidate in every one of the country's 104 constituencies, cast about for a willing victim, and eventually persuaded Mr Alban Logozure, a local bar-keeper, to stand. He was not a very active candidate, and the result was never in doubt:

C. K. Tedam, independent   6, 880
A. Logozure, CPP   950
(Registered voters, 13, 755—57 per cent poll.)

Support for Tedam cam from every part of the North constituency. At the adoption meeting of district councillors within the constituency he was proposed by the Chianapio, a Kassena chief from the west, and seconded by the Sirigunaba (naba, like pio, means 'chief') a Nankanni chief. He himself was the half-brother of the Pagapio, the most important chief in the northern section. The strength of his position lay partly through his own efforts—as we shall see, he is an indefatigable campaigner—party because of his championship of local interests against the Navropio. The argument used, and well understood, was: the Navropio, Abavana and the CPP are in league and must be checked, and Tedam is a good man to do it.

However, in the interval between the 1954 and 1956 elections the balance of forces within the constituency altered considerably. Tedam joined the Northern People's Party and began to play an active part on the opposition benches. But within his own area cracks appeared in the wall of support given him in 1954. The division was not, as might have been expected, be-tween the Kassena and Nankanni areas but between his own area, Paga, and a rival Kassena group based on Chiana. The list of candidates for the 1956 general election read:

C. K. Tedam, NPP, half-brother to Pagapio
E. K. Ayagitam, CPP, half-brother to Chianapio
V. A. Agongo, independent

The election campaign in July was fought on this basis, as a struggle for power between the Paga and Chiana peoples, the Nankanni area of Mirigu and Sirigu acting as a 'third force'. What had happened?

The outburst of Ashanti and northern 'nationalist' emotion in the period between the two elections had left the Kassena-Nankanni peoples unmoved, despite comparisons drawn by the NPP between the CPP and the slave raiders of the last century. What had impressed them was the outcome of the CPP's victory in 1954 in the south constituency. Abavana was a 'big man' in the government, and he spent much of his time when in the con-stituency impressing the local elders and chiefs with the fact of govern-ment power: there were broad hints that the Navropio would soon be recog-nised as a paramount chief, although nobody seemed to know how far his authority would extend. Such, it was pointed out, was the reward of those who supported the government. ... True, argument along these lines cut both ways: it could be said that there was now all the more reason to oppose the Navropio, and that the simplest way to do it was to go on backing Tedam. But others began to question whether it was really sensible to go on oppos-ing the CPP. Surely it was not too late to turn about? And if the Navropio was to be made a Paramount over the Nankanni area—as some suggested—perhaps there was the possibility of a similar reward in the northern Kassena chiefdoms. Quite apart from the advantages that would accrue, and the possible dangers that would be averted, by being on the side of govern-ment, a change of allegiance might have the effect of checking the Navropio by his own methods.

It was in these terms—it is alleged—and with these arguments that
the Chianapio, a comparatively young, primary-school-educated chief, was
approached and won over by the local supporters of the CPP. He thought it
improper as a chief to stand as a candidate himself but agreed to support
his brother, E. K. Ayagitam, a teacher in the local primary school. In this
way, by the time of the third general election—the second to be fought on a
constituency basis in the north—the long arm of the CPP reached into
Kassena-Nankanni, and it is instructive to note how quickly the correlation
of party and government power was made. What were Ayagitam's—and the
CPP's—chances of success?

Tedam had the weight of population on his side, for his own chiefdom,
Paga, numbered 12, 000, against Chiana's 9, 000. The Chiana people expected
to have the support of their western neighbours, the three small chiefdoms
of Kayoro, Katiu and Nakon (population 8, 000) to whom they were linked by
marriage and proximity. But Paga had *its* near neighbours, the Nankanni
chiefdoms of Mirigu and Sirigu, with over 18, 000. The Chiana camp knew,
therefore, that to succeed it must somehow divide its opponents. Its first
move was to try and gain the support of Namon, a wealthy cattle trader in
Paga, who had twice contested the chieftaincy against the present Pagapio's
family. But at this particular juncture Namon was not to be persuaded. The
Chianas, ably led by Ayagitam and an energetic fellow teacher, Patrick
Amipare, then turned to the Nankanni area. Here they had an initial triumph.
Playing on local ambitions, they persuaded the son of the Mirigu chief to
stand. In this way a serious threat developed to Tedam, who looked upon the
Nankanni chiefs as natural allies. A deputation was sent from Paga, meetings were held with the elders, the traditional gifts of kola and drinks were
offered, and the Mirigu chief was told, 'You are an old man. What will happen
to you and your family with your son away in Accra, even supposing he won?
And if, as is likely, he doesn't win, he will weaken support for Tedam. Then
you will see Chianapio become like the Navropio, always trying to assert his
authority outside his own chiefdom. Is this what you want?' With such arguments the Paga delegation persuaded the chief to withdraw his support from
his son, who then agreed to stand down.

However, the Chianas were not quite finished. A little before the closing
date for nominations they put up Mr V. A. Agongo, a Nankanni from Sirigu,
who was then clerk to the Chiana local council. Agongo stood as an independent and chose as his election symbol a white fish on a blue background.
This was thought to be a subtle move, for Tedam had used the symbol in
1954 and it was hoped that some might vote for the same symbol, believing
it to be Tedam's, in 1956.[3] It was clear by the results of the election, however, that Agongo came much too late to disturb seriously the Paga-Nankanni
alliance.

C. K. Tedam, NPP		5, 775
E. K. Ayagitam, CPP		4, 528
V. A. Agongo, independent		302
	(Registration, 17, 422—67. 4 per cent poll.)	

We turn now to the actual conduct of the campaign.

Polling was carried out over two days in both 1954 and 1956 to enable
the regional administration to make the best use of its meagre staff of pre-
siding officers and polling assistants. The effect was to intensify the campaign by allowing a concentration of effort by both sides, first in the west,
then in the north, and the thoroughness and energy with which the two party

candidates set about the campaign can be seen from the following account by one of Tedam's supporters.

> Things were not as easy in the election as they were in 1954. It was very difficult to forecast the winner.
>
> We set to work at once, called all the councillors[4] in Paga, got bicycles from the NPP Tamale headquarters. One jeep was given to us to use in the Kassena-Nankanni North and South constituencies, Builsa and Bolga.[5] We had little use for the jeep, as it is not easy to travel to the remote places with a car. The councillors and some young men of Paga helped us a great deal, expecting no reward. We made it an issue that it was a fight between the Chianas and the Pagas. We will not like the Chianas to be paramount over us. We would have to walk to Chiana for court cases and pay our levies to them; we made it known that if we allowed the Chianas to win, that means Chianapio would be made a Paramount and would dictate to our chief in Paga.
>
> Owing to this news the whole of Paga went haywire. Enthusiastic representatives from all sections volunteered to help Paga win the elections so that we might not become servants to the Chianas but masters of our own.
>
> Some of these volunteers who had their daughters married to the Nankannis and other sides tried to influence their in-laws to vote for Paga, as it would also take them a longer time to go to Chiana for their cases.
>
> Kola was sent out per leaders of groups for customary greetings... to the headmen in the district.... In the Nankanni area our aim was to convince the headmen, who were very influential. In Sirigu especially we had an assurance from the chief of support. We were not sure in Mirigu until the last two days to the elections. Most of the headmen in Mirigu supported us, but were waiting for a word from the chief, who had not made up his mind as to whom to vote for. The reason why he does not want to tell us his mind was, he said, 'the highest bidder will win the elections'. He said he heard that when they elect MPs to the Assembly we rather go to find fortune for our benefits. That for every mile we travel we claim allowance and because of that he would not tell us his mind....

It was felt to be useless to canvass in Chiana chiefdom itself, 'as they were all under Chianapio's command'. But, just as the Chiana had hoped to divide Paga and Mirigu, so Tedam and his agents tried to wean some of the Katiu, Nakon and Kayoro compounds from Chiana. A key chiefdom was Kayoro. Ayagitam had a strong foothold there through Patrick Amipare, brother of the Kayoro chief. But Amipare had at one time contested the chieftaincy against his brother, and the Pagas believed that this might help them.

> On market day we had a rally in the market with the Kayoro chief as chairman. We invited all the headmen, young men and some influential leaders in the area. We bought about three pots of pito.... The rally was a success.... We slept in the town for two days and at night called on the headmen and explained what Chianapio was trying to do....

The election was fought in acrimonious terms. Close personal ties linked the candidates and their supporters—Amipare was actually Tedam's brother-in-law; the small group of teachers, clerks and storekeepers had all been to school together in Navrongo or to the training college in Tamale; they were all Catholics, meeting together each Sunday, coming together, too, for the extra-mural class at Navrongo, or for tennis in the evening, or the rare cinema show during visits of the mass education teams. Both Ayagitam and Amipare had been active on Tedam's behalf in 1954; their defection—as it looked to Paga—in 1956 aroused bitter feeling.

The course of events after the 1956 election confirmed the worst fears of those who disliked the Navropio and his allies. Abavana, who had defeated Seyire again in Kassena-Nankanni South, was made a minister in Nkrumah's third Cabinet. Fifteen months later (1 November 1957) he was appointed the first party Regional Commissioner for Northern Ghana—a swift rise to fortune: a local schoolteacher until 1951, and six years later the political/administrative head of the largest region in the country. The Navropio did not lag behind. He was recognised by government as a paramount chief in December 1957. Then in November 1958, at the first meeting of the Northern House of Chiefs in Tamale, the Navropio (seconded by Chianapio) was elected the constitutional head of the region, defeating the once powerful Yabumwura of Gonja and the equally powerful Ya-Na of the Dagomba. The Navropio, too, had come a long way since 1951.[6]

The Bongo constituency

Although only ten miles from the large market town of Bolgatanga, the Bongo constituency is a remote one, lying off the main trunk routes. Its peoples speak one of the many cluster dialects of Frafra, and from 1932 until 1952 formed part of the Frafra confederacy of five chiefdoms as an area committee of the large Mamprusi Native Authority. In the latter year the Bongo sub-native authority was replaced by a Bongo local council as part of the Frafra subdivision of the Mamprusi District Council. At the end of 1957 the Mamprusi district was divided into three separate councils: the South Mamprusi, Kusasi, and Frafra District Councils.

The Bona—the chief of Bongo—is chosen from two 'royal' or chiefly lineages—the Anafobissi and Abagnabissi—each of which has a number of subdivisions. The earlier settled peoples live in what one might call the outer, 'rural' area of Bongo, farthest from the eponymous capital, Bongo; it is they who, subject to the chief's authority, provide the *tendaana* of the area. These lineages, with their subdivisions, are important not only in tradition but in modern party political conflicts, and something should be said of the traditions surrounding the origins of the Bongo chieftaincy.

The legend usually recited is of the itinerant warrior Awobgo, to whom the powerful chief at Nalerigu gave a horse and a boy called Anambiliga to help him in his wanderings. Leaving Nalerigu, they came to Borigo, near Bongo. The man died; they boy grew up and married a woman of the area. Later she sat under a bagne tree to rest with her bundles of firewood and there gave birth to twins: a male child whose teeth were already formed, whom she named 'Anafo', meaning 'like a cow' (that is, born with teeth), and a female, whom she named 'Abagne' after the tree. From these two children are believed to be descended the two 'royal' lineages—Anafobissi and Abagnabissi (*bissi* means 'descendants of'). Within memory, nine chiefs have come from the Anafobissi side, five from Abagnabissi; four of the latter have come from one particular subdivision—the Asankabissi of Abagnabissi.

One further point of recent history: in 1942 the Bona, Anane Salibiga, ran into misfortune. A cattle thief was caught near the township of Bongo and brought into the chief's compound. Following customary practice, all those who came to visit the chief took their turn in beating the man, who collapsed and died. The chief was held responsible, tried in the assize court at Tamale, and sentenced to a year's imprisonment with hard labour followed by ten years' exile at Bakoldo in south Mamprusi. In his absence his brother's son, Akumolga—like Anane, of the Asankabissi lineage of Abagnabissi—was appointed regent. Anane was allowed to return in 1947, although not to act as chief until 1952. The former regent, Akumolga, continued to be a powerful figure in the background as president of the native authority court.

The 1954 and 1956 elections

Forty-two delegates attended the Northern Electoral College from Mamprusi in 1951, and of these six, including Mr J. A. Ayinibisa from the neighbouring Tallensi area, were elected to the new Assembly. The election caused very little stir in Bongo and it was not until the first direct elections in June 1954 that parties and candidates appeared. The final list of nominations for the Bongo constituency was:

> W. A. Amoro, independent
> Kofi Akumolga, NPP
> D. G. Akologo, CPP

To understand the growth of party affiliations in Bongo one must go to Bolgatanga, with its great market (held every three days), its row of trading stores, district council offices, police station, hospital, middle school and Catholic mission house. A branch of the CPP was formed in 1950 by R. B. Braimah (a storekeeper) and Jerome Ayema (a letter writer) and their friends about the same time as the Frafra Youngsters' Organisation and a local branch of the People's Educational Association. The small number of educated Bongo young men used to cycle into Bolga' on market days to talk and gossip in the pito bars and to attend meetings of the FYO or an extra-mural class. They met fairly regularly each Sunday to attend mass. In this way political ideas spread into Bongo, and eventually a branch of the CPP was formed there. In these early days, however, it was more like a social club than a political organisation; it would have been difficult to say who was or who was not a member until the election in June 1954 forced this small group of teachers, clerks, traders and the local catechist into two opposing factions which looked round for support.

Kofi Akumolga, the son of the former regent and treasury clerk to the local council, listened to the arguments of Mumuni Bawumia, clerk to the Mamprusi District Council and vice-president of the newly formed Northern People's Party, liked what he heard, and sympathised with the new party's aim of defending northern interests. He wanted to stand for election and agreed to stand for the NPP in Bongo. He knew that he had the support of his father and of those who hoped to benefit should Chief Anane die and be replaced by the former regent. William Amoro also sympathised with the aims of the NPP, and might well have stood for the party but for Kofi Akumolga's prior candidature. An able, energetic former teacher, and now clerk to the Bongo local council, he too wanted to go to the new Assembly. He was also a casual member—as indeed was Kofi Akumolga—of the very loosely organised CPP branch in Bolgatanga and Bongo, but he knew that one of the arguments used with good effect by the NPP against the party was that it was 'anti-chief'. Having good hopes of enlisting the support of Chief Anane, who was sus-

picious of the Akumolga family, Amoro decided to play safe and stand as an
independent. The CPP label (in 1954) would not bring him any votes and
might lose him support. Once again, however, as in Kassena-Nankanni North,
the regional and national headquarters of the CPP decided that any candidate was better than no candidate, and they persuaded D. G. Akologo, a semi-
educated farmer in Bolgatanga, to stand. They paid his deposit and gave him
a small amount of money with which to canvass.

Akumolga and Amoro were the two most likely candidates, by their personal standing, the close relationship which existed between Akumolga and
the former regent on one side, and the alliance between Amoro and the
chief on the other. The elder Akumolga, while regent between 1942 and 1952,
had gained support in some areas by the appointment of a number of heads
of subdivisions of the two chiefly lineages; there were those, too, among the
Anafobissi—the rival royal lineage—who were willing to vote for Akumolga
rather than for the chief's candidate. Both father and son could also rely on
their own close agnates. On the other hand, Amoro had the chief on his
side, he was supported by his own Gunabissi lineage within Abagnabissi, and
he had the greater number of educated young men with him. These included
John Baptist Atubga, the catechist, perhaps the most deeply convinced supporter of the CPP in Bongo, and John Abagre, a lively, intelligent local
council employee, both of whom brought Amoro the support of their own
kin—John Baptist Atubga from the Kuyelengobissi lineage of Abagnabissi,
John Abagre from the Werigurigubissi lineage of Anafobissi. Amoro had the
additional advantage of being able to enlist support on a wide basis through
his mother, who is from the Zagsi people, in the outer 'rural' areas, from
whom the *tendaana* are drawn, and this gave him a valuable foothold among
the non-chiefly—Namoosi, Yareba and Zagsi—lineages.[7]

The picture is a bewildering, complicated pattern of lineage relationships in which the rivalry of Akumolga and Amoro was overlaid with the
older rivalry between the regent and the chief. The two royal lineages were
divided not, as one might have expected, the one against the other—for both
Amoro and Akumolga were from Abagnabissi—but between rival groups
drawn from both, and arranged round the Akumolga family on one side and
the chief's supporters on the other. The non-chiefly lineages in the more
remote part of the constituency did not vote in large numbers; but, where they
did vote, the majority supported Amoro through the influence of his mother's
kin. The educated minority supported him on personal grounds. The result was a narrow majority for Amoro and a mere handful of votes—some
quite possibly through error—for Akologo, who hardly put in an appearance
in the constituency.

W. A. Amoro, independent	2, 201
K. Akumolga, NPP	1, 856
D. G. Akologo, CPP	317

(Registered electors, 8, 208—53 per cent poll.)

A little over a year after he was elected, Amoro—with the permission of
the chief and his friends—crossed the carpet to join the CPP. Then, towards
the end of 1955, Chief Anane died, and a fierce contest for the Bongo chieftaincy took place between the two royal lineages. Three claimants came from
Abagnabissi, two from Anafobissi. Traditionally the Bongo chief is appointed
by the Na-Yiri, the Mamprusi Paramount at Nalerigu, after rival claims
have been argued out by supporters of each contestant. Three months of
canvassing and intrigue followed, with visits and traditional gifts to influential persons at Nalerigu. Finally the Na-Yiri appointed the former regent,

Akumolga. (It was immediately alleged that he had been influenced by his adviser, Mumuni Bawumia, in favour of Akumolga as the father of the NPP candidate.) Once a chief is appointed, however, there is very little the defeated families do about it except retire and bide their time.[8]

Then in May 1956, a month after the instalment of Akumolga as chief, the Prime Minister announced in the Assembly that a third general election would be held in July. Amoro was greatly disquieted. Akumolga, the father of his political rival, was chief; Kofi Akumolga was now clerk to the Bongo local council—a very influential office. Amoro was further embarrassed at this time by the government's decision not to act on its own proposal to divide the large Mamprusi district council into three separate councils. The proposal had been welcomed by Amoro and opposed by the Akumolgas, father and son. It had aroused passionate controversy throughout Mamprusi, not least in the Frafra area, most of the chiefs and elders being in favour of retaining their traditional connection with Mamprusi, most of the younger, literate citizens rather liking the idea of a greater local autonomy.[9] It was not difficult, therefore, to make Amoro and his colleagues appear as enemies of chiefly rule who had tried but failed to weaken the authority of the Na-Yiri, the Bona, and his fellow chiefs.

In Amoro's favour, however, was the fact that the Akumolga family had overreached itself. The father was already ruling with a strong hand. It could be argued that it might be unwise to add to his power by sending his son to Accra. True, Amoro had lost the backing of the chief, and this cost him some support: his vote in 1956 dropped below that for Akumolga in 1954. But the latter's vote also dropped and by a much greater extent, for some of the members of the Anafobissi lineage who had supported Kofi Akumolga in 1954 now held back. Having failed to wrest the chieftaincy from the Abagnabissi lineage in 1955, they did not see why—a year later—they should go on helping the Akumolgas and the Asankabissi division of Abagnabissi. There were others who were puzzled by the announcement that there should be a second election, for Amoro was still alive, and it hardly seemed time to change. Others again were impressed by the visit of Nkrumah during his quick pre-election tour of the north. So Amoro was again elected, although in a much reduced poll:

W. A. Amoro, CPP   1,760
K. Akumolga, NPP   1,225
     (Registered electors, 8,435—35 per cent poll.)

General conclusions

What does one need to win? This was one of the questions posed at the beginning. Is it possible now to answer for Kassena-Nankanni and Bogo?

The chief? Certainly his help is extremely useful. Tedam would have found it difficult to contest without Pagapio's support; so would Abavana in Kassena-Nankanni South without the Navropio. In these areas the chief still has authority over others and there is hardly any point in discussing whether or not chiefs should 'take part in politics': he is there to give guidance and to represent the community in everything that affects it. But it is possible, as Amoro found, to run counter to the chief's wishes and still be successful. An able candidate can use local rivalries arising from personal jealousies and long-standing rivalries between lineages. In Bongo especially, where the dispute took place within the area of a single chiefdom, Amoro was able to use a latent anti-chief attitude. The various lineages had a watchful eye

on Akumolga in 1956. He was respected, obeyed, even feared, but a jealous
suspicion was there below the surface and was used by Amoro with good
effect.

Money also is important. There is no law restricting the amount each
candidate may spend, and the regulations prohibiting 'treating' are ineffec-
tive. Most members of parliament will admit that elections are extremely
expensive: you have to spend to win, and you have to pay back what you have
borrowed whether you win or not. One estimate of election expenses in-
curred by an unsuccessful candidate in one of the northern constituencies
came to £800 in 1954 and £600 in 1956. In the south he would probably be
considered fortunate to have escaped so lightly. But money is needed not so
much to buy votes as to ensure goodwill. If a rally is held on market day
the candidate must earn the approval of a lively crowd of possible supporters
by supplying generous quantities of local beer; dancers, drummers, pipers
may be asked to perform, and the candidates must reward them. Someone
may have died—the relatives must be consoled in a practical way; someone's wife may have given birth—and the family must be honoured. These
are customary practices, except that what may have been adequate even in
recent times is no longer so today: the double handful of kola has to be
supplemented by beer or minerals or, for the 'big man', whisky. All this is
very expensive, quite apart from the cost of transport and the maintenance
of election agents. Practically nothing comes from the party headquarters—
at least in Bongo and Kassena-Nankanni—except the loan of a propaganda
van. Money for the election has to be raised locally. The area is wretchedly
poor, but there are a few comparatively rich individuals, including, of course,
the chief.

Religion? In neither election was religion of importance, except in one
minor respect in Bongo, where the formation of the Frafra Youngsters' Organisation and the CPP was probably promoted by common membership
of the Catholic Church, which helped to draw the educated and illiterate
leaders together; association meetings were often held after mass on Sunday
morning in Bolgatanga.[10] (Perhaps one should add that the Church merely
provided the opportunity for members to meet regularly together; in the
north-west, in the strongly Catholic area of Nandom, a similar development
happened *vis-à-vis* the formation of a branch of the NPP.) Despite fifty
years of strong Catholic influence, traditional animist beliefs are still
widespread. There is a belief throughout the area in sympathetic magic.
Thus every Kassena has his crocodile in the village pool at Paga. The
creatures bask fearlessly at the water's edge and, with equal confidence,
the women and children come to wash their clothes in the muddy water. It
is believed that any injury to a villager means a similar injury to his crocodile; to shoot a crocodile would mean the dealth of somebody in the village.
In the Kayoro area there is a river which has the magical property of be-
stowing wealth on any suppliant who is prepared, in exchange, to endure
childlessness. But no one is sinister or naive enough to try and use such
beliefs for political ends. When, some time after the election, I suggested
(light-heartedly) that one way to win might be for a candidate to try and
seize his opponent's crocodile and keep it in seclusion until after the election campaign, the chief laughed and said, 'No, it doesn't work like that.' Quite
clearly, like many people, the Kassena-Nankanni have learned to live in two
worlds, centuries apart in thought. Similarly Islam, although a minor political
force in some northern constituencies, played no part in either Kassena-
Nankanni or Bongo. There are perhaps thirty to forty Muslims in the two
constituencies who are either 'strangers' from Bawku or south Mamprusi,

or cattle traders who have entered Islam along with their profession. But they play no part in election politics.

Nor, surprisingly perhaps, do the women. They vote in good number. In 1954 in Kassena-Nankanni North, out of the 13,755 who registered, nearly 5,000 were women. Many of them enjoy a measure of financial independence through the sale of garden produce and pito. Brewing is a women's job. But it is asserted, even by the women, that generally speaking they vote the way the compound or village votes, the decision being left to the compound head and elders, the *tendaana*, the locally acclaimed leaders of the young men and other—male—sections of society.

Two final questions remain to be answered: the influence of parties, and the reality of elections by ballot in such areas.

Party *organisation* was a very elementary stage in both constituencies. In 1956 the party candidates had their deposits paid, and leading politicians of both sides paid visits to the two constituencies. But the candidates were still very much their own masters. Neither in Kassena-Nankanni nor in Bongo was there any formal party machinery—no office, no paid officials, no local manifestoes. Amoro was the only regularly paid-up member in Bongo in 1956—having his party subscription deducted monthly from his salary as an Assembly member. The candidates relied on personal followers who were either their kinsmen or schoolfellows (and often both). The following extract shows how one of Tedam's 'agents' went about his self-appointed task:

> In Paga the clerk to the local council, half-brother to Tedam and also a prince in Paga, acts as his agent. He is very influential. He goes round to the outlying villages on each of the market days to collect taxes from the people and takes the chance to tell the people what Tedam is doing and what would happen if they became CPPists.

Much depends also on the candidate. He too must go the rounds whenever he returns home—and in Ghana the candidate usually has his home and family in the constituency; he must visit the influential leaders of each group of compounds, hold a rally in the market place, and reward those who gave him their support.

> The chiefs, *tigatine*, the headmen and *biepio* take very little notice of what is happening in the National Assembly unless it is something concerning the Kassena-Nankanni area. They look forward to getting some presents such as drinks and cloth. The less you give the more you lose your popularity. The masses must be given pito and kola.

Thus the successful candidate must try and live up to his campaign promises: he is regarded by many of his constituents as an investment, and he will be asked for jobs or scholarships or for help in local disputes, often far beyond his capacity to satisfy all those who, having helped him to become an Assembly member, now expect something in return.

Yet parties were important. Although outwardly very similar, the two elections, from a party point of view, showed an important shift in emphasis. When, for example, Ayagitam in Kassena-Nankanni North wanted to stand for election everyone knew that he would stand for the CPP. Indeed, but for the party he might not have stood. It was recognised by 1956 that parties were more than labels, that they were avenues to power not only remotely in Accra, but in Kassena-Nankanni and Bongo. This awareness was quickened after 1956 when Amoro became a Ministerial Secretary in February 1958 and Abavana a Regional Commissioner at the end of 1957. From 1954 onwards we see the same process taking place on a small scale as took place throughout the country—we see the party rewarding its friends and making life uncomfortable for its opponents. Ideas move slowly in areas like Kassena-Nankanni and Bongo, but the understanding spread that members of parliament are important people, particularly if they are on the winning side. There were many now, including chiefs like Pagapio, who began to argue that the sensible way to behave was to show one's loyalty to the new government by joining the party. 'The CPP is strong.' 'They can do anything.' 'They are the new white men.' These were the sort of phrases used, and eventually they had their effect. In June 1958 Mumuni Bawumia, with two other NPP members from Mamprusi, crossed over to the government side. They were followed later in the year by Tedam.

Secondly, the question of understanding: did they know, in Paga and Chiana and Bongo, what they were voting for? At first sight one is inclined to say 'no': there are not more than a dozen people in Kassena-Nankanni, and less than that number in Bongo, who could have explained the difference in 1956 between what the CPP wanted and what the Ashanti National Libera- tion Movement/NPP alliance meant when it campaigned for federation. An attempt *was* made to explain the issue in Kassena-Nankanni North:

> In the 1956 election we had the backing of the NPP. We invited some of their leaders to speak—the Tolon-Na, S. D. Dombo, Mumuni Bawumia. They told the people that the CPP were against the chiefs, that the northerners are going to be used as tools for the benefit of the southerner. We should stand firm, otherwise the CPP will use us as Samory and Babatu did our forefathers in the olden days. It was the aim of our leaders to get our own Assembly where we should have full control of our money.

This was as far as the federation-unitary argument went and, as we have seen, the result in each constituency depended on conflicts born of local disputes. Amoro himself was under no delusion. Having walked out with the opposition when the Assembly debated the appointment of a Select Com- mittee on Federal Government and a Second Chamber in protest against its membership, he then decided to give evidence before it. He was at this time in the process of moving over to the government side. The following ques- tions were put to him by the committee, and his answers give a very good picture of the level of understanding in his constituency:

1302. Which constituency do you represent?... The Bongo constituency.
1303. Is this view of federalism your personal view or is it shared by your constituency?... This is my personal view.
1304. What is the feeling of your constituency with regard to this matter? ... The people of my constituency are almost all farmers and have little idea of what government involves.
1305. Are you suggesting that they do not know what is going on at all? ... No.
1306. At least there are some who can understand government, though per- haps only a few?... There may be.
1307. Are they not interested? ... The few who can understand it may be, and they may support or condemn federalism in accordance with how they have been convinced by its advocates.
1308. In your opinion which view of federalism is supported by the majority in your constituency? ... I cannot judge.

1309.   Do you mean you cannot tell us the general reaction of the people in your constituency regarding these questions?... No, I am afraid.

1310.   What happens when you, as their representative in the Legislative Assembly, go back to explain to them any Government programme; don't they do anything to indicate their approval or disapproval of the particular Government plans or measures you talk to them about?... Sometimes they feel pleased with certain matters and at other times they feel displeased.

1311.   Yes; all we want to know is what they feel about these two questions of federalism and a second Chamber?... Most of my people favour a unitary system of government.

1312.   Do you mean they agree with the views you express to them on these questions and therefore favour a unitary system of government? ... Yes.

This paints the picture admirably. But it does not make the election meaningless. The candidates knew the national issues, the electorate knew—and knew intimately—the candidates. The idea of elections as a struggle for power between rival groups was well understood. Admittedly the contest was fought within a local framework of references, quarrels between chiefdoms and lineages being given a fresh look, and with new vigour from the party conflict between Tedam and Ayagitam, Amoro and Akumolga. But these, in turn, gave depth to the struggle between the candidates. It might perhaps be argued that, even if elections are understood, the idea of representation is not; that, such is the nature of election contests in areas like Kassena-Nankanni and Bongo, the losing side, having lost, will feel that they have lost everything; that Tedam and Ayagitam, Amoro and Akumolga were protagonists in a conflict which was irreconcilable. But this, too, was probably not the case. Traditional society had a great ability to 'return to laughter' after a period of conflict, and there is no reason to doubt the ability of the Anafobissi and Abagnabissi sections, or the Paga and Chiana chiefdoms, to adjust themselves to the new fact of parliamentary contests. Already the suggestion is heard in both areas that if one section of the community supplies the members of parliament at one time, then the honour and

Table 9

	(1) Total population	(2) Aged 21 and over	(3) Registered voters	% (3) of (2)
Paga	12,707	6,811	4,732	69.5
Mirigu/Sirigu	18,594	9,996	5,015	50.2
Chiana	9,059	4,856	3,973	81.8
Katiu, Kayoro, and Nakon	7,826	4,195	3,702	88.2
	48,184	25,858	17,422	67.4

Source. Based on the 1956 *Digest of Statistics:* twenty-one and over = 53.6 per cent of the total population in the north. The population figures are, of course, subject to the approximations made in the 1948 census; the 1960 census figures are not yet available on a district basis.

office ought to go to the other side on future occasions, although whether such a solution may suit party headquarters is another matter.

Finally, a general point to be noted, of technical interest and of great importance to parties in Ghana, is the size of the electorate. Registration is not automatic: a would-be voter has to apply and make sure during the time allowed that his name is on the register. Much therefore depends on the zeal of the candidates' agents long before the election. In the 1956 Kassena-Nankanni election Tedam was out-generalled in this respect by his opponent, as may be seen from table 9.

Thus Paga and its allies, pro-Tedam, with an eligible electorate of over 16,000, registered under 10,000, or 58 per cent. The Chiana group, pro-Ayagitam, registered nearly 7,700, or 84.8 per cent, out of a possible 9,000.

In Bongo the vote is seen to be extremely small once the factor of non-registration as well as non-voting is taken into account.

1954	(1) Twenty-one and over	21,591
	(2) Registered	8,208—38%
	(3) Voters	4,374—53% of (2)
		—20% of (1)

1956	(1) Twenty-one and over	21,591
	(2) Registered	8,435—39%
	(3) Voters	2,985—35% of (2)
		14% of (1)

Amoro owed his election to a narrow majority of a very small minority vote: in 1956 to a majority of 535 in a poll of under 3,000, or approximately 14 per cent of the total eligible electorate.

There is clearly every possibility of change in both constituencies.

Postscript

The April 1960 plebiscite on the draft republican constitution, and for Dr Nkrumah or Dr Danquah as President, showed that there were still two sides to political issues in these distant constituencies.

	For the constitution	Against the constitution	For Nkrumah	For Danquah
Kassena-Nankanni North	8,489	1,244	8,524	1,156
Bongo	3,001	774	2,953	783

Notes

1   T. Hilton, Department of Geography, University College of Ghana, 1958.
2   Two other independent candidates each polled between 600 and 700 votes.
3   Tedam used the clenched-fist symbol of the NPP in 1956.
4   Of Paga Local Council.
5   I.e. Bolgatanga.
6   The Na-Yiri of Mamprusi, traditionally the most important chief in the north, was also put forward as a candidate but failed to find a seconder.

Voting was: Navropio, fifteen; Yabumwura, six, Ya-Na, six. The Chianapio, too, as a member of the regional House of Chiefs, might be considered to have done well for himself. In his inaugural address the
Navropio appealed 'not only to you, members of the House, but to each
and every one in this region to give our government his or her unfail-
ing support and loyalty in all matters. If we support the government,
the government will help us in all our needs; but if we don't, we should
not expect the government to help us. God helps those who help themselves.' The concentration of power in Kassena-Nankanni was still continuing when I revisited the district early in 1960: one of the Navropio's
relatives was the party-appointed District Commissioner, another was
the acting superintendent of the local Builders' Brigade camp, a third
was the newly appointed lay magistrate for the area.

7   But not in the Via district, where Kofi Akumolga had married the
    daughter of the Vianaba.

8   Mr Amoro himself commented on this: 'This practice of keeping mute
    even when dissatisfied is undergoing reform, and people are beginning
    to speak up for their rights.' The idea of 'destoolment' is spreading
    from the Akan area into the north under the gruesome title of 'deskin-
    ning'. Thus charges were brought in 1959 against the Ya-Na of Yendi
    and a 'deskinment case' committee of inquiry appointed to look into
    it.

9   There was a certain administrative justification behind the proposal,
    Mamprusi being a very large district council area, but it was regarded
    generally as a political move aimed at Mumuni Bawumia and the Na-
    Yiri. A commissioner was appointed to inquire into the merits of the
    case, and his recommendations that the proposal be abandoned were
    accepted by the government.

10 Bongo CPP, 1956: chairman: Joachim Agilogo, Roman Catholic illiterate
    farmer, grandson of a former chief; secretary: Felix Anongyele, Roman
    Catholic, teacher; treasurer: John Baptist Atubga, Roman Catholic,
    catechist.

VI

Ghana in 1964

Thirteen years ago the first general election was won by a nationalist party whose leader was in prison, convicted of inciting public disorder in defiance of emergency regulations. Released in February 1951, he took office immediately as Leader of Government Business, becoming Prime Minister the following year. Now in 1964 Nkrumah is President of a legally constituted Convention People's Party republic. There is this much continuity, therefore, about the Ghana scene. The same leader and party have dominated politics during the past decade, winning three general elections before independence in 1957. In addition there have been two plebiscites, one in April 1960 prior to the introduction of the republic, the other in January this year to secure approval for amendments to the 1960 constitution. The more recent plebiscite was an impressive demonstration of State power, brought to a pitch by absurdity: 'yes' votes, 2, 377, 920; 'no' votes, 2, 452. Nkrumah now has the power to dismiss judges of the Supreme Court 'at any time for reasons which appear to him sufficient' and it has been decided that there shall be only 'one national party in Ghana'—the CPP. In their beginning is their end. The former prisoner now controls the judiciary, the nationalist party has become the State. But where will they actually end ?

Despite the power of the regime, it is difficult not to wonder whether it will be able to surmount its present difficulties, which are very great. Power on this scale leaves its scars, and a list of its victims shows the extent of the damage inflicted. The Chief Justice was dismissed in December last year after the acquittal of two former Ministers and the executive secretary of the CPP on charges of conspiracy. The Commissioner of Police and nine of his senior officers have been relieved of their duties, two of them being detained in prison, presumably (though no charges were laid) on grounds of their suspected involvement in the attempt to assassinate Nkrumah on 2 January 1964. Senior members of the University of Ghana have been deported and students detained or threatened with a withdrawal of their grants. J. B. Danquah, who contested the presidential election in 1960, is back in prison under the Preventive Detention Act. Others (including a number of journalists) have been there since 1958 and must now face the prospect of a further five or ten years' detention without trial. Former CPP Ministers are in exile (e.g. Gbedemah), or in prison (e.g. Ako Adjei, formerly Foreign Minister, and Tawia Adamafio, who once seemed unassailable as Nkrumah's adviser), or dismissed (e.g. F. Dra Goka, a former Finance Minister): their duties have been absorbed by a gross enlargement of the Presidential Office. A blanket censorship exists, and the borders are closed against all three neighbouring African States.

What explanation can be suggested of this excited state of affairs? Two arguments are worth considering.

The first is that put forward by the Nkrumah and his attendant followers, some of whom are now in prison. It runs as follows. The State must be protected and the regime defended against forces seeking to undermine the independence of the country. Like most Third World countries, Ghana is a penetrated State, a potential victim of transnational power: neo-colonialism is not a mirage projected by internal fears but a reality threatened by external interests. Africa is particularly vulnerable, as may be seen from the assassination of Sylvanus Olympio in neighbouring Togo, the intervention of foreign troops in the Congo, the plight of many of the former French and Belgian colonies and the universal dependence of newly independent States on the loan agencies and capital markets of the great powers. To these external alarms have to be added local threats within Ghana itself, financed and directed from abroad. Over thirty people have been killed, more than ten times that number injured in acts of public murder at CPP meetings. There have been two attempts to assassinate Nkrumah which, if successful, would have led to tribal divisions and communal violence: development plans would then have been crippled and the dynamism for economic growth lost. Desperate ills call for desperate remedies. The CPP must mobilise the people, and if the process is painful, that is the need of the revolutionary position the party must occupy as 'the democratic instrument of the people's will and inspiration'.[1] Discipline must constrain freedom, and 'even a system based on social justice and a democratic constitution may need backing up, during the period following independence, by emergency measures of a totalitarian kind'.[2]

Against this argument may be set another. Even, it may be thought, at the level of self-interest Nkrumah and the CPP are behaving foolishly and are likely to become the authors of their own downfall. They have tried impossibly to monopolise power, the effect being to spawn a clandestine, often murderous, opposition. The cry of 'the republic in danger' and of 'the revolution betrayed' is absurd: the 'revolution' was that of a nationalist movement against a mild colonial power: it succeeded by holding in balance a number of collective interests, some traditional, some new, some institutionally based, others expressed politically through parties, unions and farmers' organisations. The skilful maintenance of this balance is much more likely to be the precondition for survival of Nkrumah and the CPP than current attempts to impose a single-party uniformity. The colonial State which the party took over in 1951 may not be a strong focus of loyalty but nor is it in any danger from those indifferent to, or distinct from, or opposed to, the CPP. The pre-independence struggle derived from the prospect of power being placed before a number of competing groups, but there are no good grounds for supposing, were even the former opposition to come to power, that it would try to dismantle the colonial structures of control. Indeed, much the greater danger lies precisely in Nkrumah's weakening of the institutions of State authority— the judiciary, the civil service, the police and the armed forces. Even interference from outside—and where is there evidence of any serious measure of 'penetration'?—is more likely to succeed in a situation of inefficient suppression than among legitimately established groups competing openly in parliament and at free elections. There is, to be sure, an argument which stresses the danger that political competition will extend popular expectation beyond the public resources of the State—an argument drawn from rather imprecise notions of breakdown in countries overburdened, or 'overloaded', with demands. Yet whatever the case may be in some Third World States, it is difficult to believe that a failure to be able to respond to all that was once predicated of the national movement presupposes the breakdown of Akan society or the Ghanaian State. There is a strong continuity of political and social life (and, one might add, a patient enduring of broken promises) at village, chiefdom and district level, the collective expression of which is quite capable of sustaining a national framework of control. To govern loosely is not necessarily to govern badly, whereas to try incompetently to rule ruthlessly from the centre is likely to produce threats to the nationalist party much more real than those it now evokes to justify the misuse of its power.[3]

Notes

1   Nkrumah, *Autobiography*, ix-x, London, 1957.
2   *Ibid.*

3   Threats primarily, of course, from the armed forces. In December 1958 there had been the mysterious, muffled attempt at what may have been a *coup*. Major Ben Awhaitey was commandant of the army camp in Accra when he confided to a junior officer that he had been approached by two members of the United Party opposition to 'organise a *coup d'état*'. He was brought before a court martial and a commission of inquiry which was unable to reach a unanimous verdict on the main charge. Awhaitey and the opposition leaders—R. R. Amponsah and M. K. Apaloo—were then held under the Preventive Detention Act. For the details see *Politics in Ghana, 1946-60*, appendix B.

VII

'Opposition' in Ghana

I

At independence in 1957 Ghana was, outwardly at least, no different from other former British colonies of that time. It was governed by a Westminster style of constitution and the interplay of two parties whose leaders had publicly declared that they would agree to differ. Thereafter there was a progression towards monopoly control as the CPP bullied its opponents out of existence to establish a situation in which Ghana was very little different from other African States. There were several points of failure during these six or seven years, but the most noticeable collapse was that of the opposition. It was resurrected, in a sense, by the *coup,* and it may benefit directly if there is a return to civilian rule; but between 1957 and the coming into force of the single-party republic it died a quick death—a remarkable collapse from its high state of fortune in 1956, when it had thirty-two seats of the 104 in parliament and 43 per cent of the votes in the last election before independence.

By opposition I do not mean the man with the gun, or the anti-party group, or the experiment in internal party competition of a limited sort in Tanzania. I mean opposition of the kind that the Westminster model implies—politically distinct, independently constituted, openly active, and with some hope of becoming one day a government. Despite the constitutions agreed to at independence, there is no such opposition party in Africa north of the Zambezi today, with the possible exception of the Gambia.

There are, to be sure, broken categories of opposition groups—minor parties, left over, as it were, from independence, without any immediate or distant prospect of office. In most States, such parties are tolerated because they are unsuccessful, and were they to look like becoming successful they might not be tolerated. One is reminded of the comment by Horace Walpole: 'one or two such victories by the Opposition, as Pyrrhus, the member for Macedonia said, will be the ruin of us; I look upon it now that the question is Downing Street or the Tower'. Examples of such frail parties are quite numerous. They include Kenya, Uganda, Madagascar, Zambia, Lesotho, Botswana and, until recently, Senegal. But the general direction is clear. It is towards a formal concentration of power in the hands of the single party or, it may be, the military junta. In addition, of course, there are the forbidden opposition parties which try to function in exile or in hiding: nothing unusual there in this modern world.

A formal concentration of power. Such is the general picture, although

Opposition in the New African States, collected seminar papers, Institute of Commonwealth Studies, London University, 1967-68, and *Government and Opposition,* II, 1967.

there is always hidden opposition within the single party—within the military too—and no doubt one could draw out a spectrum of States in which oppositional factions exist to a greater or lesser extent. In Tanzania they are allowed to function during elections. In Senegal they are said by Mr Donal O'Brien to have a recognisable identity. In Ghana, too, the outward cloak of disciplined unity under the CPP was always ragged. It was quite unable to hide the rivalry of the very many opposed groups, some ethnic, some local, some institutional, including the Assembly members versus the party bureaucracy versus the TUC versus the Farmers' Council versus the civil service, etc. As we know now, there was rivalry too between parts of the army and the President.

II

The scene can be set in this way and it does not tell us very much, except to record the almost total failure of the imported Westminster model. But that too is interesting. It seems to have been quite easy for leaders to dismiss the constitutional agreements signed at independence as irrelevant to the actual business of governing. The documents were quickly scrapped in favour of what appeared to the new Presidents to be more manageable systems, and the opposition parties were eliminated by purchase or suppression, and then legally forbidden. The situation is markedly different from that in a number of non-African Commonwealth countries which are newly (or recently) independent. Opposition parties exist in India, Malaysia and Ceylon; in Malta too, and the 'Commonwealth Caribbean'. Why not in Africa, and why did the opposition cease to exist in Ghana?

Yet there is a prior question. Why should *any* government, whether African or not, tolerate serious challenge to its rule? There is no clear answer. Suppose we turn for help to Professor Dahl.[1] He starts from the reasonable assumption that a government will (and has) always coerced its opponents except when it believes that it cannot succeed in doing so, or that 'even if the attempt were to succeed, the costs of coercion would exceed the gains'. The second hypothesis is a little doubtful, as Dahl recognises, since a government may act regardless of the consequences. What, therefore, restrains some Western and a few non-Western governments? Dahl's answer is as follows.

> Among other things, one surmises, are matters of belief, ideology, values. Costs of coercion rise, one may assume, whenever elites and the general population of a country develop a sense of nationhood that includes the opposition; a distaste for violence; a commitment to a liberal ideology; or economic and social goals that require internal stability. Finally, once a system that permits peaceful party opposition is highly institutionalised and surrounded with legal protections, the costs of destroying it are likely to be extremely high. For a government can destroy the opposition only by wrecking the constitutional system. At this stage of evolution, to destroy the opposition requires a revolution. And the costs of revolutions often run high.

It is not difficult to agree with these observations: but it seems to me that they raise more questions than they answer—a familiar reaction on my part to generalisations grounded on schematic data. Dahl's arrangement of the different forms that opposition may take, and his list of the principal causes of such variety, are interesting. I set them out in a long footnote.[2] But he is concerned primarily with the data drawn from ten 'Western

democracies', and I find it puzzling to know how to apply his classifications
to African States; for, as Dahl comments:

> These speculations as to the introduction and maintenance of a system
> of peaceful opposition suggest two further observations. First, the
> conjunction of the necessary factors depends heavily on historical
> developments over which it is difficult to exercise precise control.
> Second, the rise and conjunction of the appropriate factors take *time;*
> until now, stable systems with legal oppositions have evolved rather
> slowly. It is by no means clear whether or how the process can be
> deliberately contrived or greatly speeded up.

If Dahl is right, the task of saying anything very sensible about 'the introduction and maintenance of a system of peaceful opposition' in the newly
independent, colonial-created African States is particularly difficult. There
are no settled patterns of political belief or behaviour, and the span of
independent life is still too short to enable one to be confident about what is
likely to endure.

III

Having posted warning notices about the dangers of generalisation, let me
now try my own hand at the problem. There are, perhaps, a number of common difficulties facing the *maintenance* of a legal opposition over a large
part of the African continent.[3]

Practical difficulties

They include a lack of patronage, lack of funds, lack of access to information and to mass media. The government has so much to offer to that relatively small elite of educated citizens who dominate the political scene. It
is these (and other) practical difficulties which may account for a good deal
of the unimpressiveness of many African opposition parties even when they
are allowed to operate. The difficulties are not peculiar to Africa or to
contemporary politics. Many of them are set down in Bolingbroke's stric-
tures[4] on the shortcomings of the opposition in his day:

> They who affect to head an Opposition, or to make any considerable
> figure in it, must be equal at least, to them whom they oppose; I do not
> say in parts only, but in application and industry and the fruits of both;
> information, knowledge and a certain constant preparedness for all the
> events that may arise ... They who would engage in opposition are
> under as great obligations to prepare themselves to control, as they
> who serve the Crown are under to prepare themselves to carry on the
> administration; and a party formed for this purpose do not act like good
> citizens nor honest men unless they propose true, as well as oppose
> false, measures of government.

All very true—but it is easier said than done.

Moral difficulties

The difficulty of resistance to cajolery, thuggery and enticement, particularly in States where independent incomes are hard to come by. These
devious practices, of a sort that even relatively liberal governments are
likely to engage in, are not, of course, unique to Africa—as the long careers
of Sir Thomas Playford in South Australia[5] and Maurice Duplessis in
Quebec[6] show very well.

Inherited difficulties

(a) *Traditional rule*. The structure of traditional society, including the deep-seated desire to preserve 'tribal solidarity' by a process of consensus, and the avoidance of open competition for office, have all been evoked at one time or other to explain the movement towards single party rule. (They have also been evoked by Busia, *Africa in Search of Democracy*, to condemn single-party government.) The problems raised by such arguments are not easy to resolve: how does one transfer beliefs and actions from colonial/traditional society to the national level of party politics ? And, how does one reconcile the very large differences in traditional practice—Wolof, Hausa, Tiv, Ibo, Akan, Bemba, Tutsi ? 'Tradition' becomes a coat of many colours, useful to conceal but unconvincing as an explanation of current modes of behaviour.

(b) *Colonial government*. Here too is an old fable: the new Leader, it is said, is the old Governor in nationalist dress. If, by this, one is simply saying that for the greater part of colonial rule there was little to accustom ordinary people to the idea of opposition, including that of an alternative government, then that is probably right—although most colonial governments were more mild in their treatment of the press, political parties, trade union action, farmers' protests, etc, than most nationalist party governments have been. Moreover it is interesting that the ex-colonial States which have sustained a constitutionally protected, two- or multi-party system are those with the longest experience of British rule.

(c) *Nationalist claims and fears*. Nationalist parties, by nature, tend to be all-inclusive, laying claim to the whole nation. Opposition to the nationalist movement was equated with treachery, prior to independence, and with treason and neo-colonialism after independence had been achieved. Since there is often a powerful strain of local and/or ethnic interests in the make-up of many of the opposition parties—and in that of many internal factional groups—their leaders are also open to the charge of 'tribalism'. If one adds to this mixture of genuine and pretended fears the fondness of a number of African leaders for Marxist imagery, then neither the disappearance of the pre-independence opposition nor the attempt to suppress opposition tendencies within the single party need surprise us. When leaders rely on texts from Rousseau, Mazzini, Marx and Lenin, dressed in African nationalist garb, however clumsy the fit, there is little likelihood that open opposition will be allowed.[7]

IV

So much for the difficulties, and there are doubtless many other obstacles one could add to the list. Can one also single out specific factors which are likely to affect the existence and continuance of an opposition, or of strong internal dissent within a ruling party ? For example:

1   The ethos, history and structure of the regime ? A number of questions need to be asked. What are the social and political origins of the leaders ? How strong (or weak) is their adherence to ideology—and of what kind ? How long (and how intense) was the struggle for independence ? How close-knit or loosely woven is the structure of the ruling party ?[8]

2   The nature of the political/constitutional structure ?[1,2] I am thinking of the effect on voting patterns of the type of franchise and electoral

mechanisms used, and of the effect on party relationships of a federal
system.
3   The composition of political society—including the degree of unity or
     fragmentation in respect of regional, ethnic, urban and rural divisions,
     and the disparity in living standards between various occupational
     groups. (Again, see Dahl's list of the reasons why oppositions differ
     one from another.)
4   Size of the unit, not only in terms of the actual State itself but of the
     numbers who can be said to have been drawn into politics either
     directly as party members or by voting at elections.

V

Again, it would not be difficult to find other factors which may have affected
the success or failure of an opposition party, or of dissent within the ruling
party. Can one go further, and say that there are 'general rules of thumb'
(I avoid the notion of laws of political behaviour) which might help to guide
us through the difficulties of African politics? I cannot find them; too many
contradictions exist. For example:

1   One might argue that an arduous struggle for power is likely to diminish
     the element of division within the nationalist movement, for example
     the Algerian FLN. But there are no signs of this in Central or Southern
     Africa, and the current argument is that we must expect rival groups
     to exist in any resistance movement. On the other hand, the *rapid* rise
     to power of a new elite group (e.g. the CPP in Ghana) may breed such
     a sense of insecurity and fear, born of the instability of quick success,
     that any challenge to its authority is feared.
2   The prevalence and intensity of ethnic divisions might be thought to
     make inevitable some form of political pluralism—unless they are too
     fierce to be contained within *any* national framework of authority. But
     one can as easily argue that only when a high degree of social/ethnic
     homogeneity exists (among either the elite or the population at large)
     will leaders be found who 'trust each other' sufficiently to tolerate the
     open competition of rival parties, and who are not prepared to pay the
     full cost of coercion—as (to take quite small States) in Ceylon or Malta
     or Barbados. Yet Tanzania has a leader, who might perhaps be said to
     'have a commitment to a liberal ideology', a common national language,
     a single predominant religion, and the absence of strong tribal divi-
     sions; but it too has moved towards single-party rule.
3   Economic factors, including the distribution of private and public
     wealth, are surely important; so is the attitude of the ruling elite to-
     wards the accumulation of capital in private and State hands, or towards
     the need for local and foreign investment. But Ghana and the Ivory
     Coast, with very different economic policies, both produced a single-
     party system which was (is still in the Ivory Coast) intolerant of oppo-
     sition, while Kenya remains for the time being surprisingly tolerant of
     dissent.

     To go back to Dahl's comments on the circumstances in which opposi-
tion is likely to exist, it is certainly possible to wonder whether there is
much hope, in the stress produced by independence, and the conflict between
traditional and modern ways, of the evolution of a 'liberal ideology' which
the introduction and maintenance of opposition seem to require. In most
African States the times are out of joint; there is (it seems) widespread

anxiety at individual level, and tension born of distrust between leaders and followers, rulers and ruled. Perhaps one should try and go back to early periods in our own history in order to try and understand something of what is happening in African society, to a time when there was a 'feeling of general insecurity'... 'fear of sorcerers'... 'bad government, exactions, the cupidity and violence of the great, wars and brigandage, scarcity, misery'... I am tempted to argue that one ought to understand a book like Huizinga's *The Waning of the Middle Ages* (from which these quotations are taken) before trying to gauge political behaviour among largely peasant societies and their rulers. When I watched the passion of political quarrels between rural chiefdoms and their leaders (each much like his neighbour) in Ghana in the mid-1950s it seemed to me that I was watching something not easily described in modern terms.[9] There was a great deal of opposition at local level, as in earlier times between rival *asafo* companies; but it was also hard to see how it could operate nationally in face of the 'feeling of general insecurity' on the part of the CPP leaders. Indeed, at elite level in many African States there may perhaps be a movement out of politics—if that is possible—through disillusionment, distaste or despair; a passive opposition by withdrawal.[10] If such circumstances do occur it is hard to believe that one will see the peaceful emergence of national opposition parties.

VI

Yet, despite such forebodings, should Ghana not have been an exception? Many early observers, from Martin Wight (in that very good study of the early Legislative Council) to Kwame Nkrumah himself, once believed, or said they believed, that it might be possible to sustain both a government and an opposition in Accra. After all, Ghana is an easy State to govern, being small and compact; there is a favourable ratio of land to people; no one starves (though some may go very hungry); the annual income per head and the overall national wealth are relatively high; communications are easy, and there is a good supply of administrative talent at junior as well as senior level. Nor is the country plagued by 'tribalism'. There is a central core of Akan peoples around whom are placed related or dependent groups, none of which (with minor exceptions) declines to accept the authority of the State as a State. Only among some of the Ewe-speaking peoples is there opposition to the present boundaries.

Since 1951 opposition in Ghana has tended to be linked nationally with that distinctive category of dissent—the 'intelligentsia'. I used to think that the special feature of Ghanaian nationalism was the flood of poorly educated commoners as leaders of a homespun People's Party which engulfed the colonial administrators, chiefs and intelligentsia alike in 1949. Now I am not quite so sure. Such leaders are common enough in Africa; but there are far fewer parallels to the very small group of lawyers and businessmen who formed the United Gold Coast Convention. By the time of the first and second elections in 1951 and 1954 it looked as though their day was over. Yet they held out against the People's Party. They formed 'ghost parties' which faded almost as soon as they were named. But they also looked for allies, and found them in the local disputes which divide Ghanaian society. They then hastened to place their talents at the service of the Northern People's Party, the Ashanti National Liberation Movement, the Moslem Association Party, the Wassaw Youth Organisation, the Bekwai State Improvement Society, the Ga protest movement in Accra, the Togoland Congress movement, the Krontihene in Dormaa state, etc, etc. They gave, that is, a national focus to local protests and succeeded in winning 47 per cent of the vote in the third election of 1956 on the eve of independence. They were, of course, 'leaders of the right', if such a dimension can be envisaged in Ghana, but their support was primarily local, not ideological.

By 1966 one might indeed have supposed their day was done. The CPP's winning of the pre-independence elections under the watchful eye of the colonial-controlled administration was complemented (in a sense) by its winning the 1960 referendum and presidential election, a further referendum on the need for a single-party State in 1964, and a general election in 1965. The contest for presidential office, held simultaneously with a referendum on the change to a republican constitution, was quite clearly rigged. The 1964 referendum was farcical, reaching a 90 per cent vote of approval. The 1965 election was an absurd charade, in which 198 candidates were selected by the CPP central committee and then declared elected unopposed in each of the 198 constituencies: it was simply a non-election. By 1966 Danquah had died in prison, Busia was in exile and many were held under the 1958 Preventive Detention Act. Nor did it seem likely that their influence had left any impression. It is true that the leaders of the single party began to quarrel among themselves after 1960, and the following year Gbedemah joined Busia in exile. By 1964, after two attempts had been made to assassinate Nkrumah, the party leadership was in very poor shape, some locked up, some abroad, others watching each other intently. But the power of the party as a whole appeared formidable. From what possible quarter could opposition take on an organised form ? The trade unions had protested in 1961, but were now in disarray. Farmers were aggrieved, but powerless. The army and police had the force to act: but it was impossible to say whether, if they were to intervene, they would see their future as bound up in any way with the small opposition group of unsuccessful politicians.

Today, however, in 1967, a little over twelve months after the February 1966 *coup,* the picture is different. Fortune's wheel has turned full circle. The National Liberation Council of army and police officers has turned for help to those defeated by Nkrumah, to Busia, Akufo Addo, Victor Owusu and others of a younger generation who may still loosely be described as the 'intelligentsia'. The opposition is apparently within sight of power. And such is the nature of Ghanaian politics that the effect of the loss of the CPP has been felt up and down the country, since not every interest can have welcomed the defeat of Nkrumah. When the great wheel runs downhill it drags many with it. Chiefs have been destooled and others enstooled in their place, chiefdoms down- or upgraded, offices have changed hands, and contracts have been cancelled or transferred, while those who once joined in praising Osagyefo are now cautiously changing tune as they try to change their allegiance, although not all will succeed, if only because their opponents will be determined not to let them.

What does such a history tell us about 'opposition' in Ghana ? Its eclipse at a national level was not the result of a withering away of support for Busia's United Party, since it could always find some lodgement in the country at large by sponsoring local grievances; it happened because those in power were determined to see it blighted. It would seem reasonable, therefore, to look for the implication of the disappearance of the opposition as being the direct result of a number of decisions taken by Nkrumah and his followers, and then to go on to ask why those decisions were taken. So simple an explanation ? Is there nothing to be said for those ingenious arguments which sought to explain—and to gloss the unpleasantries of—the Nkrumah regime? I do not think there is, if only because of the uncertainty with which first one and then another line of justification was defended. An 'opposition' was not possible (it was said) because of the absence of a class situation, or because of the tradition of 'consensus' in Ghanaian political life, or because of the legacy of colonial rule, or because of the sense of national emergency after independence, or because its virtues could be preserved by the free play of criticism within the single party in power—a long recital of differing explanations, of which the most absurd has been the assumption that Ghana is a 'conflictless' society because of the absence of class divisions.

In effect, the primary question at independence was whether such conflicts as existed should be crammed within a single party or allowed to become the raw material for competing organisations. The history of the years between 1947 and 1957 shows how local quarrels can put on national dress, given the sharp rivalry among the educated elite. That such a conflict might produce not the alternation of government and opposition but government by a dominant party and the opposition of minority factions opens a new line of argument, but it has nothing to do with the notion of a monopolistic single party and its origins in a pre-industrial society.[11] How far Ghana is, or is not, divided along class lines one simply does not know. Very little economic analysis has been done to provide the data on which to judge. There are rich, poor and middle income cocoa farmers, but do they see themselves as being divided by status or by political objectives? Miss Polly Hill has shown how closely related are landowner and farmer, farmer and sharecropper, creditor and debtor. The labourers who pluck the cocoa might be thought to be among the radical dispossessed, but they are largely migrant workers from outside the country whose fortunes are closely tied to those of the farm that employs them. On the other hand, there is growing urban unemployment and the beginnings, perhaps, of a *Lumpenproletariat* in the large cities, although kinship ties are still a social bond among the majority of town dwellers.

The argument from tradition was at best obscure, at worst a pretence. There were undoubtedly restraints on the power of the chief, and early observers of the Akan states gave the same stress to the competitive nature of its society as to the corporate nature of its governments. But how could one translate the traditional values of an Akan chiefdom—politically decentralized, economically primitive—into an apparatus of control to check the power of a President, even supposing that a President like Nkrumah was prepared to accept such limitations? The CPP was actually shaped by those who were struggling to free themselves from the limitations imposed on them within the former native authorities, and they had no fear at first of concentrating power in the hands of the central government. Both the leaders and the rank and file welcomed the destruction of the opposition, in ignorance of the danger that they were sharpening a knife which might later be held against their own throats.

The equation of single-party rule with colonial government was very doubtful. Throughout the colonial period there were open struggles between rival candidates and parties in the southern municipalities (admittedly on a restricted franchise); there were sharp clashes between the intelligentsia and the chiefs within the provincial councils. There was a lively press which thought it was gagged by the colonial government until it learned after independence what gagging to the point of being choked to death could really mean. Still more naive was the argument that the single party could repro-

duce within its own ranks the benefits to be derived from the existence of
a separate opposition. The refutation was plainly there in the actual history
of single-party government after 1960, when Nkrumah became President.
Deprived of a formal enemy, the CPP turned in on itself. It was then that
Nkrumah, having used the Preventive Detention Act to cripple the United
Party, began to detain his own supporters—Quaidoo, Tawai-Adamafio and
Ako-Adjei. Far from achieving greater protection, the legalisation of the
single-party State bred further insecurity. Nor was anything done to try and
encourage competition within the CPP, either at the centre or in the constituencies. It is easy to be over-impressed by the Tanzanian device of an
enforced contest between rival TANU candidates, but at least the virtue of
public competition is recognised in Dar es Salaam. No such recognition
was made in Nkrumah's Ghana. Instead there was the mockery of the 1965
election, and a furtive manoeuvring for advantage between different sections
of the CPP and its auxiliaries which Nkrumah very quickly suppressed.

So one is driven back to asking a number of simple questions. Why did
the CPP eliminate its opponents ? Why did the opposition leaders give every
excuse to the CPP to adopt such a policy ? And what are the obstacles to an
openly competitive system within which there is room for government and
opposition, policy decisions and criticism, authority and freedom ?

I am still not very sure. But I am concerned for the moment, looking at
the two decades of party conflict between 1947 and 1967, to argue primarily
that it was always possible to draw together an aggregation of interests in
the country which was distinct from that which sustained the CPP. I would
argue further that the rivalry between these opposed groups (though sharp
and occasionally turning to local violence) did not constitute a threat to the
stability of the political system as a whole, and that Akan society was strong
enough to contain these conflicts at constituency and national level. An
irreconcilable element existed on both sides, grouped around Nkrumah and
Busia, but the main body of electoral support, and even the rank and file of
each party, were quite capable of shifting their allegiance. The United Party,
like the CPP, was a loose bundle of interests which, amoeba-like, extended
or contracted its scale of operation to take in or disgorge this or that area
of support as local issues formed and disappeared. It is true that the opposition leaders were obliged, in order to add weight to their cause, to encourage local interests to assert themselves; but that was not a bad thing in
a country like Ghana, where the horizon of ordinary people's interests is
narrow, and if one asks what 'cause' the opposition in Ghana wanted to promote, the answer is clear, and not at all sinister: they wished to replace the
CPP with themselves, and to reverse certain trends they professed to dislike.

There is one last point to make. It is fashionable at the present time in
any argument about the politics of new States to begin by dismissing the
'Westminster model' as unsuitable for those unhappy countries which were
forced by the ex-colonial power to adopt it. A world of argument is contained in such phrases. But a remark by Giovanni Sartori remains lodged
in my mind when (in a somewhat different context) he says of his students,
'They were eager to discover something new, but they knew nothing about
what had already been discovered'. It might be said of the CPP leaders
and their attitude to the framework of parliamentary government which
both Nkrumah and Busia welcomed at independence. It may be that society
in many African States is either too heterogeneous, or structured in ways
hostile to the recognition of opposed groups, and unable thereby to support
the open competition engendered by a free suffrage and a party-divided

parliament. But, for Ghana at least, other explanations must be sought for the early demolition of the Westminster model, the collapse of the opposition and the overthrow of the CPP. Perhaps the answer is so obvious that it is overlooked? What they can, men pursue advantage, and in the long run the advantage lies with the man with the gun: the CPP took a monopolist view of politics, believing that its security lay in the elimination of the opposition, and in February 1966 the soldiers came to the same conclusion *vis à vis* the CPP.

But why? Why—for example—does Dr Olivier not try to eliminate Mr Mintoff's Labour Party by breaking the rules of the parliamentary game in those little Maltese islands where a Westminster two-party system persists despite all the strains of independence? Why did the Indian Congress Party not try and move in the direction of a 'single-party monolith' from its position of dominance after 1947? Maltese mouse and Indian elephant: yet recognisably the same political animal in at least this respect. Why not Ghana too? Perhaps, however, one can begin to measure the problem by noting a particular feature of the situation.

The CPP was a successful party which came to power very early— within two years of its formation. The effect of its rapid accession to office might have been much less had the party been no more than a re-grouping of an established elite. It was not: it was the political expression of a new social group. Consider the position of Nkrumah and the CPP in, say, 1953, when all seemed plain sailing—no reefs in sight, fair weather and a contented crew. Nkrumah expressed his confidence:

> There is no conflict that I can see between our claims and the professed policy of all parties and governments of the United Kingdom. We have here in our country a stable society. Our economy is healthy, as good as any for a country our size. In many respects, we are much better off than many sovereign States. And our potentialities are large. Our people are fundamentally homogeneous, nor are we plagued with religious and tribal problems...

Then the intelligentsia rallied and local interests began to stir; the two joined together to challenge the CPP and Nkrumah was thrown off balance —an undignified position for a nationalist leader with a taste for theorising in Marxist terms. There was an obvious gap now between theory and practice. The CPP was a nationalist movement which claimed to embody a whole nation; it also laid claim to being a commoners' party which sought to represent 'the masses'. What was it to do? It might have abandoned theory for practice and settled down as a 'dominant party', reasonably tolerant of dissent. But neither Nkrumah nor the CPP would have found such a role easy to perform. Nkrumah liked to take a unique view of himself and his place in history; the other CPP leaders and the rank and file, though more sensible, were a new elite which lacked the confidence of power which the representatives of a long-established social order might have possessed. They were also faced with an opposition whose leaders, being more articulate, were generally (though often mistakenly) believed to possess superior ability. For their part the UP leaders in 1957-58 ignored the dangers of straying beyond the strict constitutional field of opposition. Out of a fierce distrust of Nkrumah, and of the party which had snatched power from their grasp, they began to talk of overthrowing the regime and gave the CPP good grounds thereby for opposing them on extra-constitutional grounds. Amidst these uncertainties, made worse by the novelty of independence in 1957, the CPP leaders clung to their mythology. They were very ready to label any opposition to themselves as unpatriotic, reactionary, tribal and/or non-existent, but they could combat the persistence of the intelligentsia opposition, and the multiplicity of local conflicts, only by employing harsh, extra-constitutional measures. This they did—and extended their power over the country until they offended the one group which had the power to resist.[12]

What the future may hold would require another article. The soldiers and police are now publicly committed to a process of disengagement not unlike that which faced the colonial officials in 1947. The interesting question is whether the 'intelligentsia'—if, indeed, they come to power sitting on the bayonets of those who put them there—will fare better or more tolerantly than those whom the soldiers destroyed.

Notes

1   R. A. Dahl, *Political Opposition in Western Democracies,* 1966.
2   Specific patterns of opposition, says Dahl, may be usefully examined in terms of their 'concentration' (How many parties are competing?), 'competitiveness' (How sharply opposed are they?), 'site' (What is the arena of competition?), 'distinctiveness', 'goals', and 'strategies'. The reason for the differences between opposition parties Dahl attributes to (i) constitutional structure and electoral systems, (ii) shared cultural premises—whether people are 'allegiant to' or 'alienated from' their polity, (iii) the 'existence of sub-cultures'—regional, linguistic, ethnic, (iv) the 'record of grievances' resulting from government action or lack of action, (v) 'social and economic cleavages'.
3   I have drawn freely on Shils's useful article in *Government and Opposition,* 'Opposition in the new States of Asia and Africa' (Vol. 1, No. 2, 1966).
4   'On the spirit of patriotism', *Works,* IV, 220-1.
5   Prime Minister 1938-65. See Katharine West, *Power in the Liberal Party,* 1966. The Labour Party was thirty two years in opposition in South Australia, and has been out of office in Canberra since 1949.
6   Prime Minister 1936-39, 1944-59. See H. F. Quinn, *The Union Nationale,* 1963.
7   The same point is made by Shils, *op. cit.,* 181.
8   *Cf.* Dahl's distinction between 'low internal party unity' and 'high internal party unity' (*op. cit.,* 335).
9   I am not, of course, saying that African political society today is comparable in every respect with late medieval Europe; but reading Madge Field's *Search for Security* on the growth of shrines in the Ghana cocoa areas, or Huizinga's account of the struggle in fourteenth century Europe to express old ideas through new forms, one becomes aware of the very different dimensions of conflict at personal and group level from what we normally encounter in our society. See too the paper by Bruce Mazlish on 'Group psychology and behaviour and their application to contemporary history', Wiener Library, 1967, and the interesting articles by Robin Horton on 'African traditional thought and Western science', *Africa,* XXXVII, 1-2.
10   No African writer has yet reached the point of despair of Eustace Deschamps in fourteenth century Burgundy, although Chinua Achebe in *Things Fall Apart* and *A Man of the People* comes near it at times:

           Pour quoy est si obscurs le temps,
           Que li uns l'autre ne cognoist,

Mais muent les gouvernements
De mal en pis, si comme on voit ?
Le temps passé trop mieulx valoit.
Que règne ? Tristesse et Ennuy;
Il ne court justice ne droit;
Je ne scé mais desquelz je suy.

Translation   Why are the times so dark
That men do not know each other,
But governments move
From bad to worse as we see ?
The past was much better.
Who reigns ? Affliction and Annoyance;
Justice nor law are current;
I know no more where I belong.

11   In this respect one might note Professor Finer's comments on the
'bad Marxism' of arguments which try to equate class with the opposed
categories, *tout court,* of the bourgeoisie and the proletariat. As Finer
observes, 'In the pre-industrial period and in the nascent stage of
capitalism Marx and Engels recognised a whole multiplicity of social
classes. For instance, in Germany in 1848 Engels counted no less than
five—the nobility, the bourgeoisie, the small-trading and shopkeeper
class, the artisan class, and the peasantry. (*Revolution and Counter-
revolution in Germany,* London, 1933, 13). Is none of these present in
Africa ? And may there not be still others, not mentioned by Marx and
Engels ?'. (*Government and Opposition, II, 4, 1967.*)

12   The 1966 February *coup* came a year too late, however, to save
Nkrumah's principal and most courageous opponent. J. B. Danquah
died in the maximum-security prison at Nsawam on 4 February 1965.

VIII

The February coup, 1966

I   The arrival of the soldiers

It was at about four o'clock in the morning of 23 February 1966 when the soldiers left Tamale to travel south across the open savannah towards the escarpment which drops down to the forest plateau of Ashanti. The ostensible reason for their journey was to take part in manoeuvres in preparation for a time when the President might decide to intervene with troops in the Rhodesian crisis, but some 150 miles south of Tamale the convoy of thirty five vehicles and 600 men halted between the small market towns of Attebubu and Ejura. There it was joined at noon by two officers from Kumasi, Major Afrifa and Colonel Kotoka. Afrifa took command, and the convoy moved south again through Kumasi to cover the remaining 250 miles to the coast; Kotoka journeyed ahead, to reach Accra by nightfall, where he was able to tell Brigadier Ocran and the Commissioner of Police, John Harlley, that the *coup d'état* which had been planned for 4 a.m. the following morning could take place. That night the police began to arrest Nkrumah's Ministers, members of parliament, regional and district commissioners, and as many officials of the ruling Convention People's Party as they could find. Major Coker Appiah was entrusted with the task of apprehending Brigadier Hassan, who was then Director of Military Intelligence, and Colonel Zanlerigu, commander of the President's Own Guard Regiment: but here the first mishap occurred. Colonel Zanlerigu escaped through a window, and succeeded in reaching Flagstaff House (Nkrumah's official residence in Accra), where he alerted the Russian-trained presidential guard. A little later the first fatality took place: the officer commanding the Ghanaian army, Major General Charles Barwah—a former Sandhurst cadet from northern Ghana—was killed while resisting an attempt to place him under arrest

Meanwhile Colonel Afrifa's convoy had reached the capital, and moved to Flagstaff House at about 5 a.m. on the 24th. Detachments of troops, which had been sent to seize the radio station, airport and cable office, had no difficulty in gaining control of these strategic points in the city; but at Flagstaff House heavy fire was encountered from the President's Own Guard Regiment. A Russian-built armoured car stationed at the entrance to the house was particularly troublesome until a little after dawn, when Colonel Afrifa's troops were reinforced by the First Reconnaissance Squadron and the Second Infantry Battalion under Brigadier Ocran; Saracen armoured cars were brought into the battle, and resistance ceased at midday when Colonel Zanlerigu surrendered and joined the rebels. So there ended fifteen years of Convention People's Party rule under Nkrumah.

Drawn together from *New Society,* May 1966, and the collected seminar papers on *Demilitarisation,* Institute of Commonwealth Studies, London University, 1967.

The President was abroad while these dramatic events were taking place, and was told of the *coup d'état* by Chou En Lai when in Peking. According to Quaison Sackey, who was his Foreign Minister, Nkrumah's first reaction to the news was one of 'stubborn nonchalence. He simply didn't believe it to be true.' One can understand his refusal, for the power of the party throughout the country had seemed absolute. Moreover he had taken special steps before leaving Accra to safeguard his position. He had imported Russian advisers to strengthen his bodyguard of Nzimas (men from his own district in south-west Ghana); he had equipped the new President's Own Guard Regiment with modern weapons, and had given them special rates of pay above those of the regular army. Had the President listened to the uneasy premonitions of his Egyptian wife he might perhaps have stayed at home, for Fathiah Nkrumah, like Calpurnia, had dreamed that 'something bad was going to happen'. Whether his presence would have averted, or scotched, the *coup* one does not know: but, once it had happened, the deposed president quickly lost support. Even those who had accompanied him to Hanoi and Peking edged away. Quaison Sackey agreed to fly from Moscow on Nkrumah's behalf to Addis Ababa, where the Foreign Ministers of the Organisation of African Unity were meeting; but he changed his plans in London and caught an aeroplane direct to Accra, where he was taken into protective custody. A few weeks later the former Minister of Defence, Kofi Baako, who had been an ardent proponent of Nkrumaism, publicly confessed his sins. 'It pains me to realise rather too late that Kwame Nkrumah, to whom I gave my service and loyalty because of the nation, was not a genuine leader but a fraud of the first order'. This swift desertion of Nkrumah brought its reward, the majority of those imprisoned being released between June and November 1966. Fathiah Nkrumah and her children settled down in Cairo; her husband went to Guinea, where Sekou Touré, remembering the help given him by Nkrumah in 1958 when French aid was withdrawn from the newly independent republic, accorded him full honours. He was proclaimed joint President (with Sekou Touré) of Guinea and—for a time—permitted to engage in radio warfare against the new leaders in Accra.

Having seized power, the military and police chiefs in Accra professed to be eager to hand it back. In a statement published in the local press on 28 February they declared that they were 'anxious to hand over power to a duly constituted representative civil government as soon as possible'. When 'genuinely free and fair elections' had been held, the army and police would 'gladly relinquish their powers to any government formed in accordance with that Constitution and as a result of the elections'. There is no reason to doubt their sincerity. Many military regimes have grown weary of political manoeuvres, and although reluctant governments have a habit of going on ruling, the Ghanaian army commanders and their allies in the police seemed genuinely to want the country to return to constitutional rule on an electoral basis. Why, then, did they intervene?

II   Justification

We might start by quoting from speeches by General Ankrah, who was placed at the head of a National Liberation Council by those who had actually carried out the *coup*. Five main charges were brought against Nkrumah, the first being that he was autocratic.

> The Ghana armed forces, in co-operation with the police, have thought it necessary to take over the reins of power.... The concentration

of power in the hands of one man had led to the abuse of individual
rights and liberty. Power has been exercised by the former president
capriciously. The operation of the laws has been suspended to the
advantage of his favourites and he has been running the country as his
own personal property. [Radio Accra announcement by the army,
24 February].

These general accusations, broadcast immediately after the *coup d'état*
on 24 February, were made more specific by General Ankrah over Radio
Accra four days later:

Until the historic *coup* last Thursday, one man had collected all power
into his own hands. ... The right of the people to vote at a free general
election for their own chosen candidates was reduced to a formal, un-
practical privilege of sanctioning the election of such candidates as
Kwame Nkrumah himself nominated. His love for the arbitrary use of
power ... led him to whittle away gradually the independence of the
judiciary and to suppress academic freedom. ...

Were the charges of autocracy valid? In 1966—yes: and perhaps it is worth
noting here that at the time of the *coup* there had been no fairly contested,
parliamentary elections for ten years; that is, since the last full year of
colonial rule. The authority of the CPP was often equated by Nkrumah with
that of the State, but the extent of its popularity was very difficult to assess.
By 1966 very few even of its own leaders had any major voice in policy
decisions, the ablest of them having been forced into exile, imprisoned, or
relegated to unimportant posts. The cloudy doctrines of Nkrumaism were
also very different in substance and style from the early nationalist beliefs
shared by the party leaders, the CPP rank and file, and the great majority
of the electorate. And in place of that early populism was the special position accorded Nkrumah as Osagyefo, and the reshaping in 1964 of the 1960
Republican Constitution in order to place very great power in his hands.

A second criticism brought by the NLC was that Nkrumah and his
followers were corrupt, and the general truth of the proposition could hardly
be questioned. So too was Ghanaian society, if by corruption was meant the
extension of the traditional custom of a bestowal of gifts and favours in
return for services. Payment of a 'dash' over and above the cost of a trans-
action was a familiar aspect of West African trade centuries before the
introduction of modern forms of government. Money had also changed hands
in colonial times in cases before the traditional courts, and the policemen
who stops a lorry on the road to inspect its licence, or to check the number
of passengers, still levies a private toll on the driver. Criticism of
Nkrumah and the CPP leaders, however, was somewhat different. It was
couched in terms of the *scale* of wealth plundered and squandered from
public funds, and the sums involved were indeed impressive. Krobo Edusei
promised the Jiagge Commission, which was appointed by the NLC to inquire
into the corrupt practices of former Ministers, that he would 'surrender to
the nation' his local and overseas assets of 'about £2 million'. Other former
Ministers and party officials confessed to having hoarded money away
totalling many hundreds of thousands of pounds. And much of this private
affluence had been acquired at a time of public hardship.

The third indictment followed from the second, that Nkrumah had found
Ghana rich and left it bankrupt. 'He brought Ghana to the brink of economic
disaster by mismanagement, waste and unwise spending. Incomes are falling, the cost of living is rising, unemployment has struck many families

(General Ankrah, broadcast, 28 February). The NLC was not alone in its accusations. Most commentators have pointed to the contrast between the situation at independence in 1957, when 'Ghana had all the ingredients for economic success', and the lamentable position reached in 1966. Bad luck in the form of low cocoa prices played its part, but a principal cause of the remarkable change in the country's fortunes, whereby reserves of £190 million at independence were transformed into external debts of £250 million, lay in the obstinate policies pursued by Nkrumah, 'regardless of the disastrous consequences which were plain for all to see'.[2]

It was said that Nkrumah's external policy had been one of a 'dangerous adventurism': that what had purported to be a policy of non-alignment had resulted in a pronounced bias towards the communist countries. 'As the National Liberation Council has already stated, Ghana will... continue to follow a policy of non-alignment. In the past, as you known, mere lip service was paid to the policy of non-alignment by the now deposed tyrant and autocrat (General Ankrah, broadcast, 28 February).

Lastly, there was the accusation that Nkrumah had weakened the position of the army and the police, first by trying to 'politicise' both services and then by establishing his own private army.

> Massive sums of money were spent every month to maintain an unnecessary large force of so-called security officers whose duty is ostensibly to provide for the security of the State but really to secure Nkrumah's own personal safety. He established a private army of his own at an annual cost of over £500, 000, in flagrant violation of a constitution which he himself had foisted on the country, to serve as a counterpoise to the Ghana armed forces. [General Ankrah, broadcast, 28 February]

It is difficult to pick out the most important of these five afflictions. Events during the previous two or three years probably had a cumulative effect, until exasperation and anxiety among the army and police spilled over into action, the occasion being Nkrumah's absence abroad. But three developments in particular seem to have upset the regular officers in the army. The first was a number of attempts to cajole them into joining the CPP, including the opening of a branch of the party within the Military Academy. The second was the conflict which arose in the Congo between the officers serving with the 2, 000 Ghanaian troops under the United Nations and the special ambassadors sent by Nkrumah with the intention of influencing the policies of the government in Leopoldville, then under Lumumba. The officers saw at first hand the rivalry of the Congolese politicians, and they blamed Nkrumah not only for over-simplifying a difficult situation but for trying to take 'an active and sinister side in the whole Congo affair',[3] obstructing the work of the United Nations operation and its Ghanaian contingent. Afrifa, for example, believed that 'forty-three Ghanaian soldiers lost their lives at Port Franqui as a result of this woeful and disastrous policy'.[4] The third, and very likely decisive, event which led to Nkrumah's overthrow was his creation of a separate President's Own Guard Regiment and the proposal to create a 'People's Militia'. On top of these developments came the virtual dismissal by Nkrumah in June 1965 of General Otu and General Ankrah on grounds that were not disclosed and for reasons which seemed to lie simply in a determination to bring the army under direct political control.[5]

The younger officers had watched this extension of party power over all the main instruments of government. They disliked the dismissal of the

Chief Justice, Sir Arku Korsah, in 1963, and the Commissioner of Police,
E. R. T. Madjitey, in January the following year. Then in 1965 came the
forced retirement of Otu and Ankrah. They saw their friends dismissed or
locked up. They heard rumours of bankruptcy. They watched the arrival
of Russian advisers in Accra. They had first-hand experience of the problems of conducting a military operation in Central Africa, and they knew
that the President would ignore any protests that the army might lodge.
Affronted, therefore, by what Nkrumah had already done, they were also
apprehensive about what he might yet do. So they acted first and laid their
plans carefully. Afrifa at least had considered using force against the
President in 1962 when he arrived back in Accra from the Congo, and again
in November 1964 when he was stationed as Acting Brigade Major in
Kumasi. The earlier *coup d'état* in Lagos in January 1964 can hardly have
occasioned that in Accra, since the one followed too closely on the other,
but the apparent success of the Nigerian officers may have emboldened
the Ghanaians. And Nkrumah's absence abroad provided them with the
opportunity to strike.
   The limited aims of the officers are worth noting. There was no
proclamation of a new order. 'Martial freedom'[6] and public liberties were
perhaps the primary aim. And the underlying assumption seems to have
been that there was nothing seriously wrong in Ghana which could not be
cured by the removal of Nkrumah and the Convention People's Party. The
impression one has from reading many of the pronouncements of the NLC
in its early months is that its members wanted to see the introduction of
'honest policies' without, if possible, having to endure the sight of party
leaders trying to implement them. So they began a familiar search for
honest men, not unlike the attempts made by the colonial government in the
early days of nationalist agitation when it too had hopes of finding a body of
responsible opinion to lead the country along a path of moderate reform.
Indeed, the NLC initially turned for support to much the same kind of people
whom the colonial officials had been forced to abandon: the intelligentsia
and the chiefs. The Council also began to think of a timetable of withdrawal,
but before drawing these interesting parallels something must be said of
the machinery of control established by the NLC.

III   The structure of control

The first task was that of demolition, and jubilant crowds helped to pull
down the large statue of Nkrumah which stood outside the National Assembly.
Streets were renamed, Kwame Nkrumah Avenue becoming Liberation
Avenue; the hut at Nkroful in the Nzima district of south-west Ghana where
Nkrumah was born (a party-ordained place of pilgrimage) was demolished
with the help of Nkrumah's own organisation, the Builders' Brigade.
Nkrumah was dismissed from office, parliament closed down, the constitution suspended, the CPP disbanded, parties were declared illegal and people
were forbidden 'to carry out political activities of any description, including
rallies, processions, propaganda campaigns and the use of party slogans and
labels'. The NLC began to rule by decree, but it tempered autocracy with
mercy. Early in April the 1968 Preventive Detention Act was abolished;
those detained by the former regime were released, and many who had been
imprisoned in the early days of the *coup* were allowed to go free.
   The overthrow of Nkrumah's government was remarkably easy to
accomplish. Fewer than twenty soldiers had been killed in the fighting
around Flagstaff House, and nearly every visitor to the country described

the public expressions of thanksgiving for Nkrumah's overthrow. The February *coup* was also unusual in that no curfew was imposed on any of the main towns; the streets of Accra, Kumasi, Cape Coast and Sekondi were crowded with men and women the day after, moving freely without fear of the army. In 1964, moved by a temptation to prophesy, the writer had tried to argue that, 'once having seized power in Accra, the replacement of the CPP commissioners in the regions by junior and senior officers was not likely to present any great difficulty to a determined army commander'.[7] So it proved. The NLC simply took over the structure of control which the CPP had inherited from the British, and replaced the former party commissioners with army and police officers. After an initial period of hesitation the NLC then began to rule as Ministers. The eight members of the Council—four army officers and four police officers—took over the portfolios of government from their CPP predecessors, reducing the number of Ministries from thirty eight to eighteen. To assist its deliberations the Council also appointed committees of civil servants for economics, foreign affairs and administration, and special commissions whose task was to expose the misdeeds of the former regime. Regional bodies were established on the same pattern—a mixed membership of army, police and civil servants, the final authority lying with the senior army officer in the region. At local level each district was placed in the charge of an administrative officer (who was obliged, however, to consult periodically with local police officers) in a way very familiar to those who had known the hierarchy of colonial commissioners under British rule.

The NLC began to make early use of the procedures whereby the CPP had bestowed its patronage on pro-government chiefdoms and denied it to others. By the end of 1966 nearly 200 chiefs had been 'destooled' and others elected (by popular assent and government pressure) in their place. The new rulers summoned a chiefs' conference in July which met briefly in Kumasi, drew up a plan for a new constitution, submitted it to the vice-chairman of the NLC, Inspector General John Harlley, and then disbanded. The regional houses of chiefs (which the CPP had refashioned out of the former chiefs' councils of colonial days) were also retained,thus demonstrating that whoever might rule from Accra—colonial officials, nationalist politicians or army commanders—the office of chief remained a permanent feature of the political scene. Other associations continued to function— trade unions, market women's groups, co-operatives—for there is a chameleon-like quality to most Ghanaian organisations, the rank and file being quick to take on the colour of the new regime. On 21 February, for example, a number of youth organisations and detachments from the Builders' Brigade had marched through 'Black Star Square' to express (in the form of a resolution) their 'unalloyed loyalty to the Party and to the nation's fount of honour, Osagyefo Dr Kwame Nkrumah'. On the 25th the new leaders of these local organisations issued a further memorandum which expressed their 'uproarious support' for the National Liberation Council. Many who once joined in a chorus of praise for Osagyefo are now trying desperately to change their tune as they begin to change their allegiance; but not all will succeed, if only because their rivals for position and favour will not let them be heard.

IV   *Demilitarisation*

Imagine oneself in place of the new rulers in Accra. It has not been too difficult to pull down the CPP government and then dismantle its ramshackle apparatus of control. Order has been imposed: the country is quiet; the people are rejoicing, for the *coup* is popular, except, of course, among those who were direct beneficiaries of the former regime. But, having established control, what should follow ? At the precise moment when the uplifted sword is held above the society it means to rule the effect is often favourable. An ordered peace replaces the turmoil of party conflict and the Saviour with the Sword is applauded on all sides: but for how long ? The simplest answer is, for as long as the soldiers can meet the demands which the politicians failed to satisfy. The primary requirement in Ghana has been easily met: the removal of the CPP. But it is difficult to believe that General Ankrah can retain popular support on that basis alone, and since he and fellow conspirators do not have any clear notion of what to do next they will have to enlist the help of others. There is often a simple belief among military men that one ought to be able to do without politicians—a corrupt, boastful set of idlers, caterpillars of the State whose disappearance would do no harm and might do immense good. But the NLC is not quite like that. Its members claim to be rulers with a conscience who are anxious to clothe their armed seizure of power in constitutional dress. Ankrah was quick to proclaim his willingness to hold elections, and the machinery of demilitarisation is already in motion. Nor do the leaders look as if they were intent on staying in power—although Afrifa has some of the mesmeric qualities of a popular hero and may acquire a taste for politics, Ankrah is an active chairman, and Harlley (it is said) is ambitious. The others seem homely men whose hobbies are 'gardening or stamp collecting'.[8]

There can be no immediate withdrawal, however, since there is no organisation as yet to take the place of the soldiers and their advisors. Between 1960 and 1966 Nkrumah effectively destroyed all formal opposition to his rule. When in power he liked to compare the CPP to 'a mighty tree with many branches', and in a sense it was true: certainly very little was allowed to grow in its shade. The NLC must devise the means, therefore, whereby it can be supplanted, as the British did in the 1950s. The machinery has already been put in motion which, *suo proprio motu,* is likely to carry the country forward through all the stages of a familiar 'transfer of power'. We must turn, therefore, to the likely consequences of a phased withdrawal by means of a Constitutional Commission, an Electoral Commissioner, the formation of parties and the holding of elections. The colonial map is being used once more to find a way through the procedures of change. And the tasks imposed by the NLC in 1967 on the new Constitutional Commission under Mr Justice Akufo Addo are strikingly similar to those entrusted by the colonial government in 1949 to the earlier commission under Mr Justice Coussey.

But strikingly similar, too, are the members of many of the new commissions. They have the old 'intelligentsia' look about them—not surprisingly, of course, since both in 1949 and 1967 the chairman of many committees are judges. But there is a continuing link too with the past through the nucleus of opposition members who are beginning to acquire not power but influence. Three of the members of the present Political Committee actually served on the former Coussey Committee—Akufo Addo, Nene Azu Mate Kole and J. A. Braimah. Others to whom the NLC has turned to for advice include K. A. Busia, Joe Appiah, R. R. Amponsah, S. D. Dombo Duori-Na, Adam Amandi, William Ofori Atta, M. K. Apaloo, Victor Owusu. They were all opponents of the CPP (some having left the party to join the opposition) and had been forced into exile or prison. Fortune now smiles upon them. Victor Owusu is Attorney General, Willie Ofori Atta chairman of the

Cocoa Marketing Board, Maxwell Owusu chairman of the Timber Marketing Board, Akufo Addo chairman of the Commercial Bank and Edward Asafu Adjaye chairman of the Ghana National Trading Company. Many of those on whom the sun of favour gleams are from that well educated, once wealthy group of businessmen and lawyers who tried year after year, through a variety of party forms—UGCC, Ghana Congress Party, the NLM, the United Party—to oppose the CPP, and it is presumably from this group that some of the NLC expect to see a future Prime Minister (Dr Busia?) emerge.

In the meantime there are economic problems to be faced by the NLC during the period of disengagement. If the upswing of prices is to be checked, the new government of soldiers and civil servants will no doubt be told by economic advisors at home and abroad of the need to cut back the expenditure indulged in by Nkrumah. The veiled criticisms of the way in which the economy was run may be found in the annual *Economic Survey*, to which the CPP government paid no attention, and in the interesting introduction by E. N. Amaboe (the government statistician) to a recent book, *The Economy of Ghana* (London, 1966). Both publications, the *Surveys* and the book, argue against the belief that Ghana was passing through the dark night of a forced industrialisation before the dawn of a self-generating prosperity. As the cocoa price declined and export earnings fell the amount spent on social services and the very inefficient and corruptly managed State corporations increased sharply, until the State was insolvent. By 1966 there was an accumulated overseas debt of £280 million, the interest payments on which absorbed between a quarter and a third of export earnings. Prices increased, as seen in the general cost-of-living index in Accra, which (from the *Economic Surveys*) stood at 100 in 1954 and 119 in 1961, rose to 130 in 1962 and to 136 in 1963. No wonder that Nkrumah feared to hold free elections in 1965. The statistics of the economy may be open to question, but not the general hardships of the closing years of the CPP regime nor the private affluence of its leaders. It is a difficult inheritance for the soldiers and the police, who are likely to be in for a longer and more troublesome period of control than they foresaw when they first intervened.

Whether such troubles as arise will force or retard the process of withdrawal remains to be seen. The move towards a new constitution and elections will have to be carried out under the watchful gaze of the soldiers themselves, and it is bound to be difficult, if only because of the wreckage left behind by the former regime through which the future politicians must carefully pick their way. There are good grounds for hope that the process of 'demilitarisation' will take place, since there are earlier precedents from the 'decolonisation' years to follow and a number of non-CPP (civilian) leaders to make use of them. Yet few countries have been wholly successful in striking a lasting balance between soldiers and politicians, or between armed authority and party rule, and the military in Accra will surely be tempted to throw the weight of its sword once more in the scale on the side of an enforced order if discontent with its successor government is widely expressed.

Notes

1   Barwah replaced Ankah as deputy commander in 1964 and was acting commander of the army at the time of the *coup*. Son of an army sergeant, he was the first soldier from the north to pass the officers' training course (in 1947).

2   David Williams, 'The Ghana economy', *The World Today*, September 1966.
3   *The Ghana Coup,* 66.
4   *Ibid.*
5   To Afrifa the removal of Otu and Ankrah was 'one of the major factors that led to the coup of 24 February'. (*Op. cit.,* 102.)
6   Geoffrey Bing's phrase, in the special number of *Venture,* March 1966.
7   *Politics in Ghana,* 420.
8   Polyphiloprogenitive, too: fifty nine children among seven of the NLC members (excluding Afrifa). General Ankrah is reported as having twenty two children. His hobby (according to *West Africa* in a somewhat guarded statement) is 'horse racing but his twenty two children shows his attachment to domestic life'.

IX

A month in the country

I   Plus ça change

I returned to Ghana in 1969 with the uneasy feeling that I had been away too long. Nothing (I thought) would be the same. Almost ten years absent! Where would be the once familiar ties of remembrance and recognition? Everthing would be different: the CPP gone, the army in command, government by decree, political life beginning to stir again and taking (surely) new forms. What was the Progress Party about which I had heard? What was the National Alliance of Liberals? *Liberalism*, in Ghana? I feared almost to return to so strange and unfamiliar a country. Would I not feel (like the hero in the rather sloppy poem by Thomas Moore)

> ... like one who treads alone,
> Some banquet hall deserted,
> Whose lights are fled,
> Whose garlands dead
> And all but he departed?

I landed at Kotoka airport. Here, too, I was taken aback by the novelty and size of the buildings, not at all like the small, friendly huts which I once entered and left *en famille* each year on holiday. I took firm hold of the new name, paid mental homage to the soldier who almost single-handed had removed Nkrumah and the party from office, and stepped into the sunshine of a Ghanaian welcome: journalists, photographers, radio and television reporters, kept at bay by my host with whom I was to spend the next few weeks.

Newspapers: the quickest guide, not to the politics of Ghana but to what its leaders would like politics to be about. I had neglected to read *West Africa*, the most sensible and informed of the West African weeklies. I turned now to the local dailies—the *Star*, the *Evening Standard*, the *Ashanti Pioneer* (resurrected in its old form), the *Ghanaian Times*, the *Daily Graphic* (in which Garth was still performing miracles of strength without joy) and rather frail publications like the *Guardian*—'an independent newspaper'.

As I read, my bewilderment grew. Where was I? 1969? Or 1949? But, really, nothing had changed! Out of Africa, it seemed, always the same. So at least one might suppose from reading the newspapers in Accra, as if one had returned to the theatre after a long absence only to hear the same actors in the same play speaking the same lines. There was K. A. Busia, earnestly recommending a policy of honest government, leader now of a Progress Party. There was Joe Appiah: *exactly* the same as in 1955, when he returned home to upset the CPP applecart, now busily engaged in much the same activitiy *vis à vis* Busia's party. There too was Gbedemah—Komla Agbeli: a little older perhaps, but not much, directing operations from his

Reproduced from six articles in *West Africa* with the permission of the editor, David Williams.

pleasant house in Accra in the same energetic style of command as I remembered him in 1951, 1954 and 1956, and then in his last campaign in 1960
during the referendum for the republican constitution and (as his opponents
now remind him) for Nkrumah as President.

Not only were the leaders the same. Many of their lieutenants and
colleagues were familiar figures from the past; Willie Ofori Atta (and a
younger, pocket edition of the great man—Dr Jones), Kwesi Lamptey (the
Hyde Park wizard of two decades ago), R. R. Amponsah, Victor Owusu, all
grouped around Busia; Modesto Apaloo, joined with Joe Appiah and H. S.
Bannerman in Accra; Ohene Djan, E. K. Dadson, and other ex-CPP figures
from the past, ranged behind Gbedemah. True, there were absent figures.
Danquah, alas, was dead; Nkrumah still in Conakry; Krobo Edusei was in
prison (as indeed he had been in 1950); Kojo Botsio, Kofi Baako, Tawia
Adamafio and others were living quietly in retirement. But it was almost
as if Nkrumah and his inner circle of friends had never existed. An election was once again in process for a new kind of self-government—independence from military rule; not decolonisation but 'demilitarisation'. And as
in 1949, so in 1969 there was an uneasy doubt (it was rumoured) on the part
of those who controlled the dying government about their successors. One
forgets now that the colonial government of the Gold Coast had not handed
power over without demur: it had locked up its opponents in 1950, it had
held up independence in 1955. Would the soldiers and the police of the
National Liberation Council also hesitate, draw back at the last from their
promise (honourably observed in every respect so far) to surrender control
by the end of September 1969? Were they in agreement still on the need to
step aside? Where would they go if they did 'withdraw to barracks'? Unlike
their colonial predecessors, they could not withdraw to a peaceful English
retirement on pension from the new government.

That was an obvious group of questions to try to answer. There were
others, too, which had to be asked, out of what one knew, or thought one knew,
about the country. Politics in Ghana (I had wearied many an audience by
repeating) were a confused and confusing mixture of two forms of conflict.
One was social, in the attempt by new groups to reach the dazzling prizes of
State power: small-time contractors, cocoa buyers, local traders, schoolteachers, clerks, transport owners and property owners, all jostling and
pushing for contracts, licences, loans, offices and jobs—status, power and
profit—which the ruling party could bestow on its followers and withhold
from its enemies. The Convention People's Party after 1949 had been precisely that kind of party, held together in its early years by the additional
and thrilling notion of independence. It had easily displaced its early rivals,
the lawyers and established businessmen of the United Gold Coast Convention, and it would no doubt have continued to absorb or ignore its opponents
had there been no armed check to is power.

Social and personal conflicts, however, were never the only struggle.
There was always that other potent cause of dispute in the rivalry of villages,
chiefdoms, districts, regions, peoples — Ashanti against the coast, the
Brongs against Asanti, the north against the south, the Ewe and the Ga
against everyone else. Within these wider spheres of competition there
were lesser circles of controversy—Wenchi against Techiman among the
Brongs, rival sections within the Adansi chiefdom in Ashanti, rivalries also
among the Ewe-speaking peoples, and between little 'village states' like
Chiana and Paga in the far north. So many local disputes, shaped by traditional quarrels over land or status, and given fresh life in modern party
terms.

What had happened to these conflicts? CCP had been born in 1949 of the hopes of a new political class determined to seize power for itself on behalf of the rest of the country. It was in terms of nationalism, commoners and the rise of the elementary school leaver that I had once loosely described the social revolution which I had thought was taking place in Ghana in the 1950s—phrases worn to death, alas, in students' essays on the 'politics of new States'. What was left of the CPP had been disbanded in the early hours of 24 February 1966, but its members and their followers—local patrons and clients—were still there up and down the country. Some had been disqualified from standing for election, others were busily disavowing their past in order, once again, to lay hands on the future. Even soldiers cannot decree the abolition of a new social class, and in each constituency there are leaders still with local powers—the chief, the trader, the lawyer, the headmaster, the sand and gravel contractor, the local produce buyer.

There was D. D. Osei, for example, at Nkawkaw, where the great central scarp suddenly thrusts itself high above the forest plateau—sixty-six miles from Kumasi, one hundred and three from Accra. Mr Osei is a former CPP District Commissioner, a former storekeeper and trader, who has his hotel and restaurant a little outside the market town. The hotel is a little shabby, perhaps, today, but it is still a friendly, comfortable and lively centre of discussion, washed down with good plain stew and beer generously provided (under payment) by Mr Osei, who must be surely a person still of influence and political skill in the Kwahu district. There are many comparable figures in Ghana—how many? How numerous is the Ghanaian elite among whom the competition for power has been re-started? Fewer certainly than ten thousand, and, as one travels about the country among friends, it is as if the whole of educated Ghanaian society knew one another through school and family ties. (Why ten thousand? One quick test is to look at the slim volume printed by the Post Office. There are one hundred and forty pages of telephone subscribers, with about a hundred entries a page, covering the whole country, from which one must deduct the pages of advertisements and the entries for government offices and foreign firms.) Which way will these local notables move, and try to influence their followers to move, on 29 August? For Busia and Progress? Or Gbedemah and NAL?

And what had happened to those older territorial conflicts? Had the suppression of national politics diverted energies and concentrated the competition for power at local level? If so, the ruling that candidates had to 'come from the local area' was likely to confirm the trend. I was told that 'tribalism' had greatly increased. But what did that mean in relation to party politics? I was also told a number of familiar stories—that what mattered, for example, in the Agona constituency was Joseph Amamoo's entrenched position in Swedru town, which had more registered electors than its smaller rivals, Nyakrom and Nkum; that the Paga and Chiana chiefdoms on the northern border were in dispute again under the rival flags of Progress and NAL instead of the former United Party and the CPP, that the fortunes of Busia and Gbedemah in the large Dagomba area were dependent on the outcome of the de-skinment case concerning the Ya Na at Yendi; and when I asked Nana Agyeman Badu, Dormahene, what was happening at Wamfie, where his Krontihene had his 'palace and court', he replied; 'The old quarrel continues.'

I was greatly comforted. Old quarrels, new forms. My spirits revived. I was on known ground, with familiar signposts. I was able to grope my way forward, ready now to listen to the closing stages of the Constituent Assembly in Accra, where arguments over the inclusion of God in the preamble, and the detailed wording of article 71 in the constitution, were prolonging debate.

But first I thought that I should go quickly to Ashanti to pay my respects to former colleagues and to renew old friendships.

II   Vengeance?

At home again in Kumasi, drinking soberly in the Hotel de Kingsway with Sam Arthur, Willie Boatin and others, I was told an interesting, amusing story which seemed to me later to be full of gloomy omens. There sat Mr Collinwoode Williams, hardly a day older (in appearance) than in the great days of the *Ashanti Pioneer* when the hotel was a marvellous centre of gossip and news; here was the long bar, band, and open dance floor where (it is said) the editor of *West Africa* once slept in a camp bed under a mosquito net to the sound of high-life music. And this was the story I was given.

Mr X was a loyal CPP member and had been for many years. He voted CPP, when elections were permitted; he turned up at rallies (when they were held), and he spent what he had to on entertaining party officials, donations to the party treasurer, subscriptions to funds sponsored by Osagyefo, and other worthy causes. His complaint was that the rewards which came his way were disproportionate to his loyalty. What was to be done? He multiplied his activities and enlarged the scale of his donations. The prize he sought was simple enough, to be made a District Commissioner in order to reap the benefits of a powerful local office. His wife (a sensible woman) protested; she was uneasy. 'Why change from what we are? More money means more trouble. We have the store, we have local contracts. I beg you not to do what you are doing.' In the long run, however—and it was quite a long run—he was successful, and was told to be prepared to take up his appointment as District Commissioner at Z in Brong Ahafo. He made the journey to his district, returned delighted, called his wife, calmed her fears, announced that their troubles were over, and returned to give orders to the local masons and joiners for a number of improvements to the Commissioner's bungalow which awaited him; then he journeyed home to collect his family, slept soundly, woke early, ready to move, listened to the morning's news, and heard with dismay turning to grief and fear that the army had proclaimed the overthrow of Nkrumah and the party. His wife was loud in her recriminations. Mr X ran round in circles, protesting that he had never wanted to be a District Commissioner and indeed had never really been appointed—all in vain. The police arrived, in he went (for a few weeks only); and he came out of prison bereft of contracts, money, hope and—almost—wife and family. Alas, poor villain!

If all power in Ghana corrupts, the loss of power is an absolute calamity. A minor difficulty in the teaching of government at Manchester (or at any other university in Britain) is how to convey to students the very real dangers—the enormity of the penalties as well as the prizes —of political life throughout much of world. After all, it is a long time since party leaders at Westminster had to worry about the outcome of an election in terms of 'Downing Street or the Tower'. That is not so in Ghana, where it is very easy to meet politicians and less innocent victims of the post-independence years who knew almost total defeat and indefinite imprisonment in Ussher Fort or Nsawam, Fortune smiles on the successful, but frowns very grimly indeed on the defeated.

That was certainly true of the first Republic from July 1960 to February 1966. There was then a great fear among those who had won of forfeiting what they had gained, particularly if those who had lost in 1954, 1956 and 1960 came to power. Fear of revenge and the desire for revenge led very quickly to the Preventive Detention Act and the assassination plots which twice came near to success. No wonder that Nkrumah became fearful ... To while away the flight to Accra I had read Sallust's account of the war against Jugurtha[1] and his description of the king's terror as the plots against his life multiplied. 'From that moment, Jugurtha never knew a day's nor a night's peace. Every place, person or time became equally suspect; he feared his fellow countrymen as much as the enemy, peered apprehensively into every corner and started at every sound. Every night be moved to new quarters, often to places which were quite out of keeping with his dignity as a king.' Was Nkrumah haunted by such fears? In 1951 hopes were high, and confidence unclouded. But seven years later the first political prisoners were detained. The law was distorted, and the pleasure of revenge given full reign.

We who seven years ago
Talked of honour and of truth,
Shriek with pleasure if we show
The weasel's twist, the weasel's tooth.

Will politics in Ghana once again take the form of plots, reprisals, conspiracies and revenge?

I motored back to the capital, and the following morning, as we went to listen to the Constituent Assembly, I also remembered a story (in similar vein) that was once told me long ago, in the wicked colonial past, about a northern paramount chief. He was discovered, it seems, by the local (British) District Commissioner, mercilessly beating a sub-chief who had offended him.

'Enough,' said the District Commissioner. 'Enough. He has been punished enough; and remember, you should never kick a man when he is down.'

'But,' protested the chief through an interpreter, 'that is the best time to kick him—otherwise he might get up.'

The closing stages of the Constituent Assembly seemed a long way at first from these primitive notions of revenge and punishment. The Assembly met in the former parliament—the old King George V Memorial Hall. The officials of the Ghana parliament were in charge; the admirable Joe Welsing edited the printed proceedings which appeared—corrected and approved—within twenty-four hours of debate. Members fell quickly and easily into parliamentary habits, bowed to the Chair on entering and leaving the chamber, and referred 'with respect to my learned friend'; the 'Ministers' were the chairmen of the various sub-committees appointed to examine sections of the draft constitution. Westminster had reasserted itself not only in the procedure—there were first, second and third readings—but also in the style of debate and the arrangement of the benches. The undivided semi-circular chamber of the single-party Republic had been reconstructed left and right of the Speaker, although members sat according to personal preference rather than in party or proto-party groups. Joe Appiah, for example, sat in friendship alongside R. R. Amponsah, despite their rivalry as members of the UNP and Progress. Thus seated, each could goad the other:

Mr R. R. Amponsah. Mr Speaker, I should like to say that I agree with
the amendment ... except that I would like reference to Art. 70.
Mr Speaker. That is why we are taking 70 first.
Mr Joe Appiah. He was away campaigning at Nkoranza for the elections.
Mr Amponsah. The member knows I do not need to campaign to win the
elections. We will win in any case. (Uproar.)
Mr Joe Appiah. In this world the cheapest thing is to hope. (Laughter.)

As I listened to the debates—at times very expert, at times ragged to
the point of incomprehension—and renewed old friendship with those I had
thought never to see again I was moved almost to tears. The remaking of
a constitution, in an attempt to bring back what had been lost of freedom and
justice, was, after all, a solemn occasion. It was rare also for the same
generation of leaders to be given so dramatic a second chance to repair the
mistakes of the past, and to be given that second chance by the very people
who had put a violent end to the first attempt at parliamentary government.
One could argue that the NLC, and the civilian members of the Constituent
Assembly, over and above the rancour and differences which often divided
them, were concerned to refute the dictum that politics comes out of the
barrel of a gun. For the present at least, the soldiers' guns in Ghana had
restored the ballot box, and it had been decree No. 299 of the NLC which had
opened the Constituent Assembly 'on 31 December 1968 at nine o'clock in
the forenoon in the third year of the Administration of the National Liberation Council'.
    As the early debates drew to a close it was difficult, nonetheless, to con-
ceal a growing doubt. Not at first, since by far the greater part of the constitution was accepted without serious division. True, there were those who
were uneasy (rightly in my view) about the notion of 'unamendable' as well
as entrenched clauses, but in its basic form the constitution once again
bears the stamp of Westminster, garnished by provisions which seek to
prevent a monopoly of power by any one person or party, and in so far as a
constitution can shape the political life of a country the new Ghana republic
now has a sensible framework of rules and provisions. Other forms of
help were enlisted. Towards the end of the Assembly God was put at the
head of the preamble and 'chiefs' were added to 'the people'; so that the
opening phrases of the constitution in its final form now read: 'In the name
of the Almighty God to whom all actions both of man and States must be
referred We the Chiefs and People of Ghana Having experienced a regime
of tyranny ...'
    Fine words. But there was a sour side to the constitution-making as
well. It derived from Article 71 (2) (b) (ii) of the draft constitution which
was the subject of a rancorous debate within and outside the Assembly.
The sub-clause dealt with the disqualification of members of a future
parliament and government, and was quite clearly concerned with one person in particular: K. A. Gbedemah, leader of the National Alliance of Liberals (NAL) and almost certainly either the future Prime Minister or the
future leader of the opposition unless prevented by decree from being one
or the other.

III *Good guys and bad guys*

There could be little doubt in one's mind after listening to the closing debate in the Constituent Assembly that an element of revenge is present at
all levels in the parties now entering the final stages of the election. Why

that should be so is easy enough to understand. The past is too close for comfort, and what one party is unwilling to remember the other is unable to forget. In this sense, too, perhaps Ghana has joined the modern world, sharing (in a mild way) the discomfort experienced by countries whose citizens once condoned what they now condemn. The events of the past twenty years have also provided ammunition for each of the main parties, which, when attacked, defends itself by reminding its opponents of their own past misdeeds.

Listen to an extract again from the Constituent Assembly debates. On 11 June Gbedemah made a silly mistake in his paper, the *Evening Standard,* by asserting that there was no quorum for the Assembly's debate on the disqualification clause in article 71 of the draft constitution. He had written a little pompously:

> A Constitution, if it is to be meaningful, must endure through time ... [and] there is yet to be in all human history, a constitution with one man as an object of fear of the constitution makers to be removed by hook or by crook.

Then came the accusation that there had been too few members present when the Assembly decided to include the article (under which Gbedemah might be disqualified) in the constitution.

On 24 June Joe Appiah and Jones Ofori Atta moved that the offending article and its author be brought before the Privileges Committee:

> *Joe Appiah.* ... If people who call themselves leaders and who expect people in this country to vote for them, will themselves show such gross stupidity and ignorance of the work of Parliament, and seek to scandalise the Constituent Assembly and hope to get away with it, such people who in their blind arrogance think that they have a divine right to rule this country—Mr Speaker, my attention has been drawn to—
>
> *Mr Ayiku.* On a point of order, Mr Speaker. It appears that this House is taking a new form—our work is right now degenerating into party politics and—[Uproar—Sit down!] ...
>
> *Dr Jones Ofori Atta.* I beg to second the Motion because I think if you read carefully through the statement, it is a calculated attempt to undermine the integrity of this House and it affronts the Constitution which we are trying to write. I think for a leader of this country to indulge in such an activity which is really aimed at overthrowing the Constitution which we are at the moment making is a very dangerous thing indeed ...

Such a fuss! But there was also un unpleasant note of vindictiveness to this unctuous defence of propriety, and a month later, when the Assembly was debating the disqualification clauses, Mr Justice Azu Crabbe tried to set the record straight. He recalled 'the very chequered career' of sub-clause (2) (ii) (b) of article 71 and warned members that 'if we as responsible citizens of this country are not careful, this debate will surely bring the House into disrepute'. He was given a rough reception. When Nene Azu Mate Kole II, for thirty years Konor of Manyo Krobo, tried to plead for an end to the acrimony which disfigured the debate, he was given short shrift:

> *Joe Appiah.* On a point of order, sir. Mr Speaker, some of us are getting fed up with this pontification.

The upshot was that Article 71, clause 2, was written into the constitution

over the protests of a minority of the Assembly members, whereupon the
NAL contingent—led by E. H. Boohene, Sam Okudzeto, and Dr Obed Asamoah—
walked out before the close of proceedings.

There was, to be sure, a very difficult problem behind these charges
and counter-charges. A majority of Ghanaians would probably agree that
there are good guys and bad guys, and that the latter should be prevented
from becoming MPs. Both Busia and Gbedemah would agree that Nkrumah
ought to be excluded. Lunatics, too, are thought to be inappropriate members of a future parliament. And criminals. But what and who is a 'criminal'
Suppose a person were convicted of theft before the court, surely he should
be disqualified—even for a petty crime, say, shoplifting? But what about a
person who was called before one of the very many commissions of inquiry,
asked to account for certain properties (including money) acquired during
the Nkrumah regime, and was then unable to satisfy the commission? Should
he too be disqualified? And suppost such a person to be Gbedemah? What
then?

His defenders argued as follows: that a commission of inquiry, under
which such findings might be reached, is not a constituted court, its evidence
often being hearsay and inadmissible in law; nor was there usually a right
of appeal from its findings. Moreover to disqualify a person from becoming
an MP on the findings of a commission of inquiry might be to establish an
ugly precedent, since a wicked government could pack its commissions and
thus dispose of awkward opponents. There was also the problem of the
date of commencement of such a disqualification. Should it be from the
beginning of the second Republic, or from the period of NLC rule; should it
also include the findings of commissions lawfully established under the
first (Nkrumah) Republic? If the latter, then many of those who were now
calling for such a ruling would be affected. Such were the arguments ad-
vanced on Gbedemah's behalf *ad hominem,* Gbedemah having been found by
the Jiagge Commission not to be able to account for a relatively small
amount of his total 'assets'.

The NAL response to this attempt to disqualify its leader has also been
to attack. The Progress Party (it is said) is simply the Old United Party
scrambling for office once again, this time under the hidden protection of
the NLC. Its leaders are those who once formed the Ashanti NLM, the
Northern People's Party, and the Togoland Congress, plus the old intelligentsia, all of whom wanted in 1954 to divide the country into federal units
on a semi-tribal base. As for Joe Appiah and the so-called United Nationalist Party, they are simply the former Ga Shifimo Kpee movement which had
sought to redress the grievances of the Ga-speaking people in and around
Accra, plus outsiders; hence the party's slogan— *ababase*.[2] The truly national
party, therefore—so the argument runs—is NAL, which has genuinely sought
to recruit new talent on a national basis.

When such arguments are put to the Progress Party members they are
quickly rebutted. Gbedemah (one is reminded) not only agreed to the introduction of the Preventive Detention Bill in 1958: he also defended its use
against—whom? Among others: R. R. Amponsah of Progress and M. K.
Apaloo of the United Nationalist Party. And Gbedemah has no cause to talk
of sectionalism: he is cursed with the albatross of tribalism around his own
neck, since his party is Ewe-led, Ewe-based and Ewe-motivated, except
where it has been forced to recruit from among former CPP members. The
bulk of the party outside the Volta region is no more than the old corrupt
CPP shorn of its most notorious characters, and it is bereft of those members only because they have been caught out and barred from taking an open

part in the election. And why (they say) should we in Progress be forgiving towards Gbedemah? We have rejected a number of former CPP members who wanted to be Progress candidates precisely because of their past, and are we now to condone in our rivals what we refuse to accept in our supporters?

There are minor parties and individual candidates who reject both Progress and NAL. Gbedemah (they say) brings too much of the past with him. Busia (they say) forfeited support in 1959, when he 'ran away' from Ghana, leaving others to fight and suffer: he is a would-be general who deserted his troops. Each of these minor parties has a local stronghold: the UNP among the Ga people of Accra, the People's Action Party (PAP) among the northerners working in the south; and their hope is not of winning but of being king-makers—holding the balance between NAL and Progress should the final result fail to produce an absolute majority for any one party.

It seems perfectly clear, however, that there are two main parties, each broadly based among the new Ghana elite and each with its own stronghold. NAL has recaptured some of the loyalty once given to the CPP as a party of commoners-on-the-make; it is also firmly rooted in the Volta region and wherever there are sizable pockets of Ewe-speaking migrants. Progress has benefited from the very considerable discontent up and down the country with the Nkrumah regime; it too has a particular appeal in certain districts because of the old United Party base in Ashanti and in parts of Upper Ghana. Even to the most casual onlooker, it is the rivalry of the NAL and Progress propaganda vans which dominates the scene—gaudily painted and gaily festooned with one or other of two rival symbols.[3] Each side has its war cries—'Victory, victory, victory' for NAL, its followers saluting each other with a 'V' sign for victory; 'Pro, Pro, Pro' for Progress, with a clenched fist, presumably meant to be a demonstration of defiance and confidence. The struggle for power has brought a division between these two main contestants, each built up from local concentrations of support under the leadership of many who broke from earlier attempts at a Third Force (and a new start in politics) simply in order to gain access to power at the centre. The symbol is the party, and the party is the network of support drawn together painstakingly by Busia or Gbedemah.

Who will win? The decisive area (as always) is the Akan-speaking south. Each constituency wants, of course, to be on the winning side, particularly when the rewards of winning are so lucrative, and until recently there was the general assumption that it would be Busia and Progress, who were first in the field, and who represent the clearest break with the past. Hence the scramble which took place to stand on the Progress ticket, a jostling for office which the party headquarters had great difficulty in resolving. Now there is rather less certainty about the outcome, and this fact alone explains the bitterness of the opposition to Gbedemah who has the advantage (as is feared by his opponents) of considerable resources of political skill born of a long apprenticeship in the art of electioneering. Progress seemed likely to win, therefore, but none of the politcally knowledgable friends of whom I made such inquiries were willing to write NAL off as a negligible force.

Envoi. One last reflection. I talked to officials at both party headquarters and was assured that the administration of the election would be fair and honest. Each party ought, therefore, to accept the outcome as a just reflection of the wishes of the two and a half million electors. Other legal and constitutional measures may be used after the election to try and reverse the verdict at the polls. But, for the present, the election itself is something to be wondered at, the fact that it is actually taking place, in what used to be Nkrumah's Ghana, in tropical Africa, in 1969.

V   Bad guys don't eat

The results of the election which were announced this week are a very substantial victory for Busia and Progress. And perhaps it should have been expected, although many were uncertain even among those who publicly declared their confidence in one side or the other. Why did Progress win? For two general reasons. Firstly on *practical* grounds, because many local leaders in the non-Ewe, non-Ga constituencies thought that the party would win, and joined to secure the advantages of being on the winning side. (It was interesting to discover how many intelligent politically alert individuals, of whom my most kindly host J. G. Amamoo was a representative figure, having scrutinised the political scene, and after carefully weighing the chances of both parties, had come down when they could on the side of Progress.) Secondly on *moral* grounds, because a substantial section of the electorate outside the Volta region thought that Busia and Progress *ought* to win, as the leader and party who had been opposed to the CPP and Nkrumah. A similar phenomenon had happened in 1951, bringing the CPP to power, in opposition to the British, the chiefs and the UGCC. Progress has now repeated the old CPP success of winning almost every seat in the south among (no doubt) the same electors. Nor is it difficult (now that we know the result) to list the particular advantages which Busia is said to have over his opponents—advantages, that is, over the only opponent who mattered.

In the first place, Busia was first in the field. It is not all that important to be first, as Danquah and the old UGCC learned to their cost in 1951: but it helps, particularly if your opponent arrives on the scene too late to persuade a sufficient number of local notables that he has a reasonable following. Busia had the further advantages of being known over a large part of the country, not only as a person distinguished in his own right but as chairman of the Centre for Civic Education. He was active, therefore, in a way which carried with it the notion of a 'leader' during the critical period of the prelude to the election, some time before parties were legalised.

Secondly, I was told that Progress had benefited from the early period of registration of electors, when many of those (former CPP supporters) who might have turned to Gbedemah held back from anything to do with politics for fear of reprisals. I am not sure how valid such an argument is. Looking at the numbers of registered electors—about two and a half million—I would argue that the figure is quite high, particularly when compared with 1, 459, 743 in 1956; and 2, 098, 651 in 1960. Many, of course, did not register and many did not go to the polls, but that has always been true of Ghana, and there is still no very satisfactory explanation of the fact of non-registration and non-voting.

Thirdly, it is said that Progress won because it was clearly opposed to the former civilian regime. Gbedemah and NAL were, too, of course; Gbedemah had said so frequently from exile; but still he carried too much of the CPP past with him, and his opponents who remembered his departure in September 1961 were able to argue that Gbedemah was a would-be CPP rival to Nkrumah, not—as were Amponsah, Appiah, Owusu and others—a reformed character who had seen the light and who had turned away virtuously from a corrupt regime. One might have thought that Gbedemah would have picked up support from those who had benefited from the CPP, but too much had happened since 1966 for any simple formulation of that kind to take place. The former leaders were still in disgrace, while others had been busily transferring their allegiance to what seemed more hopeful prospects—primarily to Busia and Progress. And they could tidy up their discredited past by seizing hold of Busia's promise of magnanimity—that Progress would be 'a new party ... open to all citizens, and already its membership includes former United Party members, former CPP members, and those who belonged to neither'.

Therein, I think, lies a cogent explanation of why Busia won. He seemed all along to have the mantle of victory upon him. His early appearance on the political scene as the most influential member of the old opposition, his close and cordial relationship with the majority members of the NLC (particularly Afrifa), his ability to attract the support of senior members of the administration like Richard Quarshie and J. H. Mensah: all these factors helped to weave the mantle for him. Power and the prospect of power (as said earlier) are marvellous magnets of attraction in countries like Ghana where so much is at risk, and here was the heir apparent to a government which would once again have the power to employ, disburse and reward. Such, very likely, were the conclusions reached by local leaders of position in the early months prior to the election, particularly in the thick cluster of constituencies in southern Ghana. In addition, the fact that Busia is an Akan—a 'Brong' from Wenchi—and Gbedemah an Anlo Ewe was an enormously helpful bonus to Busia, since it meant that there was no national figure to capture the old Ashanti-Fanti, Ashanti-Brong rivalry.

And yet one ought not, in fairness to many ordinary Ghanaians, semi-literate as well as literate, to leave out of account those who voted for Busia and Progress because they believed that he at least, and perhaps the party he led, were the furthest removed from the corruption and bullying of the Nkrumah regime. It is easy to say that many became disenchanted with the corruption of the CPP government because they were excluded from it. The fact remains that many too were offended by its ostentatious display of private wealth, particularly at a time of public hardship, and were opposed to measures like the Preventive Detention Act because either they or those they knew, had suffered cruelly from its enactment. Another anecdote: I sat one evening in Joseph Amamoo's house in Accra and was told a memorable story by a Stool elder from Agona Swedru. 'Oh yes, ' he said, 'I was detained. A policeman came to my farm one day and told me I should go to Winneba to see the inspector. So I went, not making any preparations, and was told I should accompany him to Accra. I went to Accra, and the superintendent said that there was a van outside to take me to Ussher Fort. I asked him; "Why? What are the charges?" And he told me: "Old man, you are annoying Kwame Nkrumah with your UP propaganda and you must go inside." "For how long?" "Five years." So I went inside.'

Somewhat foolishly, I asked him what it was like. He scratched his ear, held his hands to his head, and said, 'It was bad: four of us in the small cell, one latrine bucket, no work to do, no work at all. Six o'clock, they open the door and you can go into the yard to talk. No newspapers to read, only the Bible. And six o'clock again at night, back in the cell. Mosquitoes? Very bad. No net, only a blanket on the floor. And bad rice with poor kenkey full of gravel. I got sick. Many were sick and some died. Then one day when my time had come I was called to see the prison superintendent, and he said, "Old man, you go back to your cell. I have heard from the government. Five more years."'

'So how many years were you there?' I asked.

'Five years, eight months, twenty days!'

'And you were released?'

'Yes, because of the soldiers, and but for that I would be sitting there still. I know that very well. One morning they did not let us from the cell, and we stayed there until nine. Opposite was a high room with bars. I lifted up my eyes and there I saw some CPP Ministers—Kofi Baako and E.K. Bensah, the MP for Agona. Then they opened our cell and said we could go free. So we went, only the superintendent called us back and said we must sign for our belongings. Then we came out.'

I asked him, finally, what he had done to warrant such punishment, and he said, 'I was CPP, then I changed to NLM and UP, and that is why I suffered.'

Stories like this are common enough in Ghana, and those who underwent detention have not looked kindly on arguments for tolerance towards their opponents.

What happens now? To examine this second question needs a separate article. But at least one can express a hope that what has begun well will continue well. Can a competitive party system work satisfactorily in Ghana under such old-fashioned concepts as a government and opposition? Certainly the *mechanics* of the election worked. All honour to the administration. The present voting method, borrowed from earlier French African elections, is probably a better system than the method formerly used of multiple ballot boxes concealed behind a voting screen. But the administration of an election is at best only half the story. There has to be an acceptance of the result by the winner and the losers, including acceptance of the essentially plural nature of Ghanaian society. It does not look as though the politics of compromise and restraint are agreeable to either side in the light of Busia's overwhelming victory. His position now is that of a leader of a dominant party which is opposed 'at the edges' by minority groups. Will he and those around him refrain from trying to enforce their will on the minority when discontent begins to be voiced not only outside but within the over-large ranks of their own party? Will Gbedemah and his followers, wherever they are located, patiently accept their defeat, if defeat weighs heavily upon them?

Judging by the debates in the Constituent Assembly, some at least of the Progress leaders are unlikely to be very tolerant; judging from Busia's comments after the election, it may be that a line will now be drawn across the past, and all its misdeeds consigned to oblivion: but sub-clause 2 (b) (ii) of article 71 is there still, and will be there even if a right of appeal is added. There was, perhaps, only a small rift in the lute between PP and NAL perhaps no bigger than Gbedemah. But:

It is the little rift within the lute
That by and by may make the music mute!

VI *Caesar's laurel crown*

Combing through the election results, one can begin to see the boundaries of Busia's victory and the limits of Gbedemah's defeat. Once again, the parallel that comes to mind is 1951, in the sweeping victory of Nkrumah and the CPP in the first general election. Are Busia and his supporters heirs of the old nationalist movement? It must be so. Nor should we be surprised. The conditions being similar, the outcome is also similar. As in 1951, so in 1969, a new start has been made after the near-paralysis of political life under the first Republic and the NLC: nine years in all. In 1969, as in 1951, popular emotion and private interests have come down overwhelmingly on the side of the party which seemed most likely to make a new beginning, and in 1969, as in 1951, the main check to the triumphal march of Progress has been the trans-Volta vote—east and north—among the non-Akan. There is every reason, also, to suspect that history will repeat itself in the sense that at the next election (if there is a next election) Progress, like the old CPP, may find itself troubled as much by internal differences as by external enemies. Success has its dangers in almost equal measure with the bitterness of defeat, and Busia's head may lie very uneasily crowned with such a wealth of laurel.

There are dissimilarities, of course, between 1951 and 1969, quite apart from the difference between Nkrumah and Busia. The Progress Party's victory among the Akan-speaking peoples of Brong-Ahafo, Ashanti, and the south, was even more impressive than that of the CPP nearly twenty years ago: partly, no doubt, because Busia, an Akan, was challenged directly by Gbedemah, an Ewe; partly because many of the minority groups—Ewe, Ga, Nzima—drew together in 1969 for protection against the dominance. How can one set this down?

Seats in the predominantly Akan area

	Progress	NAL	Others:
Brong Ahafo	13	0	0
Ashanti	22	0	0
Western region	10	0	3
Central region	15	0	0
Eastern region	18	4	0

Note: NAL candidates forfeited their deposit, having failed to win one-eighth of the total vote, in nineteen constituencies.

Staggering as this picture is of the overall dominance of Progress, the party was actually stronger in the Akan areas than appears from the table. It lost seats only in three small areas: in the extreme west among the Nzimas, who—still mourning the loss of their great patron, Kwame Nkrumah—voted against Progress *and* NAL; at Amenfi, where Mr P.K.K. Quaidoo has his isolated stronghold; and (3) in the extreme east, where the Akan shade off into the Ga Adangbe, who voted for Gbedemah. The NAL vote was often derisory, as in the three Amansie constituencies in central Ashanti:

Amansie Central:

PP	11,040
NAL	953
Others	375

The only areas where NAL could enlist substantial support (it is probably right to argue) was from among non-Akan immigrants. In two of the Kumasi City constituencies, for example, the NAL vote reached a respectable size:

Asukwa:	Progress	10,283
	NAL	6,450
	Others	749
Subin:	Progress	9,714
	NAL	4,695
	Others	1,312

In both constituencies there are considerable numbers of non-Akan (including Anlo-Ewe families) who must have helped to bring the NAL vote up.

Move now to the much smaller Volta region of sixteen seats and the picture is the same the other way round.

Volta Region:

NAL	14
PP	2
Others	0

Note: Progress candidates forfeited their deposits in six constituencies.

Again, the exception served only to emphasise the extent of Ewe solidarity. Progress won its two seats in the northern part of the region, in what used to be known as 'Akan Krachi', where the population is a mixture of Akan, Ewe and northerners. The result was a narrow victory:

Krachi:

Progress	4,968
NAL	4,250
Others	426

compared with the massive NAL vote in the wholly Ewe constituencies:

Avenor:

NAL	6,598
PP	245

North Tongu:

NAL	10,088
PP	767
UNP	668

In Anlo, for example, the fight (in so far as it existed) lay between the NAL candidate and M.K. Apaloo (an Ewe) who had been detained when Gbedemah was still CPP Minister of Finance; but the collective voice of NAL as a Ewe party proved the stronger, while the Progress candidate (despite his being an Ewe) was beaten into the ground.

Anlo:

NAL (S.R. Tetteh)	5,062
UNP (M.K. Apaloo)	1,700
PP (K. Ahiabor)	156

The overall picture of Akan-Progress, Ewe-NAL is necessarily modified by the way in which the voters were divided in the two northern regions, and by the apparent readiness of the people of Accra to vote for every party: Progress, NAL, PAP, UNP. There was, however, a strong collective Ga vote in Accra which helped the UNP to victory in the Ga and Ashiedu-Keteke constituencies—a reminder of the former Ga Shifimo Kpee movement which troubled the CPP in 1957-58.[4] There was a group voting, too, in the north but within the narrow boundaries of a lineage (competing against other lineages) or a local chiefdom (in rivalry with a neighbouring chiefdom). These communal groups and their notables were wooed by the parties, and Progress was better placed, by and large, in this courtship because of the old ties of association among the leaders of the former United Party: Busia, S.D. Dombo, B K. Adama, Abayifaa Karbo,[5] Adam Amandi and others.

So it was 'tribal voting' in the south? And 'collective group voting' at district and 'village voting' in the north? Well, yes, in a sense it was. But one must also enter a double *caveat* against too simple an interpretation.

Firstly, there were unusual features about the election (as in 1951) which may not recur. It was, after all, the first—ushering in a civilian regime after military rule, as that of 1951 brought in a nationalist regime after colonial rule. If elections continue to take place, they are unlikely to have an overriding issue from which one party can draw maximum benefit. Secondly, if one looks still more closely at the election results it is also possible to see the outline of familiar disputes beneath the immediate dominance of Busia's party. They were there, not only in the north and Accra but in the Akan areas too. There is no space here to argue the case at length, but at Sekyere, for example, in Ashanti, Progress was weakened by local rivalries between different chiefdoms; and at Suhum, in the south, there was a sizable anti-Progress vote which probably reflected the old conflict between 'local indigenous Akims' and 'immigrant settler groups'. It is worth noticing, too, that nowhere in the central region, only at Abetifi in the eastern region, and only in the extreme west of the western region, did the NAL candidates forfeit their deposits. Most were able to find some support among local quarrels of one kind or another.[6] After all, NAL picked up over 30 per cent of the vote against 59 per cent for Progress. Given time, and the struggle of the new government to meet the conditions of economic stringency which face its leaders, dissatisfaction is bound to grow, and to find support from these local grievances.

A surprising and disagreeable novelty of the election was the extraordinary anti-Ewe sentiment that was expressed in conversation with many of those who were against Gbedemah and his party. One can explain this very strong animus not simply by a dislike of Gbedemah's reappearance in political life but in relation to events after the 1966 *coup*. Suddenly there were the soldiers, and the police, and everyone burst out singing, but when the music died away it was noticed that the NLC was commanded (it seemed) by minorities: Ewe and Ga. When Ankrah (a Ga) was moved out, and charges were brought over-hastily by Harlley against the Chief of the Defence Staff, Michael Otu, the evidence to many was overwhelming. It was all an Ewe plot. Soon Ghana would be run for the benefit of an energetic minority, operating first within the armed forces, and now behind Gbedemah. 'Appoint an Ewe to a public corporation or to a government department and within a year the entire hierarchy down to the messenger will be Ewe.' So the argument ran. And there was always some evidence for it, since the Ewe, deprived of any natural wealth in their own barren region, have for many years been energetic in seizing the opportunities of public employment, including positions in the army and police, which wealthier communities (like the Akan) did not wish to occupy. In practice, looking through the list of senior officers in government departments and the public corporations, the evidence is certainly not clear of any Ewe domination: it could hardly be so in view of their number. But a belief does not, of course, have to be true for people to hold it fervently.

Now there is an Akan-dominated government of an Akan-dominated society. Were I to become, by some improbable change of fate, leader of the governing party I would be much less apprehensive of my Ewe opponents in front than of the large and expectant following behind. I would be fearful too of the ambitions of those now excluded from power, remembering the *Songs of Innocence* that:

The strongest poison ever known
Came from Caesar's laurel crown

VII   *Saviours without a sword*

All the party argument in the world cannot alter the fact that the authors
of the new Ghana government are the soldiers and the police. Busia and
Gbedemah, Progress and NAL, ordinary citizens and friendly observers,
have all paid their respects to the memory of Kotoka and have praised his
fellow conspirators. Quite rightly so, and if the new Progress government
can agree to govern in conjunction with a 'troika presidency' for a further
limited period after the formal dissolution of the NLC on 1 October all may
be well. It should help to ease the old government out, and ease the new one
in. One almost forgets now, in the excitement of the election, that it has
been the military which has governed Ghana for over three and a half
years, although it was impossible not to be aware of its existence during
the pre-election period as an armed shadow over the party battleground,
and the recent disturbances at Yendi point to the need for a very careful
relationship between soldiers and politicians under the new civilian government.

One is beginning to forget, too, how rough a passage the NLC had after
1966: Kotoka killed, Ankrah removed, the Otu affair, rumours and counter
rumours of rivalries within the NLC, financial embarrassment, international
difficulties about recognition, international problems of indebtedness.[7] Many
of the NLC members must have complained that when troubles come they
come not single spies but in battalions, and in 1967-69 it began to look almost like a copybook exercise in the 'politicisation' of the armed forces:
the army turns out the politicians who have their revenge when politics
begins to infiltrate the army. Nor could the NLC be sure who their civilian
successors would be if an election were held. So much greater perhaps
should the tribute be to Afrifa, Harlley, Ocran, Deku and Yakubu in their
pursuit of a return to civilian rule. True, the army still has to disengage
fully, and it still remains to be seen whether it can remain wholly detached
from politics once it has disengaged. A full disengagement may not be easy,
should the politicians once again offend the soldiers.

Turn now to the new saviours without a sword. Already one or two
distinctive features of Dr Busia's government are worth noting. For example, it is not openly ideological. That much at least Progress has in common with the National Alliance of Liberals. Neither of the party manifestos
laid claim to a philosophy of government: and 'socialism' is not merely out
of favour, it is apparently held in distaste. Such is the fate of the purveyor
of second-hand ideas: the market turns against them— for a time—and what
was once in vogue is now despised. The prevailing sentiment in Ghana
when I talked to both parties was rather like that satirised in Brecht's
Threepenny Opera, 'eats, not morals' and a quotation from an earlier play—
Drums in the Night—seemed to me an apt comment on the mood of the electorate at the end of the Nkrumah period: 'Do you think I am going to rot in
the gutter so that what you call the Idea can keep on the up and up? What's
the matter with you: drunk?' Nor were such sentiments restricted to the
older generation. Shortly after I left Ghana I received a charming letter
from a young Ghanaian whose father I had met, quite casually, at the Liberation Circle[8] near Barclay's Bank in Accra. After saying how much he
wanted to study in Manchester, he mentioned—in passing—the forthcoming
election.

'The contest,'he said , 'is now between Progress Party which is led
by Professor K. A. Busia, an eminent and internationally known Ghanaian, and
the National Alliance of Liberals, led by Mr. K. A. Gbedemah ... who helped

the ousted President, Dr Kwame Nkrumah, to dupe Ghana and turn Ghana into a socialist state, a form of government which Ghanaians despise. The party which is going to win, surely sure, and I assure you, sir, with an over-whelming victory, is the Progress Party. Thank you!'

The letter was written one week before the election, and was a great deal more accurate than forecasts by migrant editors and visiting profes-sors. Perhaps the letter would not be worth quoting but for the fact that the writer was youthful enough to have been a CPP Young Pioneer on whom, presumably, the daily chanted slogans and weekly catechisms of Nkrumaism were so much water off a duck's back.

How the UGCC would have rejoiced! Its proper heritage gained at last ... But will the new Cabinet also work well? In one respect at least it may be better placed than the former CPP government. With members like J. H. Mensah and Richard Quarshie it ought to be able to work easily with the administration, a useful combination rarely achieved in newly independent States, where the party apparatus of power is often at odds with the admini-strative structure of planning and control.[9] And its relations with the elec-torate? It is bound to move down from its present position: a fate suffered in turn by the colonial government, the CPP and NLC, and—surely sure— Progress. One quotation alone from J. H. Mensah's budget speech of 15 July 1969 (when he was still Commissioner responsible for finance) is enough to make one cautious about what can and cannot be done in Ghana by any government in 1969-70. 'The modest increase in the volume of economic transactions in Ghana in 1968 was not accompanied by an improve-ment in the employment situation.' Expectation sits high in Ghana at this time, as in 1951, but the economy of the country in the 1970s is likely to be very different, and much worse, than in the boom years of the '50s. So dis-content will grow and look for new outlet

What will follow? Parties in the triumphant position held by Busia and Progress slip very easily into the belief that minority opinions are either negligible or wilful. The leaders look at the number of seats in parliament, not at the actual votes cast, and their hold on what they have won seems doubly assured. That is what happened to Nkrumah and the CPP when arro-gance became married to neglect. A good case can be made out today for a prudent restraint by the new government in the use of its powers, and it may be that the Progress Party under Busia will be more sensitive than the CPP was under Nkrumah. But who can tell? Academics love to propose: it is the new State politicians and soldiers who dispose. The politicians have returned to office, the soldiers must retire; and the electorate, which waited so patiently and expectantly to record its votes, must abide by its decision until (as one may hope) it is asked to vote again in 1974.

Notes

1   In the translation by Ian Scott-Kilvert, New English Library, 1962
2   A Ga expression translated very loosely as 'those in front will come back'.
3   NAL: a yellow sun with nine zigzag flashes of light for the nine regions of Ghana, and the party cry: 'Say it loud, I'm NAL, I'm proud'. Progress: a white sun rising above a red horizon on a black background, and the party cry: 'Pro, Pro, Pro' or 'Sure, sure, sure'.
4   It may have been Joe Appiah's association with UNP which led to his defeat in his Ashanti constituency—that and neglect of his own area in his effort to find a national following.

5   Now Chief of Lawra (Lawra-Na) and clearly of enormous help in the
      local constituency:
      PP   13, 909
      NAL   2, 030
      UNP   808
6   At Abetifi NAL chose the wrong candidate and dropped to third place
      behind an independent.
7   The most serious event during the NLC's rule was the attempt by
      Lieutenant Arthur, Lieutenant Yeboah and Second Lieutenant Poku to
      seize control in Accra. They headed a small detachment of about
      100 men of the Reconnaissance Squadron, travelled the ninety-nine
      miles from their base at Ho to the capital, and captured the radio
      station, after killing Kotoka and three junior officers. Their motive
      was simple. They wanted promotion and they hoped for glory. The
      attempt was suppressed, and Arthur and Yeboah were publicly executed.
      In November 1967 Air Vice-Marshal Michael Otu, Chief of the Defence
      Staff of the Ghana Armed Forces, and his *aide-de-campe* Lieutenant
      Kwapong, were accused of subversion and dismissed. (Otu was sub-
      sequently reinstated by Busia.) In April 1969 Ankrah was forced to
      resign and was replaced as Head of State and chairman of the NLC by
      Afrifa.
8   Formerly 'Kwame Nkrumah Circle' and, for a brief, hilarious twenty-
      four hours in March 1957, 'Kwame Nkrumah Circus', spelled out in neon
      lights, a mistake of the signwriters which was quickly put right.
9   This prediction was wrong; see below, p. 153.

X

The 1969 election

An unexpected and nostalgic sight: propaganda vans combing the urban and rural areas in search of voters, abusing each other peacefully, campaigning for Busia's Progress Party—'Pro, Pro, Pro'; or for Gbedemah's National Alliance of Liberals (NAL)—'Victory, victory, victory'; or for PAP, or APRP or UNP.[1] Pamphlets, manifestos, party papers, party broadcasts and telecasts, political debates in the constituent Assembly which finished its work shortly before the election, party quarrels in the small drinking bars which make life so pleasant in the towns and tolerable in the villages. Unexpected because the holding of a free election is a not very common occurrence in Africa in 1969, nostalgic because it recalled memories of earlier contests in the 1950s when the Convention People's Party was engaged in similar campaigns against its opponents until they were eliminated early in 1964. Then the CPP was suppressed early in 1966 by the army and police. Were there other parallels between the late 1950s and the late 1960s? The British had claimed to prepare the country for self-government, and were dismayed by the appearance of a single-party republic. Would the soldiers who had paved the way for the return of party politics be similarly dismayed by the outcome of an election held under their protection?

Matters of fact

1.   The election was conducted in the familiar British fashion of single-member constituencies and a 'first past the post' outcome. The style of voting was changed from that of earlier contests. Electors were given coloured voting slips corresponding to the number of party of independent candidates in the constituency; they selected the ballot paper they favoured, and dropped it in the ballot box, casting the others into a bowl of acid. It says much for the pertinacity of the administration and the vigilance of the police that the election was conducted without incident throughout the country on a single day, 29 August, or almost throughout the country, for the weather turned against the election in the far north, and in one constituency— Chiana Paga—voting had to be held a few days later after the floods had receded. I have used the word pertinacity rather than efficiency since there were reports from some constituencies that polling was delayed until midday, ballot boxes having arrived late, and polling and party agents being muddled about what to do; but, somehow, the election was got through, and those who were defeated could find nothing substantial to bring against the conduct of the election, though of course they complained that they had lost.

2.   There were 140 constituencies, of which only two were unopposed— Agona Kwabre in Ashanti, taken by Progress; and South Tongu in the Volta region, taken by NAL. Of the 138 contests only twenty-six were straight-fights—a phenomenon of less significance than one might suppose because of

Africa Quarterly. Delhi, IX, 3, October-December 1969.

the very many heavy majorities achieved by the successful candidates. Both Progress and NAL contested all the 138 disputed constituencies.

   3. At first reading, the turnout was reasonably high:

Registered voters	*Votes cast*	%
2, 351, 658	1, 493, 371	63·5

But one must remember (what many forget) that this is a percentage only of those who registered and not of those eligible to register. A rough calculation can be made as follows:

   Total population: 8 million?
   Total adult population: 3 million? (i.e. Ghanaians over twenty-one.)
   Those who registered: 78 per cent of the adult population?
   Those who voted: 49·9 per cent of the adult population?

There is therefore still a large untapped reservoir of votes.

   4. The percentage poll was uneven throughout the country, the highest being in Accra—70·41 per cent; the lowest being in the north—52·99 per cent; but of course the poll may be high where the registration is low.

   5. Seats were divided regionally as follows:

Ashanti	22
Western region	13
Central region	15
Eastern region	22
Brong-Ahafo	13
Upper region	16
Northern region	14
Accra region	9
Volta region	16
	140

   6. Who won? Progress—handsomely:

Progress	105
NAL	29
Others	6

   7. Handsomely—yes: but there was one ugly fact about the result, namely the predominantly Akan basis of the party's victory, and the predominantly Ewe basis of the main opposition to Progress. By 'Akan' I mean the main areas of Ashanti, Brong-Ahafo, and the three southern regions. By 'Ewe' I mean the main areas of the Volta region (viz. table 10).

Table 10

Region	Seats	Progress	NAL	Others
Ashanti	(22)	22	0	0
Brong-Ahafo	(13)	13	0	0
Central region	(15)	15	0	0
Western region	(13)	10	0	3
Eastern region	(22)	18	4	0
Volta region	(16)	2	14	0

8. Indeed, this Akan-Ewe division is sharper than appears even from the table. Of the seven seats lost by Progress in the Akan-dominated Western and Eastern regions, two are in the extreme south-west, where the Nzima people are still mourning the loss of their patron, Kwame Nkrumah,[2] four are in the eastern part of the Eastern region where the Akan are outnumbered by Krobo, Akwamu and Ga-Adangbe peoples.[3] The one remaining seat (Amenfi) which the party failed to win went to a strong local candidate, P. K. K. Quaidoo.[4]

Similarly, the two seats lost by NAL in the Ewe-dominated Volta region are in the border constituencies where the Ewe people are outnumbered by the Akan.[5]

The percentage voting pattern in the Volta (Ewe) region, and in the five predominantly Akan regions, tells its own story (table 11). The result is that NAL and its allies, in opposition, represent minorities—Ewe, Ga, Nzima and a number of northern groups; but these minorities are not concentrated wholly in one region, and NAL picked up some support throughout the country as a whole.

Table 11 (all figures are percentages)

	Ashanti	Brong-Ahafo	Central	Western	Eastern	Volta
Progress	78	85	71	53	61	18
NAL	17	14	19	16	34	77

(b) Progress won a higher percentage of seats in parliament than of votes in the country. As usual, to him that hath is given (table 12).

Table 12

	Votes	%	Seats	%*
Progress	876,378	58·7	105	75
NAL	454,646	30·4	29	21
Others	162,347	10·9	6	4
Total	1,493,371	100	140	100

* On a strict system of proportional representation the allocation of seats would be: Progress, eighty-two; NAL, forty-three; others, fifteen.

9. What can be said to lighten this sombre picture?

(a) The two northern regions and the nine Greater Accra constituencies were divided more evenly between the parties (table 13, overleaf).

(b) The vote of 876,378 for Progress is more than double that given to the Convention People's Party in the last free election in 1956:

CPP   398,141: 57% of the vote in a 60% poll.
Opposition 299,116: 33% of the vote in a 60% poll.

But the percentage of the total vote given to Busia and Progress (58·7) is not much more than that once given to the CPP. Progress is in a dominant position, therefore, but it falls a long way short of being a *parti unique*. Even if one eliminates the votes in the Volta region, the non-Progress vote

Table 13

	Upper		Northern		Accra	
	Seats	% votes	Seats	% votes	Seats	% votes
Progress	13	56	9	48	3	36
NAL	3	32	5	42	3	32
Others	0	12	0	10	3	32

remains quite high: 487, 820, or 36·4 percent of a total vote of 1, 335, 707—
higher, that is, than the pro-CPP vote a decade earlier.

(c) The 1969 election was possibly something special. It brought a
return to civilian government, as that of 1951 brought in a nationalist
regime after colonial rule. The CPP then, Progress in 1969, was the chief
beneficiary of a dominant political desire, but a quite different pattern of
politics may take shape once that desire loses its full force.

We are moving from facts to conjecture. So:

Questions of opinion

1. Do Ghanaians vote collectively—by family, village, district, region,
community? Yes: but these collectivities may be opposed *inter se;* and what
appears to be an alliance at one time—e.g. the Akan in 1969—can easily
divide—as the Akan were divided in 1956. There are many 'territorial'
conflicts between rival chiefdoms, many traditional conflicts, as in the
Dagomba skin dispute, many local rivalries for jobs and contracts, and
some proto-class conflicts in the main towns. NAL picked up nearly 200, 000
votes in the 'Akan-dominated' regions and it would be absurd to argue that
they reflect no more than the non-Akan minority in these regions. It was
able to feed on local disputes of one kind or another—territorial and social—
in addition to Akan/non-Akan differences.

2. Do Ghanaians vote 'for the winning side' on the Akan principle *Obi
nni sono akyi mmoro huasu?*[6] I do not dispute the fact that Ghanians like
to be on the winning side, or that the victorious end of the seesaw tends to
come down with a bump because of the rush to that end of would-be clients
looking for opportunity: contractors, job hunters, small-time traders looking
for a market-stall allocation, large-scale traders looking for an import
licence, etc, etc. That's the stuff of urban and small-town politics. I have
argued elsewhere that a primary reason why Busia and Progress won is
that 'he seemed all along to have the mantle of victory upon him'. 'His
early appearance on the political scene as the most influential member of
the old opposition, his close and cordial relationship with the majority members of the NLC (particularly Afrifa), his ability to attract the support of
senior members of the administration like Richard Quarshie and J. H.
Mensah: all these factors helped to weave the mantle for him.'[7] But now,
upon reflection, I am not quite so sure, on a number of grounds:

(a) The vote in the small Chiana-Paga constituency was held after the
main election results were known, yet the result was still very close.[8]
True, it can be argued that Progress might have lost in this northern constituency had it not been known that Busia had won: the fact remains that
6, 879 (a majority of those who went to the polls) voted against the party

which was now to form the government. Why? Because of local lineage and inter-village disputes within the Kassena chiefdoms—a common enough phenomenon throughout the country, there being no room on the winning side to accommodate all the 'polyarchies' of which so large an area of Ghanaian society is composed.

(*b*) Communal solidarity is easily fractured—as among the Ga in Accra, who voted in almost equal measure for Progress, NAL, the 'local party', UNP and an independent.

(*c*) Once again—the anti-Progress vote (which I had not seen when I wrote the articles in *West Africa*) was really quite high.

(*d*) I should like a longer run than one election before passing judgement on the likelihood of those in power staying there. And, as I say, the 1969 election—like that of 1951—was in a somewhat special category.

3. Why, then, did Progress win?

(*a*) Not, surely, because of 'charisma', although Busia and his followers *did* have a certain moral appeal for those who dislike the bullying and corruption of the previous civilian regime.

(*b*) Not because of the programmes of the two main parties. They said much the same thing: a return to civilian rule and a better life for everyone. And that was all. Earlier ideologies had taken flight.

(*c*) I would argue that Progress won for four good reasons:

(i)   The election was focused on a single issue—the return to civilian rule—and Busia and Progress were seen to represent that issue, Busia because of the part he played during the interim period of transition, Progress because it contained a number of leaders who were also in the public eye during the quasi-military, quasi-civilian administration period. Busia and Progress were the obvious alternatives to the CPP. It was in a simple sense well understood by Ghanaians 'their turn to rule'.

(ii) Gbedemah and his followers were identified too closely still—despite their avowals—with the former CPP regime and its defects: 'chopping money' and 'locking people up'. Certainly it was easy for Busia and Progress to tie these labels round their opponents' neck, and it almost choked them.

(iii) The fact that Busia is an Akan, Gbedemah an Ewe, was a useful talking point which reinforced the appeal of voting for Progress.

(iv) The 'mantle of victory argument' probably did persuade a number of local notables to declare their support for Busia: again a very useful bonus.

4. Why did the army withdraw? Perhaps for the very reason it intervened: to protect its autonomy and unity of command? Nkrumah interfered with the army and police, so they interfered with him, but in ruling Ghana they found that they were becoming politicised—a horrid fate. There is probably a good deal of force in such arguments, since by 1969 the NLC was was looking very ragged. It held together, but only just. When Lieutenant Arthur challenged his superior officers, when General Ankrah fell out with his fellow Council members, when the Chief of the Defence Staff, Michael Otu, had to resign, when Harlley quarrelled publicly with Afrifa, and when mutual accusations of intrigue were bandied about between Ewe and Akan officers, one began to understand how the army and police were themselves mirrors of society as a whole. When the soldier-administrators took control of Ministries and departments they professed still to prefer the life of the barracks, and they are now making good their original promise to trans-

fer control. Yet it still remains to be seen whether they can in fact 'take the army permanently out of politics', or 'politics for ever out of the army'.

For the present, the NLC has yielded to strong civilian pressures for change, pressures which include a large degree of self-interest among— whom? Time and again when I was in Ghana the election and the re-entry of the politicians were talked of not as innovations but as the restoration of what had once existed and had been lost. But restored to whom, and lost by what section of society? Who are the beneficiaries of the *coup* and the return to civilian rule? At first sight the answer is clear: the soldiers and the new Progress Party government; and that, of course, is true. The change in leadership after February 1966 is striking, and if an analysis were made of the social background and educational attainment of the new Cabinet it would, I am sure, be very different from the social origins of the former leaders of the Convention People's Party. The 'intelligentsia' are in power—that small group of professional men whose post-war leader was Dr J. B. Danquah and whose new prototype is Professor Busia. The difference between Nkrumah's entourage and Busia's immediate colleagues is not absolute. R. R. Amponsah, now Minister of National Resources, and Victor Owusu, now Minister of Foreign Affairs, were CPP members until they resigned early in 1955. None the less, the style, outlook, and policy of the new govern- ment are probably going to be unlike those of the Nkrumah regime: more cautious, less dramatic, more tolerant of traditional networks of power, more tender towards local entrepreneurs.

Was the *coup*, therefore, and the election, in any sense a counter- revolution, reversing the victory of the CPP in 1951 when it first came to power as a nationalist People's Party? One would still like to know much more about the nature of that revolution. Dr Rathbone and others have added considerably to the early picture I once drew of a divided yet com- posite class of small traders, stallholders, petty contractors, lorry owners, cocoa factors, schoolteachers and clerks whose rank-and-file membership of the CPP gave the party its election victories between 1951 and 1957, and whose rank-and-file membership (one should add) of the main opposition parties also gave the nationalist movement its close-fought battles of that time. Such a social category of economic interests cannot have been des- troyed by so mild a change as that from Nkrumah to Kotoka, or from Afrifa to Busia. They are there still, and those who worked and voted for Progress and NAL must have been drawn from the same kind of interests, now con- siderably expanded in number, which comprise the local networks of support in each constituency. The present holders of power are not very different therefore, from what they were in the 1950s in the little market centres and towns of the central and southern regions—that is, in the main areas of power in Ghana. Some chiefs have gone, others have taken their place; those who were too prominent in the CPP have lost both position and influence (and very likely a large part of their wealth as well). But many of those who were active supporters of the CPP, and benefited from the party in power, have quite clearly turned to Progress in 1969 and are benefitting from the new office holders. Would they have gone on voting for the CPP if Nkrumah were still there, and if elections were allowed? Perhaps. But one cannot be sure. Many that I talked to spoke of a rank-and-file disenchantment with the CPP leaders because of three prime factors. Firstly, the reduced activity of the party at rank-and-file level after 1960, most noticeable in the absurd election of 1965. Secondly, the increasingly difficult economic position in the 1960s and the disparagement of 'local capitalism' by those who had learned to talk 'Nkrumaism'. (It was interesting how both parties in 1969

shunned the word socialism, and it may be that these local traders, contractors, shopkeepers, transport owners and so forth have at last got the
party they want.) Thirdly, there was—and it is worth stating once again—an
uneasy disapproval, even among those who had profitted from the former
regime, of the harsh measures used to suppress those who voiced such
criticisms.

Statistical note on the elections

The first general elections after the *coup* were the most costly (officially
estimated at £1 million sterling) and most keenly contested in the political
history of Ghana. In all, five political parties took part, namely the Progress
Party (PP); National Alliance of Liberals (NAL); United Nationalist Party
(UNP), having Dr H. S. Bannermann, a medical practitioner, as its chairman;
All People's Republican Party (APRP), under the leadership of Dr E. V. C. de
Graft-Johnson, an Accra barrister; and the People's Action Party (PAP), with
Ayarna Imoru, a northern business man, resident in Accra, as its leader.
There was also a sprinkling of independents.

The elections were carefully planned. An eighteen-member Constitutional Commission, under the chairmanship of Akufo-Addo, the Chief
Justice of Ghana, was appointed by the NLC on 24 August 1966 'to ascertain
as far as possible the wishes of all sections of the people of Ghana on the
question of what type of constitution would be most suitable for adoption by
Ghana', following the abolition of the republican constitution of 1960. After
some months of work, proposals for a constitution for Ghana were produced
and presented to the NLC. A Constituent Assembly of 150 members, made up
of individuals and representatives of 'identified bodies', was then brought
together and, under R. S. Blay (a former Supreme Court judge) as Speaker
and Nene Azu Mate Kole as Deputy Speaker, drew up a draft constitution
which, duly signed by all the members, was presented to the NLC. The
Assembly was later empowered by the NLC to enact the constitution, and
accordingly, on 22 August 1969, a new constitution for Ghana was promulgated to usher in the second Republic.

One outcome of the new constitution was the setting up of a three-man
Presidential Commission to function for a period not exceeding three years.
The Presidential Commission, inaugurated on 2 September 1969, comprised
Brigadier A. A. Afrifa (chairman), Mr J. W. K. Harlley, Inspector General
of Police (deputy chairman), and Major-General A. K. Ocran, Acting Chief of
Defence Staff.

A sixteen-man Electoral Commission, under the chairmanship of
Justice J. N. Siriboe, was appointed on 22 December 1966 to examine and
make recommendations on the qualifications and disqualifications of electors
and parliamentary candidates, the registration of electors, and the division of
Ghana into electoral districts. One of the principal recommendations was the
creation of an independent body to see to the conduct of elections in Ghana,
namely the Electoral Commission, and in March 1968 V. C. R. A. C. Crabbe,
a High Court judge, was appointed to the office of Interim Electoral Commissioner and charged with the responsibility of organising elections, provision-
ally set for 29 August 1969, in readiness for the formal transfer of power on
30 September 1969.

On 1 May 1969 the ban on political activities was lifted. There emerged
a plethora of political parties, numbering sixteen at the outset. By the time
of the election only five had survived, several of the splinter groups having
joined forces with the stronger parties or fallen out. The right of a political

party to function was dependent on the securing of a certificate of registration from the Electoral Commission and on the submission to the commissioner, within a given time, of a statement indicating the assets and sources of income of the party concerned. No foreign organisations or individuals were permitted to give financial support to any political party or candidate contesting the elections.

A total of 479 candidates filed nomination papers. The breakdown of the candidates in the regions was as follows: Ashanti, eighty-two; Eastern, seventy-eight; Upper, fifty-four; Central, fifty-three; Volta, fifty-one; Northern, forty-five; Greater Accra, thirty-three; Brong-Ahafo, thirty. About twenty candidates stood as independents. There were seven women candidates, one of them an independent. The Progress Party and the National Alliance of Liberals each presented 138 candidates; the United Nationalist Party eighty-six; People's Action Party fifty-two; and the All People's Republican Party forty-five. Of the total number of candidates, eighty were barristers and twenty medical practitioners. There were also ten university lecturers, eight journalists, four former ambassadors and twenty former parliamentarians. 140 seats in the parliament (corresponding to the electoral divisions of the country) were contested, spread regionally as follows: Ashanti, twenty-two; Eastern, twenty-two; Upper, sixteen; Central fifteen; Northern, fourteen; Brong-Ahafo, thirteen; Western, thirteen; Greater Accra, 9.

More than 8,000 polling booths were opened at vantage points in all the constituencies. In the urban areas one polling booth was allocated to 1,000 voters, while in the rural areas the ratio was one to 500 voters. Voting started at seven o'clock in the morning and ended at 5 p.m., though there were a few delays which necessitated the extension of time in certain areas.

To ensure orderly elections, no drinking bars were permitted to open near polling stations on election day. Voting started at a slow pace in constituencies, but increased gradually in the course of the day. Voters were in good humour and waited patiently for their turn in the long, winding queues which formed long before the actual time of the voting. About 64 per cent of the registered voters went to the polls.

Leaders of the parties who succeeded included K. A. Busia; K. A. Gbedemah[9] and Fred Segbefia, leader and first deputy leader of NAL, as well as Ibrahim Mahama, the party's general secretary; Dr H. S. Bannerman, chairman of UNP; P. K. K. Quaidoo, chairman of APRP, who was the only candidate of his party to win a seat. Veteran politicians, notably S. D. Dombo, William Ofori-Atta and R. R. Amponsah (all PP) were returned. Harry Sawyerr was the only independent candidate who won. Four NLC commissioners who stood on the ticket of the Progress Party were returned: J. H. Mensah (Finance); R. A. Quarshie (Trade and Industries); N. Y. B. Adade (Attorney General); and K. G. Osei-Bonsu, the first Commissioner of Information.

Party leaders who lost their seats included Dr E. V. C. de Graft-Johnson (APRP), J. F. Cobbina (chairman of NAL), Ayarna Imoru (PAP), Joe Appiah and M. K. Apaloo, both of UNP, and E. H. Boohene and E. K. Dadson of NAL. Professor T. F. Sai (PP), formerly Head of the Department of Preventive and Social Medicine, Ghana Medical School, S. G. Antor (PP), a veteran politician, and Issifu Ali (NAL), formerly Commissioner of Information, were also unsuccessful.

Victor Owusu, formerly Attorney General (PP), and Dr G. K. Agama, lecturer at the University of Ghana Legon (NAL), were elected unopposed.

Three of the eight journalists won their seats—C. D. Reindorf, J. G. Amamoo and Daniel Bayensi—all of whom stood for the Progress Party.

Out of eighty barristers who stood for the elections, forty-five lost their seats; while a total of about 250 candidates, mainly from the smaller parties and the independents, failed to secure one eighth of the total votes cast in their respective constituencies and as a result forfeited their deposits.

Notes

1   PAP: People's Action Party; APRP: All People's Republican Party; UNP: United Nationalist Party.
2   Nzima East, Nzima West, both going to the People's Action Party.
3   Ada, Yilo/Osudoku, Krobo, Manya: all to NAL.
4   The voting was: Quaidoo, 4, 282; Progress, 3, 682; NAL, 686; PAP, 109.
5   The Krachi and Nkwanta constituencies.
6   'He who follows an elephant does not get wet from the dew.'
7   'A month in the country', *West Africa,* 6 September 1969. See chapter IX.
8   Progress, 5, 343, NAL; 4, 839; others, 2, 040. See below, chapter XI.
9   Only to be unseated after the election, following an action in the High Court under article 71(2)(b)(ii) of the new constitution. See above, p. 116.

Table 14

Regional breakdown of the political parties

(a) Number of seats contested

Region	G. Accra	Eastern	Central	Western	B. Ahafo	Ashanti	Volta	Northern	Upper	Total
No. of constituencies	9	22	15	13	13	22	16	14	16	140
PP	9	22	14	13	13	22	16	14	15	138
NAL	8	22	15	13	13	21	16	14	16	138
UNP	8	16	8	5	4	18	14	7	6	86
PAP	7	3	5	12	0	10	3	5	7	52
APRP	0	9	10	7	0	8	1	4	6	45
Independents	1	6	1	3	0	3	1	1	4	20
Total No. of candidates	33	78	53	53	30	82	51	45	54	479

(b) Number of votes obtained. No. = number of votes, % = percentage of total votes

	Greater Accra		Eastern		Central		Western		Brong-Ahafo		Asahnti		Volta		Northern		Upper		Total	
	No.	%	No.	%	No.	%	No.	%	No.	%	No.	%	No.	%	No.	%	No.	%	No.	%
PP	43,608	2·92	130,275	8·72	114,734	7·68	71,240	4·77	127,707	8·55	215,707	14·45	28,491	1·91	50,301	3·37	94,315	6·32	876,378	58·68
NAL	39,145	2·62	73,321	4·91	29,962	2·01	21,646	1·45	21,745	1·46	47,835	3·20	121,606	8·14	44,643	2·99	54,743	3·66	454,646	30·44
UNP	28,456	1·91	3,888	0·26	4,165	0·27	1,381	0·09	1,387	0·09	5,049	0·34	4,991	0·33	2,488	0·17	4,874	0·33	56,680	3·80
PAP	4,328	0·29	1,429	0·10	3,227	0·22	27,979	1·88	—	—	2,688	0·18	1,555	0·11	2,624	0·17	7,293	0·49	51,123	3·43
APRP	—	—	1,342	0·09	9,420	0·63	9,896	0·66	—	—	—	—	91	0·01	2,756	0·18	3,201	0·21	27,328	1·83
Independents	6,174	0·41	4,156	0·28	71	0·01	2,991	0·20	—	—	5,288	0·35	929	0·06	2,381	0·16	5,286	0·35	27,216	1·82
Total No. of votes	121,711	8·15	214,411	14·36	161,579	10·82	135,133	9·05	150,839	10·10	277,129	18·56	157,644	10·56	105,193	7·04	169,712	11·36	1,493,371	100

Table 15 Number of seats won

Region	G. Accra	Eastern	Central	Western	B. Ahafo	Ashanti	Volta	Northern	Upper	Total
No. of constituencies	9	22	15	13	13	22	16	14	16	140
PP	3	18	15	10	13	22	2	9	13	105
NAL	3	4	0	0	0	0	14	5	3	29
UNP	2	0	0	0	0	0	0	0	0	2
PAP	0	0	0	2	0	0	0	0	0	2
APRP	0	0	0	1	0	0	0	0	0	1
Independents	1	0	0	0	0	0	0	0	0	1
Total No. of candidates	9	22	15	13	13	22	16	14	16	140

XI

A northern contest

At the northern crossing of the great Volta lake the Yeji ferry now has to thread its way through a cemetery of dead trees, still rooted in the drowned soil, in order to reach the distant landing stage and the road to Salaga and Tamale. Ten years ago there was only the swift current of the river and a brief transit into the northern regions. The benefits of modernity, cast adrift on the empty waters of the lake, have divided Northern and Upper Ghana from its southern neighbours to a greater extent than for many years past. It seemed possible, therefore, that there would be a response to the 1969 election on the part of the 200, 000 northern electors different from that of their southern counterpart, since there was no prime reason why a northerner should prefer a predominantly Akan-based Progress Party to a predominantly Ewe-based NAL. To some extent that proved true. The constituencies of Northern and Upper Ghana were more evenly divided between the parties than the southern and Volta regions (table 16).

Yet despite the barrier of the lake, and the apparent freedom to choose, the north remained closely linked to the south. It was to Busia and Gbedemah that local leaders in the two regions turned in the end, jettisoning earlier attempts to create a separate movement, and ignoring the appeal of the northern-based PAP. In this way entry was afforded to the two national parties because of the readiness of the north to accept their help, although the traffic was not at all one-sided, since, if Progress and NAL had benefits to bestow, the north had votes to deliver. The question no one before the election could answer was which of the two parties would be the more attractive proposition.

In considering the question the reader may be misled into supposing that Progress or NAL were free agents in an open bargaining situation—independent buyers and sellers in the political market. But it was not so. A different analogy might be that of a game of chess between PP and NAL, in which moves across one part of the board were necessarily countered by rival moves across other squares. But that too ignores the fact that the pieces themselves were very alive to the efforts made to move and capture them. Indeed, to be in the north in 1969 and look south was to feel that NAL and Progress were themselves being manoeuvred by village players intent on seizing advantages in the never-ending conflicts of local politics. In moving north across the Volta both parties were entering regions of an intense patriotism where loyalties to homestead, village, clan and chiefdom were woven into the fabric of society, not only among the grouped homesteads of the Sissala, Kassena, Nankani, Lobi and Dagarti but in the larger chiefdoms of the Mamprussi, Dagomba, Wala and Gonja. The gathering of support by outside interests among these northern peoples

---

Written in conjunction with Mr Lobaza Allen, 1970; hitherto unpublished.

extended the horizon of their demands, but it did not alter substantially the pattern of local allegiance, of which the lines of division among the people at large were essentially 'traditional'.

Table 16

	Northern	Upper
Registered electors	198,586	302,807
Voters	105,193	169,712
Percentage of electors voting	53	56
PP		
Votes	50,301	94,315
Seats	9	13
NAL		
Votes	44,643	54,743
Seats	5	3
APRP		
Votes	2,756	3,201
Seats	0	0
PAP		
Votes	2,624	7,293
Seats	0	0
UNP		
Votes	2,488	4,874
Seats	0	0
Independent		
Votes	2,381	5,286
Seats	0	0

An earlier article discussed the substance of northern politics in the period before independence, including the rise of the Northern People's Party and its merger into the UP opposition. It looked too at the kind of conflicts which enabled party leaders in Accra and Kumasi to find support at local level, as between the opposed 'gates' of the Yendi Skin, the Muslim quarrels in Wa, the Catholic influence at Nandom, and the quarrels between village chiefdoms among the Kassena-Nankani in the Chiana-Paga constituency. In this present essay we go back now to the same area of Upper Ghana, on the northern boundary of the country, where Mr Lobaza Allen was an active figure in Kassena-Nankani politics, and we begin by restating a number of aphorisms about political life in this remote and friendly district which were repeated to us time and again. The language is retained as recorded (by notebook and pen).

Elections are interpreted in this area and the most part of the Northern and Upper regions to mean a personality struggle. The election results confirm the pride of the winning faction. National politics as such have no meaning, and no candidate can go far without bringing in local issues. The elders and people give support to the one they think will help them in solving their day-to-day problems, someone they can approach easily and understand. Votes will go to those who command respect of the elders and people. The people are concerned more with local events than happenings at national levels. Their own leaders are the ones who matter and who

talk of government politics to suit their local activities. The success
of a party rests on the square shoulders of these local leaders who
direct or misdirect the people to suit their plans. Since they are
respected they are supported, whatever party they join. The chiefs
and people have no choice about parties.
Not much account is taken of southern politics. The activities of the
Centre for Civic Education, for example, were not known in the
constituency. It died when it was to be born. The launching of the
centre for civic education in my district never came up. It rained
heavily on that day. The people kept away. The officers who came
to launch it went to the Mission house, had fine lunch, drank coffee
and left without a word. That was the end of the beginning of the
Centre for Civic Education. Since then we have never seen them
before the voting.

The primary effect of 'national politics' coming into the north from
outside is to sharpen ambition, and to breed faction. It is true that some
kind of integrative process may be detected in the closer contacts between
groups, districts and regions, but it is usually the contact of conflict. And
since the notion of a class struggle, as social categories of opposed economic interests, is very remote, the rivalry (which is endemic) is either territorial (between villages) or communal (between lineages). When the
word 'class' is employed, it is used very loosely to describe a community
which has succeeded or failed to get its local candidate elected, when those
who fail see themselves in danger of becoming 'second-class citizens'
bossed about by those who have won.

Response to the registration of voters was encouraged not so much by
the Government Information Department but by the young, ambitious,
would-be politicians who felt it was their turn and their section's turn
to get to power. The electorates are influenced locally by the would-be
politicians in their civic responsibilities of voting for power on behalf
of sectional, divisional, tribal interests.
Some time after the *coup* and before the ban on party politics was
lifted, sectional groups based on tribal or divisional sentiments were
set up. Their main aim was political, to consolidate their position as
a unit to compete against other units. As one association put it,
'Kassena, hands off Nankani area. We have had enough domination.
We want our own son to represent us.'
In the clash between village and village the loser dropped to second
class. This class superiority struggle continued under the CPP, with
the winners leading in everything.

There is another sense in which class is used: to describe the difference between those who are 'established' and those who are not, a distinction usually drawn between the former politicians of the NPP and the more
recently educated leaders, although it is doubtful whether so sharp a contrast substantially exists throughout the two regions.

There are two classes of leadership. The young educated who benefited during the CPP era by way of scholarship and political appointments. They include young school leavers. The other class comprise
old politicians of the opposition (NPP) with support from the chiefs,
elders and farmers. Whereas the latter live with the people, the
revolutionary youth are mostly government-employed or students
living in other regions and visiting only on holidays. The established
leaders look on the ambitious Youth with contempt.

The daily round of the great majority of the people in the two northern
regions is determined by the seasons for millet, rice, sorghum and ground-
nuts. For seven months of the year the life of the peasant farmer is harsh:
then the harvest is over and there are months of leisure when baskets are
woven or leather goods fashioned. A limited irrigation produces a few dry
season vegetables, and the young men migrate to work on the southern
cocoa farms or in the cities. Among those brought into contact with the
south—and by extension to those around them—a sense of being 'northern
and different' is very marked, reinforced both by the crowded life in the
poorer 'Zongo' quarters of the towns in Ashanti and the south and by the
shared educational background of those who went to the rather good secondary schools and training colleges in Tamale, Navrongo, Pusiga and Wa.
It was in these circumstances of a desire to protect and advance a 'northern unity'—evoked especially by the introduction of adult suffrage—that the
Northern People's Party was brought together in 1954 and flourished
throughout the then undivided north. Under inducements offered by the
central government to come within the generous embrace of the 'party in
power', the NPP lost many of its leaders (notably Mumuni Bawumia)
although it survived as a section of the United Party, until that too was
extinguished by the declaration in 1964 that Ghana was a single-party
republic.

By the time of the first military *coup* Ghanaians in these two northern
regions were very alert to the advantages as well as the dangers of
politics. The *coup* also saw the drawing together of local threads of
support ready for the time when party politics might be re-started by
permission of the military. Such were the origins of a Northern Youth
Association, and we look at its genesis before turning to the party align-
ments which divided the north during the election. Again we quote local
accounts of what is said to have happened.

> Before the lifting of the ban on politics there were movements and
> associations. One was the NYA. All northerners all over the country
> embraced it. It brought northern brothers and sisters together in the
> south and the north, and there was a cross-section of top police and
> army officers, agriculturalists, lawyers, journalists, clerks, teachers,
> nurses, midwives. It also included young and old politicians, and
> meetings were held in regional capitals. The NYA gained good
> strength from the support given by the NLC commissioners in
> Northern and Upper Ghana. One interesting point was that all the
> executive members were from the revolutionary youth, made up
> mostly of lawyers, journalists and trade unionists. The old brigade
> of the defunct NPP were not in the executive. But they gave support,
> because its aims and objects were those of the old party.

As the date of the return to civilian politics drew near the NYA fell
apart—or rather it was torn by the struggle between those who had been
in power (including a number who had suffered as a consequence) and
those who now wanted their share of the benefits. By a natural consequence the struggle took on something of the character of the 'old and
established' versus the 'young and radical'—one hungry generation trying
to tread down another.

> An internal struggle unfolded between the old brigade, made up of the
> former NPP politicians, and the new force from the Youth. The
> latter were either in primary or middle school in earlier days and

had benefited from the special scholarship schemes for northerners in the days of the CPP Ministers. These young budding politicians naturally inclined to the CPP, reborn as NAL, and stood a good chance to win in constituencies where the old CPP leaders could no longer stand, being disqualified. But it was no surprise that the old NPP brigade suspected that the young brigade wanted to oust them. The young felt that they were more educationally qualified, and could stand up for the north against the south better than the former NPP leaders. They stood for revolutionary actions and grabbed all the seats on the NYA. So the older leaders withdrew and started to organise in the familiar way through chiefs, and for Progress. They won, although the Youth and NAL put up a good fight. The old order is changing.

Perhaps it is. But such quarrels were fought out among a very small number of educated leaders who could put together a following only by enlisting the help of the chiefs and elders of these northern chiefdoms. Where NAL succeeded it was for the same reasons, and on the same basis of support, as Progress—because its local leaders in the constituency were able to produce a majority from among the scattered homesteads and their traditional heads. In such enterprises one must know intimately—and the examples are taken almost at random—the twists and turns of traditional politics within the labyrinthine intrigues of the royals of the Dagomba Skin at Yendi, Mion, Karaga and Savelugu and among the Muslim leaders in Tamale; or to know intimately (because one is to the manner born) the struggle between rival lineages among the Frafra and Tallensi communities. The 'revolutionary youth' who turned to NAL as the reincarnation of the CPP, or the 'conservative brigade' who joined Progress as the continuation of the NPP and UP, had to weave their support together in identical ways. Where there were differences in the style of leadership the explanation was usually, as we shall see, because one party or the other had a dominant hold on the constituency, thus forcing its opponent into less traditional—and less successful—mannerisms; but such differences in no sense reflected a substantially different appeal to the substantially different body of electors. How could it be otherwise? 'Party appeal' is invariably no more, and no less, than the simple programme of reform which every candidate endorsed: 'Elect me and I will advance the interests of our people' as a village or a clan or chiefdom.

The election

Any notion of a joint Northern Youth Association candidate for the Paga constituency faded quickly. To the old division between Paga and Chiana, each with its own Youth Association, there appeared a third element, the Nankani chiefdoms and a Nankani East Literates' Association. Each of the three areas was strongly in support of a local candidate, but not *totally* in support. In Paga, for example, the Progress Party nominee

> came from the royal ruling family and therefore was opposed by other factions from rival class and families. The rivalry came from chieftaincy disputes, marriage quarrels and superiority struggles. The litigants against the chief form the minority but they are a force to reckon with in almost every district in the constituency.

These quasi-traditional disputes afforded every opportunity to an ener-

getic canvasser (appropriately supplied with gifts) to widen or heal each
local rift.

> After the greetings and counter-greetings, the canvasser asks the
> chief's permission to allow him to speak to his subjects in the market
> place where the Boys have already been sent to organise the people
> and keep the place lively by drumming and merrymaking until his
> arrival. The first speaker is usually the chief's linguist or a re-
> spected elder. The local chairman tells the people why the other
> opponents were standing and why they choosed to go with that par-
> ticular party. The people are given a full history of the opposing
> candidates—their behaviour in the society, their sincerity and honesty
> and whether they would help them if they had them not at heart. Most
> part of the speech is directed personally against the opposing candi-
> dates.
>
> The people were then educated on the party's symbol and how to
> vote. After the rally, the drummers take over to entertain the people.
> Invited guests are served with local drinks. The candidate goes back
> to the chief and expresses his thanks. The candidate gives account of
> the response of the people. This system of lobbying for votes con-
> tinues until the election day. Sometimes the candidate is forced to
> visit a particular chief or area two or three times in a week when
> the going is difficult or as demanded by the agents. The agents are
> given pocket money ranging from N₵ 10· 00 to N₵ 50· 00 for the
> greetings, buying of cola, drinks and for hiring of bicycles. A good,
> reliable and respected agent can work miracles by getting support.
> The rest is left to Mother Luck.

Tedam, who had agreed to the change from NPP to the United Party,
had later gone over to the CPP. He now proposed to stand for, and was
endorsed (after some dispute) by, the Progress Party. The National
Alliance of Liberals secured an able candidate, A. A. Luguterah, the only
lawyer, then recently qualified, in the constituency. Other candidates and
parties did what they could to secure positions of local advantage. (It was
interesting to see how quickly the two major national parties were sought
out by the strongest local candidates throughout both the northern regions.)
Luguterah was unopposed as the NAL nominee: who would contest a lawyer
and a man of growing influence far beyond the Kassena-Nankani area?

> He was actually one of the brains behind the formation of the NYA. He
> also knew the ins and outs of the constituency. He organised meetings
> when most of the ex-CPP politicians, including Tedam, were in pro-
> tective custody. He later won the confidence of the NLC, and was put
> on commissions and made chairman of the Ghana Upper Volta boun-
> dary demarcation. Being a lawyer, it was alleged he could work for
> the enskinment of aggrieved candidates in place of the present chiefs.

Quite drastic steps were needed to combat so strong a candidate. When a
local Progress Party organiser returned from Accra and toured the constituency, he

> noticed to his surprise that the NAL had strong following, as against
> the belief that PP was going to have an easy win. Knowing very well
> the people's thinking, he went to the Paga market on market day, bought
> a shirt of NAL colours and symbols. He announced to the market that
> he had returned with news from Accra. Brothers and sisters there

(he said) were denouncing the NAL party as being too tribalistic.
Those who have come to realise this have been burning their party
dresses and symbols, as was done to the CPP colours and party cards
after the *coup*.

When the crowd thickened, he requested two boys to hold the NAL
shirt high on two sticks to the general view of the people. He lighted
the shirt into flames. It burnt into ashes. The people were surprised
at the lawyer's (NAL) party shirt being burnt without a challenge.
Soon words spread out to the homes and outlying villages that a son
has come from Accra to burn lawyer's shirt and that lawyer had no
power to challenge him.

The burning of the NAL Party shirt went well to demonstrate
that actually lawyers couldn't do everything. His message to the
people went through.

The independent candidate, on the other hand, 'did not canvass or hold
any rally. He alone was the only person who knew what he was about',
whereas 'the two serious candidates spent the days and nights talking their
way to the heart of their electorates'. The PP candidate

used his personal influence and that of the leaders of the former NPP,
like Chief Dombo, Jatoe Kaleo, B. K. Adama. The NAL candidate used
his position as the only local lawyer. Some were of the opinion they
would not lose a case in court if they supported him. On both sides
money changed hands, and gifts were offered. There was a shortage
of millet in the North and Upper regions, and food gifts were priceless.

The election itself was unusual, and in one sense, in the counting of the
ballot papers, it was extraordinary. Again we use the words of one of the
election agents:

The election was fairly conducted. There was one major drawback
which reduced the voting power. Ballot papers were delayed, due to
poor communication, and voting was held three days late. The electors
were so eager to vote, they came on election day, turned up the following Saturday, were disappointed, and on Sunday again they turned up
without voting. It was not until 1st September that the election was
held.

The counting of the votes started at 9 p.m. same day (1 September
1969) and continued without break until 2 p.m. the following day (seventeen hours of counting). During the counting and recounting the NAL
agents challenged almost everything that was being done in the counting, sometimes three or four times. All their requests were granted;
hence the counting of 12, 222 ballot papers went through the night, the
following morning and into the afternoon. Eventually, when the final
results were to be announced, the NAL counting agents requested that
they would like the boxes to be re-opened and counted again. This
request was too much, taking into account the pains the counting
officers had taken. However, the Returning Officer upheld their request and suspended the announcement of the results. Recounting
would be done at 4 p.m., after two hours' break to allow some who
had not taken their previous supper, breakfast and lunch to do so. The
officials who did the counting felt it was too much and asked to be
relieved. They retired and left the boxes in the counting centre under
police guard. The PP agents returned at 4 p.m. to the counting centre.
The Returning Officer, with six new counting officers, were also there

ready for the recounting. But not until 5.15 p.m. did the NAL candidate and his counting agents turn up. The Returning Officer, a Forestry Officer by occupation, got up and announced as follows: I promised to recount the votes cast at 4 p.m. on the request of the NAL candidate and his agents. I have with me here new officers for the recounting. We have waited for more than an hour, without the showing of those who requested for the recounting. I don't think I can do more than this, I have had enough patience. I am satisfied with the counting and I announce as follows: C.K. Tedam, PP, 5, 343; A.A. Luguterah, NAL, 4, 839; Edward Atiyoori, PAP, 1, 652, and A.F. Adda, Independent, 388.

The statistical details of this picture show the balance of support within each of the three main areas (table 17).

Table 17

	Registered voters	PP	NAL	PAP	Ind.	% poll	% PP vote
Paga	5, 570	2, 348	1, 250	23	71	66	63·5
Chiana	6, 971	1, 577	2, 583	52	113	62	36·4
Mirigu/Sirigu	8, 266	1, 400	992	1, 576	198	50	33·6
Special voters (election officers, etc)	—	18	14	1	6	—	—
Total	20, 807	5, 343	4, 839	1, 652	388	58·7	43·7

Clearly, the heavy Progress vote in the closely populated Paga chiefdom, plus the party's minority support in the neighbouring two areas, determined the result. If we look more closely still at the critical area of Mirigu/Sirigu we can begin to see the basic elements of election contests in the north. We see how village-chiefdom disputes are tied into national party conflicts which both use and are used by these local factions. The group loyalties of family, clan and village determine the weight of electoral support, but they cannot secure a monopoly of the votes. The Mirigu/Sirigu wards were a tiny universe of feuding groups in which the contestants struggled to put together a following, each succeeding most where he was personally best connected (table 18).

Table 18

Wards	Registered voters	PP	NAL	PAP	Ind.
Kandiga	2, 966	352	110	1, 068	58
Mirigu	1, 946	472	495	51	61
Sirigu	1, 690	235	193	280	39
Nabago	1, 664	341	194	177	40
Total	8, 266	1, 400	992	1, 576	198

The heavy voting for the People's Action Party in the Kandiga ward could easily be explained by the fact that the party's candidate was born in and grew up in Kandiga. Similarly, by one last picture—as close as we can get—we can show the attractive strength of a 'local son' in part of the small Mirigu chiefdom (table 19).

Table 19

Wards	Registered voters	PP	NAL	PAP	Ind.
		104	48	21	12
Achobisi	971	72	36	4	12
		135	28	12	11
Kengio/Kasselengo	614	44	294*	7	6
Gonem	361	117	89	7	20
Total	1,946	472	495	51	61

* 'The NAL agent for the party comes from this ward and is the prince who contested the Mirigu Skin. He therefore organised against the party (PP) which the chief supported and brought more votes for NAL because of his influence.'

The March by-election

There was an unexpected sequel to the September contest. The NAL candidate appealed against the results of the election; that failed, but a writ taken out in the Supreme Court against Tedam under section 71 of the constitution succeeded. The Progress Party MP was disqualified (as the NAL leader, Gbedemah, had been *before* the election) on the grounds that he had been a CPP member of parliament and a member of the regional steering committee of the outlawed party. A by-election was ordered, therefore, and both parties re-entered the fight.

Luguterah stood again for NAL. The local Progress Party executive narrowed its choice to two possible candidates, both women, one a young teacher training college tutor who had studied at the University College of Cape Coast, whose father was an influential Catholic catechist and an elder of the Sirigu Skin. The other was Tedam's niece, Miss C.K.Tedam, a young Certificate 'A' teacher, from Paga. The Paga faction carried the day, and 'Miss Tedam was informed of her nomination, to her surprise' the night before her papers were filed. The candidate was then kept in the background during the election, and

> was seen only when elders and chiefs demanded to see her. In each case she spoke briefly on the role and importance of women in society. On many occasions on party campaigns she was left in the house to rebuild her strength ...

But to balance the legal and personal setback of having its original candidate disqualified, progress now had the immense advantage of being the 'party in power', and good use was made of the fact.

Miss Tedam's party was the one in power, and some development projects planned by the NLC were then being executed by the PP government. Big durbars were held to celebrate the occasions. In one section it was arranged that a tanker with water should be sent to a notorious drought area. The chief spoke and said he realised it was only the PP government which could help them. A retired army sergeant and chairman of NAL announced that he and his people were now supporting Progress.'

The PAP candidate declined to stand, and was persuaded to try and swing the Kandiga and Sirigu villages behind Progress. (The net result was to diminish the overall vote in those wards: turnout dropped considerably, to a quarter of those registered, of whom a majority now voted for Progress.) Luguterah suffered the indignity of being arrested two weeks before the election and charged before the local court with stealing, but was released on bail to enable him to continue his campaign. The overall vote was low compared with the general election: 44 per cent of the registered electors, against 59 per cent in 1969, part of the explanation being the absence of a local candidate in Sirigu/Mirigu and, no doubt, a sense among NAL supporters in the Chiana area of having to struggle against a 'government party'. Yet the contest was closely fought, and the outcome was in no sense predetermined:

Miss C. K. Tedam   5, 567
A. A. Luguterah   3, 636

Table 20

Districts	Registered electors	Votes for:		% turnout
		PP	NAL	
Paga	5, 570	2, 294	1, 032	59·7
Chiana	6, 971	2, 001	1, 776	47·8
Mirigu/Sirigu	8, 266	1, 272	828	25·3
Total	20, 807	5, 567	3, 636	44·2

A final comment

Much is made by many commentators of the inability of African communities to understand the idea of opposition, and of the lack of national focus for those who live in the more remote areas of 'new States'. Neither characteristic was evident in 1969-70 in Kassena-Nankani. The area is certainly remote from Accra, but despite the distance, despite the sense of being 'northern and different', despite the barrier of the lake and the slow ferry, neither of the two national parties had any difficulty in finding candidates in the constituency. On the contrary, the leading contestants were quick to seek out the national parties, and both sides—parties and candidates—traded briskly with each other to what they believed would be their mutual advantage. As for the notion of opposition, the district was shot through with majority and minority factions whose members were

very much aware of their relevant positions, which they sought constantly
to augment in traditional quarrels, district conflicts, regional politics
and, in 1969-70, two parliamentary elections.

XII

Progress in Ghana

Re-reading Dr Kofi Busia's book *Africa in Search of Democracy* (London, 1967) and revisiting Ghana was a sobering experience. Certainly I found it so. How easy it is to be in search of good government; how hard it is to achieve it! Everything in the book is so persuasive, including a great deal of criticism of many African governments for failing to live up to the ideals their leaders proclaimed. One wondered even then, in 1967, how Kofi the leader would compare with Kofi the writer. Then in October 1969 the Ghanaian army and police handed control of the country back to civilian leaders, and Busia became Prime Minister after his Progress Party had won the first general election to be held under the new constitution. Six months of office is not a long period by which to judge the performance of Dr Busia's government, but the early decisions of a new regime often establish the style if not the conduct of its rule. And so it may be with Busia and Progress. What can be said about them, particularly in the light of Busia's own observations prior to the election?

There is everything to be said for his ideals. They are impeccable. So, too, in general was the manner of his party's arrival in office. I saw the run-up to the election in August 1969: there was nothing of substance to criticise. It was an admirable and moving renewal of democratic procedures—neutrally conducted, peacefully contested. And if Africa really is in search of democracy, one might argue that Ghana rediscovered its virtues last year. It now has a Prime Minister publicly devoted to maining freedom and justice: twin ideals of the Ghana republic. But look closer and the picture is much more obscure: more murky, if only because of the involved nature of Ghanaian politics, whether under Busia or Nkrumah, which may as often hinder as promote the virtues proclaimed by its leaders.

Consider, for example, the vexed problem of tribalism.[1] It is a term of criticism applied to others: the Ewe are 'tribalistic,' say the Progress leaders—look at the election results, look at the way the NLC under Harlley and Kotoka began to pack their kinsmen into the special branch of the police and into dominant positions on bodies like the Ghana Trading Company and other public corporations. The Ewe for their part either deny such accusations or justify their 'clannishness' by stressing Akan hostility to minorities in the country. And Dr Busia? We have his reflections on the problem of tribalism and national unity. They revolved—when in exile—around the notion of 'a nation of different tribes, possessing a diversity of traditions and even cultures'. Misguided leaders, said Busia, seek to combat traditionalism: but, 'as we see it, the social realities suggest that a sounder approach to the problem of tribalism in Africa is to accept the

International Journal, **XXV**, 3, 1970.

fact of pluralism'. Ethnic associations are 'not necessarily incompatible with the building of a democratic nation'. They may even afford 'better prospects for democracy in consonance with group interests'. How? By the encouragement of regional and local government, since 'tribalism, whether it is manifested by an ethnic group large enough to be a region or only by a small one occupying a village, offers opportunities in local self-government'. Fine words, which must have come readily to a trained sociologist, and to a party leader in exile whose primary base of support between 1954 and 1959 had been among the Ashanti traditionalists, in alliance with Ewe, Ga and northern minorities. But they do not fit very easily into the present concept of a dominant party government most of whose supporters not only disliked the Ewe and Ga majority on the NLC in 1966 but, since they took office, have been very critical of the Ewe-based opposition.

Consider, too, the problem of the single-party State. Considerable care was given in the Constituent Assembly to safeguards against single-party rule. Busia, too, wrote nobly against its evils. In practice, however, Busia may very soon find himself Prime Minister of a *de facto* single-party State, since, outside the Volta region, the present handful of opposition members are unlikely to improve their position at the next election. What happens then? Busia was critical of Tanzania's experiment with single-party elections, since it offered only a limited choice to the electorate. He was also critical of British colonial rule in its closing stages, since he believed that (in Ghana) it gave too much support to Nkrumah and the CPP, too little to the opposition—and himself. 'The British teach that an opposition is an essential part of the parliamentary democratic system; yet their policy for helping the institution of the parliamentary system at this final stage never included any official help to the opposition, (who) had to fend for themselves, without any help'. And today? The Ghana opposition is represented at national level in the Council of State.[3] But one may doubt whether it is likely to receive any practical help from the triumphant Progress Party in office. Indeed, the first leader of the opposition, K. A. Gbedemah, was unseated by his local opponent, who brought an action in the High Court under article 71 of the constitution: a provision deliberately added to the constitution (it is reasonable to argue) in order to prevent Gbedemah's continuance in parliament.[4]

Consider, again, the problem of the relationship of party and State. Nothing is more strongly stressed in Busia's book than the 'rule of law' and the 'dignity of man'. John Stuart Mill shines through the pages of his belief in democracy: freedom for the individual, protected in his liberties by an independent judiciary and an impartial, incorrupt civil service—a freedom denied to the people of Ghana by Nkrumah, who in 1963 dismissed the Chief Justice, bullied the civil service and subordinated the courts to the needs of his party.

And in 1970? *Plus ça change, plus c'est la même chose?* Not quite, perhaps: but the resemblance is sometimes very close. At the end of last year the newly appointed Progress government acted precipitately against the large number of foreign nationals in the country, hastening a process begun by the NLC. The move was popular because of the opportunity it gave local traders and businessmen to take over the positions hitherto held by Nigerians, Syrians, Malians and others,[5] and because it was also widely believed that the expulsion of aliens who were not exempted from the provisions of the order would lower the urban crime rate, provide employment for Ghanaians and diminish the (illegal) flow of capital from the country. Harshly and inefficiently administered, the order led to a great deal of suffering, mitigated by the degree to which the order was evaded; nor is it at all clear that the kind of jobs carried out by many foreigners can or will be done as efficiently by Ghanaians. Why was it done? Perhaps because it was popular among Ghanaians generally, perhaps because it rewarded those who had supported the party: but, whatever the reason, the act was a poor testimony to the tolerance of a government presided over by a leader who had once set great store by its practice.

Early in 1970 the government turned against the administration, dismissing 568 officers in the civil service and public corporations, ostensibly on grounds of inefficiency, by a cumbersome process of damnation round the Cabinet table—rather like Caesar, Anthony and Lepidus, who marked down those they disliked by mutual bargaining and consent. Then in April the government was challenged in the courts by Mr E. K. Sallah, a dismissed manager of the Ghana National Trading Corporation. A sorry pantomime followed. When judgement was about to be given the Attorney General tried to object to two of the panel of five High Court judges (sitting as the Supreme Court) who had sat to hear Sallah's application; the objection was dismissed on Friday 17 April by a four-to-one majority of the Supreme Court, and the original panel then delivered its opinion the following Monday, upholding (by three-to-one) Sallah's claim that he was wrongfully dismissed by the government under section 9 (i) of the Transitional Provisions of the constitution.[6] The case was a difficult one of interpretation, complicated by the remarkable refusal of one of the judges to take part in the Sallah judgement, since he disagreed with the Supreme Court's dismissal of the Attorney General's objection to two of his colleagues on the panel. And there the matter might have rested, but for a still more remarkable speech on television by the Prime Minister, who flatly refused to accept the judgement of the court. 'My government', said Busia, 'will exercise its right to employ only those whom it wishes to employ'. One trembles to think what Dr Busia would have said about Nkrumah had the former president attacked the judiciary as follows:

> Some of the judges appeared to have been more concerned with saving their colleagues from embarrassment than with upholding the established principles of a fair trial ... There are some who think they can use the courts politically to change the people's choice so clearly and so massively made in fair and free elections last August ...
> They are wrong. They cannot succeed. I did not react not because, as some have taunted, the government is weak, but because I respect the principle that the executive should not interfere with the judiciary in the proper exercise of its functions. But if the judges want to play politics, I am quite ready to take them on ...
> What I have come to say tonight to the nation is this: that as long as I remain the Prime Minister of this country, I shall do my best, with the co-operation of my Cabinet, to uphold the highest standards of democracy as I understand it, whether in the legislature, or the executive, or the judiciary.
> I cannot be tempted to dismiss any judge. I shall neither honour nor defy anyone with martyrdom; but I will say this, that the judiciary is not going to hold or exercise any supervisory powers not given to it by the constitution...[7]

Rhetoric? Perhaps, and there are sentences which suggest that the Prime Minister was possibly reacting not only against the judiciary but

against charges from within his own ranks that he was too weak and mild
a leader. Indeed, there may be a sense in which many of the acts of the
new Progress government have been taken less on their merits than under
the compulsion of *seeming to do something*. The government is clearly
under great pressure since its election victory. Unemployment is high,
expectation is still higher. Yet few are likely to be satisfied, given the
external restraints on the economy. True, the new government is en-
deavouring to set the entrepreneurs free. Encouragement is being given
to local, Ghanaian businessmen alongside efforts to increase food produc-
tion and raise farming incomes. The progress Party election manifesto
had promised its 'support for and confidence in private enterprise' and
the new government had proposed legislation to advance the take-over by
Ghanaian of small-to-medium foreign-owned concerns. If there is a
distinct style of government to emerge during these first six months of
office it probably lies in this: in clumsy efforts to open the economy to
local skills, a Victorian belief in self-help, coupled with a recognition that
the State must enable private enterprise to grow. The flavour is very
different, therefore, from the socialist preaching of the previous regime,
although the kind of people likely to prosper under Progress are not likely
to be very different from those who made money under Nkrumah, and the
role of the government in the direction of the economy is unlikely to be
markedly less than under Nkrumah. For the present, however, a certain
lack of bluster is noticeable: a lack of heroic posturing abroad, less dogma
at home. Political life in these first months of office appears more re-
laxed than in the last feverish days of the first Republic, although the poor
still live miserably and it is very doubtful whether their plight is likely to
grow less. It is argued that increases in wages have fallen behind increases in the cost of living over the entire decade 1959-69, and that farm
wages and cocoa incomes are lower in real terms than they were a decade
ago.
     When one considers the pressure of population on natural resources,
or the demand for rewards on the scarcity of political prizes, and the very
little room open to the leaders for manoeuvre within the economy, the
future is not a very welcoming prospect. Alas for the new States! If God
wants to put his angels to a test, all he has to do is to send them to govern
a newly independent country! So at least one may conclude from the first
six months of Dr Busia's government in Ghana—a government of bewildered
men, not recording angels.

Notes

1   More sensitive readers may prefer 'ethnicity' or 'primordialism'.
    I am employing the word commonly used by Ghanaians.
2   *Africa in Search of Democracy,* chapter 7, 'Tribalism'.
3   An advisory body of twelve members, among them being the Prime
    Minister, the Speaker, the Asantehene (as president of the national
    house of chiefs), the leader of the opposition, and eight leading
    citizens.
4   Article 71—approved after bitter debate in the Constituent Assembly—
    disqualifies persons, against whom adverse findings have been made
    by a commission of inquiry, from holding public office for five years.
    Gbedemah was known to be affected by such a provision, and was (as
    noted earlier) unseated after the election through an action in the High
    Court. See above, pp. 116-18.

5   When, for example, market stall traders were expelled from the
     northern town of Bawku, local traders took their place and set a
     placard over the stalls which read 'Nangodi Busia Stall—Thank-you
     Busia Stall'.
6   The question at issue was whether section 9 (i) of the Transitional
     Provisions, which were effective for a six-month period and which
     empowered the government to dismiss members of the civil service,
     could be held to apply to the whole of the public service, including
     public corporations, or only to offices created by the NLC.
7   20 April 1970.

XIII

The return to military rule, 1972

I

There is an element of black comedy in the renewed intervention of the
soldiers in Accra. The champions of yesterday are discredited, labelled
villains, and replaced by new heroes whose virtues are proclaimed like
angels trumpet-tongued as the scene changes and a new government is
installed—unless, of course, the attempt fails. When the first *coup* succeeded in February 1966 success was crowned with laurel. The record
of the National Liberation Council's brief regime was commemorated in
words of self-esteem. It is to be hoped, said the soldiers, that 'some day,
when the evolutional history of Ghana is written, the part so nobly and
admirably played by the NLC could be recorded in characters of gold'.
Treason had prospered, unlike the tragic comedy of Lieutenant Arthur and
his rebellious troops in April 1967, who tried and failed to stage a second
coup against the makers of the first. Kotoka was killed, Arthur executed
publicly, and the NLC dismissed the attempt as a wicked action of 'a few
selfish and misguided soldiers'. Now Colonel Acheampong has succeeded
where Arthur failed. What will be said of the new coup? It depends, I suppose, on who next writes the history. But perhaps we shall all have to
rewrite some of the history of Ghana, for what kind of society and State is
it that can so easily be captured and held?
    The weakness of political institutions at a national level is certainly
in marked contrast to the permanence of local structures. In the early,
confident days of the Convention People's Party Krobo Edusei used to like
to quote Shelley: 'Kings are like stars,' he would declaim from the party
platform. 'They rise, they set.' Yet kings in Ghana, and certainly the office
they hold, are nothing like as ephemeral as politicians, parties, parliaments
and the scrupulously defined constitutions on which so much legal care is
spent. A further ironic note was sounded in what was probably Dr Busia's
last public speech before his departure for London and the overthrow of
his Progress government. He was addressing, a little like the headmaster
the prefects, the National Assembly of Chiefs in Kumasi. The gathering of
traditional leaders was a familiar sight, different, no doubt, from the
assembly of chiefs which met to treat with Bowdich or Dupuis or (at the
end of the nineteenth century) with Governor Hodson, yet very likely much
less so than the purveyors of the concept of 'modernisation' would have
us believe. At the meeting with Busia the new Asantehene could look back
over his predecessor's long reign and note that the late Otumfuo, Nana Sir
Osei Agyeman Prempeh II, KBE, had survived four decades of change, including the restoration of the Ashanti Confederacy, the manoeuvres of the
British in their retreat from empire, the advent of a People's Party, the

hopes of the National Liberation Movement, the claims of Osagyefo Dr
Kwame Nkrumah, the arrival of the soldiers, and the triumph of Progress.
Busia, however, was much concerned to give advice. Chiefs were urged to
examine and reform their institutions. According to the report in the local
party newspaper, Dr Busia 'stressed that the institution of Chieftaincy as
part of the social system should work, grow and function to secure the
basic needs of the people. He therefore called on the Chiefs to be forward
looking, and adapt themselves to the situations of today.' It was in line
with the discreet bullying which had come to mark the style and substance
of Progress government that the Prime Minister added, 'in certain circumstances it was for the Government to judge who should be a chief.'

But what sort of national institutions are needed to 'work, grow and
function to secure the basic needs of the people'? Ghana has almost run
out of samples—colonial government, multi-party competition, single-party
control, military-administrative government, dominant party rule, government by the elementary schools leavers in 1951, and by the graduates in
1969; and now, once again, a new saviour with the sword. What is there
left to try? Throughout it all the majority of the population—who once
obeyed the British, cheered Nkrumah, and queued to elect Busia and
Progress—watched passively the removal of their national leaders. Only
at local level have popular emotions been stirred to direct action by the
threat to institutions which retain their allegiance. Despite the apparent
revolt of 'the commoners' in the early nationalist years, the *nkwankwaa*
(that fabled group) have remained a passive majority in national politics,
acted upon rather than acting. A mainspring of politics in Ghana has been
local conflict, and the ordering of society in the village or chiefdom or
district. No party politician or military ruler has dared to proclaim the
republic of the common man at village level, or to abolish the office of
chief; and ordinary illiterate Ghanaians have indeed been moved to violent
action in defence of 'rights'—in Yendi, or Jacobu, or Anlo, or Wamfie—when
local loyalties have been passionately aroused.

Are we to see a total discontinuity, therefore, between national and
local politics? Power at the centre, without consent; legitimacy in the
village without power? That can hardly be true, however difficult it is to
describe the linkages between them. Social groups are not sharply differ-
entiated, although they may be easily recognisable; there is no rigid division
between property owners and peasants, nor between educated and unlettered.
If there is a pervasive concept in Ghanaian politics considered nationally
it is that of 'patronage', conveying the notion of dependence. Big men are
patrons with followers, although wealth is often the index, not the deter-
minate, of status, and personal loyalty to individuals and the 'collectivity of
the tribe' (however that is defined) is very strong still. Such lines of
patronage radiate out through fine-spun webs of influence from the centre
to the districts, and from the local up to the national level, in a search for
mutual benefits. People—that is to say, individuals, families or the majority
in a village, chiefdom, district or even region—give their support to those
who can look after them. Hence the widespread acceptance of any 'government of the day', since the central administration in Accra is the greatest
of all patrons. There are well tested grounds for such beliefs. The
Brong-Ahafo chiefdoms were a good example of qualified support for the
government, first for the CPP in 1956 and then for Progress in 1969. Most
local groups saw the benefits of obtaining, and then of retaining, a separate
Brong-Ahafo region, and were able to trade their support for Nkrumah
and Busia in exchange for the creation and retention of a separate region.

But support at national level is not affection beyond the point of benefits received and services given: unconditional loyalty is reserved for the village or family group or the local community.

Here is one explanation of the failure of the CPP and the Progress Party, and of the way in which these party regimes collapsed without a hand being raised to save them, or a hand raised even to wipe away a tear of regret except by those who were the direct beneficiaries of a particular regime. It is an explanation based on profit and loss, and rests on the assumption that politics at a national level, and at the intersection of national and local interests, is simply the politics of the market place. When the goods run out, the traders are discredited. They lose not only their customers but the trust that the customers once placed in them. It is one of the main themes of Maxwell Owusu's interesting account of politics in Agona Swedru,[1] from which one can argue that no ordinary elector in Ghana is going to risk his security, let alone his life, to defend a governing elite which fails to provide sufficient 'benefits', including the material comforts of a high-import economy—tinned milk, corned beef, sardines, cloth, cutlasses, petrol and motor tyres at reasonable prices. Least of all is he likely to do so when public hardship is accompanied by private wealth openly demonstrated. Admittedly such displays are common. There is a flamboyant and generous enjoyment of the beneficence to be derived from wealth and power. The sins of the rich in Ghana, at least up to the end of 1971, have always had a great deal more to do with the Prodigal than the Miser.[2] But they are often seen as sins, none the less, and it was easy to understand the complaint of a disillusioned Progress supporter who remarked; 'I could see the need for austerity in July last year, but was it really necessary for Ministers to arrive at Parliament House in large Mercedes cars to announce the fact?' In the absence of an identifiable loyalty to institutions and ideas at a national level, the political market has to depend on demand and supply, and the ease with which the electorate accepted the overthrow of the CPP in 1966 and of Progress in 1972 may be no more than disenchantment with a party machine which had failed to keep its early promises. But since no foreseeable regime in Accra is likely to do *that*, the prospect is gloomy.

Is it right to argue that Progress at the end of 1971 was in much the same position as the CPP at the beginning of 1966? If so, in what sense was it true? Is it also correct to equate the seizure of power by Acheampong with that by Kotoka and Harlley six years ealier? Kotoka could point to the way in which Nkrumah had closed the door very firmly on any possibility of change under the CPP. Acheampong hardly waited until the second Republic was established, and the 1969 election was over, before planning the second *coup*. The NLC could look at the mockery of the 1965 election and conclude that change could be brought about only by force. The NRC can hardly justify *its* rule by the conduct or outcome of the 1969 election. But there were of course 'professional reasons' for both interventions; and Colonel Acheampong (like Colonel Kotoka) was correct in assuming that his *coup* would be either approved or, at worst, not resisted. Perhaps, then, we have to conclude that national forms of rule in Ghana are constantly at risk as much from the indifference of the ordinary elector as from the malignity of those who want to change them.

II

Those who commented at the time on Nkrumah's overthrow in 1966 were fairly confident about what had happened. The CPP (it was argued) had

forfeited its support and had shrunk to a narrow base of self-indulgence.
Far from being a 'mobilisational party' within the taxonomy of terms
much liked by American writers, the CPP was sitting heavily and (it
seemed) irremovably on everything and anyone who disagreed with it.
Since, like most new-State governments, the party was too rudimentary
a structure for total control, it was also incapable of fashioning a single
apparat of power. So it lapsed into an inefficient despotism by which the
leaders tried deliberately to limit, rather than to enforce, political action.
The charade of the 1965 election, when nearly two hundred candidates were
'elected' unopposed, offered only one example of the extent to which the
CPP had become suspicious of its own followers and distrustful of an
electorate which had once rallied in considerable numbers to its appeal.
The party had achieved its aims; it was in power, and it had no notion of
what to do with it other than self-enrichment and public exhortation
through the press. Government (it was said) had become a private monopoly of the newly rich, and the single party was simply the organised
expression of a new political class on the make which was determined to
use the authority of the State to establish a secure economic foundation
for its own continuance.

It was a sorry end, since at its inception in 1949 the CPP had given
some promise of being able to reflect the society it governed and of keeping within manageable distance of its problems. It was loosely constructed,
popularly based, open to all the disputes which divided local society yet
able to use such divisions in order to maintain control. By contrast, at its
end the CPP was struggling to survive not by open competition, and the
skilful use of its powers as a party in office, but by imprisoning its opponents in the name of 'Nkrumaism' or (even) 'African socialism'. No wonder,
then, that by 1966 the army saw an opportunity to intervene.

But, surely, it may be asked, the position of the Progress Party at the
end of 1971 was very different? After all, it had been in power for only
two years. Can distaste for its rule have grown so quickly? It had also
been elected by an overwhelming vote in a free election and by a higher
proportion of a large electorate than the CPP had managed to achieve even
in the high noon of its existence. Was the electorate really so fickle as to
have turned away from the party so early?

Perhaps it was, since the PP leaders had almost gone out of their way
to offend those who were most likely to sustain them in office. It was not
simply that the political market had run out of goods but that the traders
had offended the customers. The Progress Party, as it was put together
in 1968-69, had exercised a distinct appeal for a number of sectional
groups over and above its more general stance as an Akan party, including
its appeal to a more honest government than that of the last years of CPP
rule. It could also claim to represent 'the new intelligentsia', including
the judges, lawyers, university teachers and senior civil servants; and it
was supported by the growing number of Ghanaian businessmen and a
broad section of the better-paid industrial workers. The lawyers and
judges had been the architects of the 1969 constitution which had brought
about the return of civilian politics. The civil servants had served the
NLC under Ankrah and Afrifa very loyally, and could look to Busia's
government as the continuation of the NLC's rule in civilian dress. The
businessmen had similar expectations of a policy favourable to local
enterprise, the trade unions looked not only for a continued improvement
in the level of wages but for an influential position *vis à vis* the new
government through Bentum as general secretary of the TUC. The popu-

lation at large seems to have believed that Progress and Busia offered at
least a change of masters.

   With remarkable fortitude, however, the Progress government engaged
in battle with each section of its supporters. There was more than a touch
of the old intelligentsia in the assumptions which many of the leaders
brought to their rule. They seemed almost to believe that they were riding
aloof above the partisan battles, protected as much by a righteous display
of *amour-propre* as by a massive parliamentary majority. Very early
after taking office in October 1969 they clashed first with the civil service
and then with the judiciary in their stubborn pursuit of the Sallah case,
ending in the Prime Minister's appearance on television to browbeat the
judges.[3] By 1970 restraints on the economy were already cutting back the
privileges of the well-to-do, and by 1971 the hardship was widespread.
The trade unions protested, there were strikes and violence, and the
government rushed legislation through parliament under a certificate of
emergency in order to disband the TUC. As if to ensure that there would
be no shortage of opponents, the government also upset the students by
making them pay (by way of loans) for board and accommodation, and the
sick and injured by imposing hospital charges.

   Meanwhile those who had believed that Busia and Progress would be
a considerable improvement over both the CPP and the military, as a
party prepared to defend 'Freedom and justice', watched with some dismay
the erosion of those high principles defended in Busia's own account of
Africa in Search of Democracy. They did not much like the harsh and
summary expulsion of non-Ghanaians, nor the Bill (again under a certificate of emergency) to forbid the advocacy of 'Nkrumaism', nor the proposal to protect the Prime Minister by legislation 'from insult', nor the
brushing aside of General Ocran's insistence that MPs ought not to delay
over complying with the constitutional requirement to declare their
assets, nor the rough handling of the dismissed civil servants, the universities, the judges, the opposition press, and the TUC. There was nothing
in the Progress record of the capricious cruelty of the last years of
Nkrumah's government, but there was enough done to enable the party's
opponents to say (and its friends to wonder whether) it was moving in the
same direction. And while the leaders were concerned with the supposed
dangers of a revival of Nkrumaism—never a very plausible phenomenon—
discontent was gathering among those, including the soldiers, whom they
assumed to be on their side.

   Of course it is easy now to be wise after the worst has happened, to
list the defects of the Busia administration, and to raise a knowledgeable
eyebrow at the folly of a government which behaved so inexpertly as
politicians. Perhaps it was never likely that a government led by the old
intelligentsia opposition, reinforced by a new generation of intellectuals,
would be very skilful at the art of the possible. It was also very likely
unwise to expect any government in Ghana not to conform to the general
pattern of belief that power—like justice—needs not only to be used but
publicly demonstrated, and used on occasions in full measure, pressed
down and running over. But when all is added up in criticism of Dr Busia's
government, a good deal remains still on the other side, not only in its
favour but in extenuation of its mistakes.

   Freely elected, it was one of the few African governments which held
out the promise of further elections—a re-registration of electors was
carried out in 1971 for local elections the following year and for future
contests at national level. For good or bad, Ghanaians (outside the Volta

region) had a government they themselves had chosen, and a large proportion of the electorate was certainly delighted with the nationalist stance
adopted by Busia's administration, including the expulsion of foreign
traders and the promotion of Ghanaian business.

Many of the misfortunes of the Progress government came with the
misfortunes once again of cocoa. In 1966 the fall in price prior to the
coup, and its rise after Nkrumah had been removed, enabled students of
neo-colonialism to detect the white hand of the chocolate manufacturer at
work in the manipulation of the Ghanaian economy. But Busia too encountered the same difficulties, in an indebted country, of falling export
prices and rising import costs. The economic measures introduced after
July 1971, like those of 1961, were very harsh, and the massive devaluation of 44 per cent at the end of the year put an abrupt end to what was
left of those earlier hopes in 1969-70 that the economy could be rescued
from its very low level of performance. Until we have a proper study of
the Ghanaian economy it is hard to know what difference the CPP/Nkrumah,
as against the NLC/Busia, mix of State and private enterprise actually
made to the development of the economy as a whole. Probably very little,
given the general predicament of its external dependence on world markets.[4] Different army commanders in 1966 and 1972 made no distinction
between Left and Right when they intervened to 'restore the economy',
and it may be that the coincidence of military governments and higher
cocoa prices (if both continue) may reconcile the ordinary Ghanaian votes
to military rule. But still—but still, when the economic argument is fully
made, whether against Nkrumah or Busia, the political difference between
the CPP in 1966 and Progress in 1972 remains. The former had stifled
political competition, and had adopted a constitution which ensured the
suppression of dissent. Busia's government had behaved arrogantly and
often foolishly, and had spoken in bullying tones about its opponents; but
it was still under a form of constitution which offered some hope of representative rule and peaceful change—a hope which it would certainly be
impertinent to suppose that very many Ghanaians do not still entertain.

At this point the careful observer of the post-colonial scene might
well think that he had had enough of such arguments. *Coups* are made by
soldiers and soldiers have guns. It is in that single fact that *coups* have
their origin. Colonel Acheampong's success is the measure of his power,
and power comes from the barrel of a gun ... But will it remain that
simple?

III

For a brief period after 1969 it began to look as if the military and the
politicians in Ghana had succeeded where so many others had failed. The
soldiers had filled the stage in 1966, but were then escorted off three and
a half years later, almost without protest, by the party leaders. A new
Horatian ode seemed needed to Progress, and to Busia's return from
England. Now, however, the truth of Marvell's closing stanzas has been
reasserted:

> And for the last effect
> Still keep the sword erect ...

> The same arts that did gain
> A power, must it maintain.

How did such a situation come about? The danger of a further *coup* seems never to have worried the 1966 military junta, nor the Constituent Assembly, nor the politicians, despite Lt. Arthur's abortive *coup* in 1967 and the experience of neighbouring and more distant States. The main concern was to prevent the return of a single-party dictatorship, not a renewed militarism. The break in constitutionality occasioned by the first *coup* was thought to have been healed by a new constitution under a popular seal of approval. Yet what was to prevent the man with the gun from having his way a second or a third or fourth time?

There is a sense, of course, in which the makers of the 1969 constitution were over-conscious of the danger. They hustled the soldiers off the stage in order to 'demilitarise' fully and finally. A major issue which worried members of the Constituent Assembly in its closing sessions was the relationship between the future politicians and the retiring members of what was then the National Liberation Council. Should the soldiers and police continue to hold office, or should there be a civilian President? It was on a motion introduced by Nana Agyeman Badu, a very shrewd man indeed, that debate sprang up over the NLC's suggestion of a troika presidency of two soldiers and a policeman. And for a time the NLC had its way. A triumvirate was established consisting of Lieutenant General Afrifa, Inspector General John Harlley and Major General Ocran (who was then Acting Chief of Defence Staff) as an interim Presidential Commission. The original intention was that it should act for three years, but so keen were the future politicians, grouped around Busia, to be free of the soldiers, and of any taint of puppetry, that the proposal was amended in order that the soon-to-be elected parliament could replace the military Presidential Commission with a civilian President. Within eighteen months the change was made when Akufo Adde became Head of State.

The Constituent Assembly went still further. It insisted on complete civilian control over the army and police under the new constitution, removing the General Officer Commanding the Armed Forces from the proposed Council of State and reducing the representation of the army and police on the Armed Forces Council. Indeed, the army and police were removed so thoroughly from the political scene that the politicians ceased to be aware of what the soldiers might be up to off stage—until their re-entry.

Precisely why Colonel Acheampong has intervened is still not fully clear. Very likely it was through a combination of particular grievances because of reduced expenditure on the army, and a general sense of exasperation because of the sorry state of the economy, leading to a personal resolve to 'step in and clear up the mess' in January 1972, as earlier heroes had done in February 1966. Perhaps one needs to add to this professional discontent an ambition to rule? Having been a regional commissioner under the NLC and then denied access to power at the centre because of the coming to office of Busia in 1969, Acheampong may simply have wanted to try his own hand at governing.[5] The earlier *coup* had been easy: why should a second not succeed? But what happens now?

In 1957 the British transferred power to the CPP because it was there to receive it. In 1969 the NLC was able to believe that Busia and the Progress Party were rightful inheritors of the period of military rule. In both instances there was a willing disposition on the part of the withdrawing power to transfer control. The British were in no mood any longer to run a colonial empire. General Afrifa, too, one may guess, had had enough. Few soldiers believe at first that politics are real. There is the comfortable assumption that they can be put into cold storage, under armed guard, along with the party slogans and the platform rhetoric, but inevitably under such circumstances, as the NLC found under its non-party rule, political demands and pressures take on new forms and seek new channels of influence *vis à vis* the military. So, no doubt, it will be for Colonel Acheampong, until, eventually, the point is reached, however far distant it may seem today, when fresh elections and a new constitution and civilian leaders are contemplated. The future timetable of change is now quite impossible to foresee, since there is no identifiable leader or group with whom the new military government can begin to negotiate. But one day changes in that direction may take place. Can anything be done to smooth the way?

Understandably, the best gift that could be bestowed on the country, on the military and civilians alike, would be a strong upward movement of cocoa prices for the next decade, a generous attitude overseas towards the regime's external debts, and an unprecedented reduction in the price of Ghanaian imports. Then indeed we might reach Andrew Marvell's happy world, when Ghanaians might

> that sweet militia restore
> When gardens only had their towers
> And all the garrisons were flowers.

Vain hopes: Colonel Acheampong will need to bear arms for a good while longer. One must also expect that there will be more plots among supporters of Busia, defenders of Nkrumah, ambitious soldiers and discontented politicians, more treason trials and a frightened reaction by the NRC. But is there no advice that a hesitant political scientist can offer? In the first of these three articles it was said that, Ghana having tried everything—parliamentary government, single-party rule, military administration—nothing now remained on offer. Perhaps that was not quite accurate. Twenty years ago it was possible to comb through the multitude of blueprints, which the Colonial Office obligingly prepared, for an almost infinite variety of would-be independent States—mixed assemblies, a qualified franchise, unitary constitutions, federal constitutions, executive presidents, republics, monarchies, city States, associated States. Other advisers must be found today. Yet there is no shortage of remedies for the ills of the post-colonial States, for the literature of such inquiries into 'military rule' is already vast, and in recent months a comprehensive guide to the 'typologies of civil-military relations' has been on offer.[6]

Dr Luckham would place Ghana in the category of a 'guardian State', one out of nine possible situations (he says) in which the civil and military authorities of a country may find themselves—excluding an ominous tenth category of 'political vacuum'.[7] In such a guardian State, it is said, the distinction between the military and the civil power is clear; but no clear pattern of control by one over the other exists. Then it is that the army (and Dr Luckham may certainly say that again) has 'a degree of self-steering capacity' leaving it 'free to define its own relations with its environment in the absence of constraints from strong civil institutions'.

The whole passage is worth reproducing, in which Dr Luckham argues that the political role of (for example) the Ghanaian army is

> to uphold and extend support to 'The State' internally as well as
> externally. Ideologically, therefore, it is disposed to regard itself
> as the Platonic custodian of a vaguely defined 'national interest'. On

those occasions that it does put coercion to political use, this occurs because of a dispute with other elites as to the definition or methods of pursuit of the national will, rather than because it acts as the agent of particular interests or power groups. In so far as any special interests are invoked they derive from the professional imperatives of the military establishment.

Having intervened, however, the army is faced with the questions, how long should it rule and how can it withdraw? Here is an old, much discussed problem.[8] It may, says Luckham, exercise a 'direct guardianship' for a time, governing through the military or the civil service; or it may move in and out of office—'an alternating guardianship', moving in when its concern for the national interest is aroused, moving out under civilian pressure or because of the officers' desire to protect the cohesion of their army. In certain circumstances the army may simply act as a guardian catalyst, bringing about changes in the civilian order; or it may exert a 'covert guardianship', when its control is very indirect but is there still as a factor to be reckoned with. Should it remain in power too long, however, then it may itself be infected. A 'Praetorian State' comes into existence, in which 'military organisations lose their unity of purpose and action, and fragments of the armed forces split off, each with their particular alliances with outside groups'. Once this occurs, the army will 'find it very hard to extricate itself from the political miasma'.

These are, of course, analytical categories, not actual situations in which one or more of the type situations may be blurred. But the relevance for the Ghanaian army is clear. If it stays in power too long, it may lapse into factionalism. If it withdraws too far, it may be able to exercise its guardianship role only by intervening disruptively in force once again.

Is there, then, no half-way house in which the army can remain close to civilian politics in order to protect whatever view of the national interests its officers are determined to preserve, yet sufficiently detached to keep its boundaries intact and to enable it to preserve a unity of command free of too gross an interference from civilian politics?

I had thought at first that the Progress government should have retained the guardianship of the NLC in 1969 and have insisted on a qualified return to civilian rule. Colonel Afrifa might then perhaps have kept a closer eye on Colonel Acheampong? But I was told in Accra by former Progress supporters that the device was unlikely to have worked, since the former triumvirate soon lost touch with the field command of the army over which Acheampong retained control. Soldier-administrators quickly drift away from those who have guns, although if army rule is one day to be diminished the way forward must surely lie in the direction of some mode of compromise between the military and fresh party leaders, whoever they may be. Compromise is not unknown to the military, since the soldiers have been too few to govern directly. In 1972, as in 1966, army rule has necessarily been government by delegation to civil servants under such supervision as the army leaders can impose. Compromise with politicians, however, raises problems of a quite different order, and Ghanaians may one day find themselves back again in the complicated procedures of diarchy: an overlapping division between party and army commands.

It will not be as simple in the future as it was in 1968-69, since the NRC will surely wish to weight the scales of any future mixed government heavily in the army's favour, having to risk the dangers of politics entering the army in order not to lose control. The balance will have to be a matter of very delicate negotiation, unless, of course, the soldiers, or one among their number, tries to find his own civilian base of authority through a controlled political organisation, not in order to remove the bulk of the army from politics but to keep it on reserve, hooded perhaps, but ready still to act. It will not be at all easy. For to end where we began, with Marvell, we need to ask: who will be the falconer to lure the falcon to its perch? Can Colonel Acheampong really play the dual role of civilian Lord Protector and army commander? Only perhaps if it could be argued that the soldiers represent a 'class' in the sense that Karl Marx once explained the case ironically in respect of Louis Napoleon. The quotation is familiar, but it becomes still more cogent if it is altered slightly:

> Acheampong represents a class—the most numerous of Ghanaian society—the Ghanaian peasant smallholders ... The great mass of Ghanaian society is formed by the simple addition of homologous multitudes, much as potatoes in a sack are simply a sack of potatoes ... And is so far as there is merely a local interrelationship among the peasant smallholders whereby the identity of their interests gives rise to neither community nor national bond nor political organisation they do not form a class. They are unable therefore to enforce their class interests in their own name ... and must be represented by an unlimited governmental power which protects them ... and which subordinates society to itself ...[9]

Superficially attractive? By suppressing the hostile political elites of warring parties the army can represent the millions of peasant small-holders by defending the State for them? There is a distant echo here of the former colonial government in its role as 'trustee' for the illiterate rural population against the few Westernised elite. But where is the evidence for such claims? In 1966 the army tried to cast itself in the modest role of catalyst, effecting change. Today Acheampong has begun to claim much more, but it is surely open to question (not least by the peasant smallholder whose labours sustain whoever rules in Accra) whether the National Redemption Council represents more than itself. Moreover, not only may the price of its protection be high: the protection itself may become illusory. The army absorbs resources, including a large foreign exchange component. Yet it may increasingly be unable to perform even its self-appointed task of imposing order as plots and *'coups* to change the *coup'* begin to multiply against its rule.[10]

Notes

1   *Uses and Abuses of Political Power,* Chicago, 1971.
2   I am thinking of Pope's lines:

> 'Tis strange, the Miser should his Cares employ
> To gain those Riches he can ne'er enjoy.
> Is it less strange, the Prodigal should waste
> His wealth, to purchase what he ne'er can taste?

3   See above, p. 153.
4   Among newly independent countries, as among older established States, there is of course always the possibility of unexpected good fortune. Oil in Nigeria has become manna from the underworld to

break the circle of indebtedness, although the sudden access to new wealth can hardly be said to have had a stabilising effect on Nigerian politics.

5   Vagueness in military *coups* is a common enough aspect. See, for example, the account by Maxime Rodison of the degree of irresolution in the 1952 revolution in Egypt, in P. J. Vatikiotis, *Egypt since the Revolution*, London, 1968.

6   By Dr Robin Luckham in the quarterly journal *Government and Opposition*, VI, 1, winter 1971. Dr Luckham taught for a time in Nigeria and Ghana, wrote an extremely good book on the Nigerian army, and is joint editor of *Politicians and Soldiers in Ghana, 1966-72*, London, 1975.

7   The nine categories (with examples) are: objective control (Western Europe and the US), constabulary control (Sweden), *apparat* control (USSR), the nation in arms (Israel), the revolutionary nation in arms (North Vietnam), subjective control (possibly the Vietcong), the garrison State (Greece, Jordan), the guardian State, the Praetorian State (Dahomey, Sierra Leone after 1967).

8   For which the best analyses are still: S. E. Finer, *The Man on Horseback*, London, 1962, and M. Janowitz, *The Military in the Political Development of New Nations*, Chicago, 1964.

9   *The Eighteenth Brumaire, Works*, Moscow, 1958. For Ghana, of course, read France; for Acheampong read Louis Napoleon.

10   See below, p. 189. The original composition of the NRC took shape from the early band of conspirators: Colonel Acheampong, Major Agbo, Major Baah and Major Selormey. (See Valerie P. Bennett, 'Motivation for military intervention: Ghana', *Western Political Quarterly*, XXVII, 1973.) In 1975 these three early companions resigned their commissions when a new Supreme Military Council was drawn together round Acheampong.

Epilogue

Et in Arcadia ego: politics and learning in Ghana

Fragments of an autobiography are of little interest in themselves, but they may be of help in putting together the history of the times from which they are remembered. In the pages which follow, which include such fragments, I have tried to pursue a simple theme. It is that of the export of ideas and institutions from Britain to a colonial country, and the difficulties which arose from their import into Ghana. I was no more than half conscious of such problems during the 1950s, when I was engaged in adult education. I was too busy enjoying myself in as devoted a way as I could under the aegis of the Department of Extra-mural Studies, and the questions which troubled others became—for me—of academic interest only later when I began to look back at the relationship between the university at Legon and the government in Accra. What that relationship was and what it is today reflect a familiar theme. It can be re-stated by noting that the location of political power in Ghana after the first election in 1951, as under the present military Redemption Council, was out of line with the very high social status accorded the educated elite of the universities. Admittedly, there was nothing very new in that: the correspondence between political and social power is rarely exact. It is also easy—as Professor Mackenzie once pointed out—for observers to mistake one for the other, to look at institutions and the powers vested in them without noticing the sometimes rival, sometimes complementary, strength of a social hierarchy in which power may rest on a very different footing.[1] In Ghana, however, in the decade before and after independence, the educated elite and the political leadership were sharply opposed. They were opposed in a very broad sense as 'rival colonists'. From 1945 onwards, graduates from the universities had begun to enter the public service, local government, the professions and business enterprises, replacing the British, and becoming a new administrative elite with direct access to the resources of the State. But in laying hold of the proto-independent State, they were opposed by the power of a nationalist party in the hands of a 'political class on the make' which was certainly no less determined to exploit the resources they were beginning to control. Of course, such differences were often blurred by expediency and common sense: but they were encapsulated, so to speak, in the opposition of the university as an institution of privilege to the nationalist—and today the military—government as an apparatus of control. These differences were sharpened by envy, and enlarged by what passed as ideology. Successive governments looked jealously at the intellectual pretensions of an academic elite, many of whom could hardly bear to endure their exclusion from office: it tormented them. The ideology was usually diffuse and cloudy. But at the centre of a good deal of rancour there have been interesting argu-

Minerva, XIII, 2, Summer 1975, 236-69.

ments over the idea of an African university or, at least, of a university which should somehow distance itself from its expatriate origins.

These are the loosely connected themes which I hope to be able to illustrate from time to time through memories of my extra-mural students and their efforts to reach out for some form of higher education. It may be asked whether Ghana is very different from many other countries in having to endure a conflict between State and university? Perhaps not, although conflict—like unhappiness—is always uniquely interesting. Moreover a sense of antagonism between the 'intelligentsia' and the 'party in office'—whether it was under colonial or nationalist or military control—is very much a Ghanaian theme, and it was there, in Accra and throughout the country, that I was witness to it. The reader may also observe that by 'university' is often meant only the University of Ghana at Legon, and not the two sister institutions at Kumasi and Cape Coast, but in this respect I can make amends for so narrow a vision only by apologising: time and the material were not available for me to extend the view.

How they became available to the limited extent illustrated here was simply a matter of good fortune when, early in January 1974, I was invited to attent the silver jubilee of the holding of the first New Year School in January 1950—the tropical equivalent of the Oxford summer schools. I was unsure, as I travelled comfortably to Accra by Ghanaian Airways, whether the full span of twenty-five years had really passed, but incidents of chronology are rarely exact in African tradition and I was certainly not disposed to cavil. I was grateful for the opportunity to revisit the university, and I used the occasion to read through the *Reports* of vice-chancellors and the proceedings of convocation of the past quarter of a century.

Our reunion went off without mishap, but in February 1974 all three universities were closed for a time by the military. That too was becoming a general pattern, which was certainly not confined to the 'Third World'; but there were—I thought—particular problems in the relationship between the university at Legon and the government in Accra which had not been adequately explored. One was common enough—that of 'autonomy' and 'control'. Another was the charge made by successive governments, against all three universities, of 'elitism'. A third was the familiar post-colonial problem of 'identity'. In a general sense they could all be brought under the broad question borrowed by Colonel Acheampong from Lord Annan: 'What are our universities for, anyway?' But it is probably sensible to take them one by one.

The university under Dr Nkrumah

The watchword of the university at Legon is on its coat of arms: *Integri procedamus*. It mirrors very well and emblematically the ability of faculties and departments to move forward under their own authority. But of course it opens the university to the charge that it is claiming too great an autonomy compatible with the amount of public money required to sustain it. The accusation has varied very interestingly over time but only at one brief point—and then perhaps disastrously—has the university been in harmony with the government in Accra. The more usual experience has been one of suspicion alternating with tolerance. Mr Justice Apaloo remarked, as chairman of the council of the University of Ghana in March 1972:

> Since the birth of this university, four successive governments have come and gone. Emerging from a period of partisan politics that has

seen the rise of two military regimes, this nation is ... just beginning to grope towards the foundations of the Third Republic in the not too distant future. We in this university have had our differences with some governments. But it is equally true to say that we have also enjoyed security and academic freedom in fair measure under others.

I can remember feeling the weight of such differences as a tutor in the Department of Extra-mural Studies, which, being out and about in the country, was always in the front line of any attack which was attempted, whether mildly by the colonial government, or severely by Dr Nkrumah, or —long after I had ceased to teach under its control—obliquely by rival bodies like the Centre for Civic Education.[2] None of the governments with which the university has so far been in dispute—neither the Convention People's Party at its most frenetic, nor the NRC at its most soldierly—have quite reached the position advocated by one of the delegates, Fr Torralba, to a meeting in Paris in 1973 of the International Association of Universities, who argued that 'relations between the university and the government should be those of docility and intelligent subservience';[3] but the problem, if it is a problem, of control versus autonomy has never been very far from the debate. Differences, often quite sharp differences, have arisen. Perhaps they were unavoidable, yet that is not to say that they need have been quite so painful. In times of nationalist assertion and financial restraint, the desire of a newly established government for control has often been matched not only by its determination to rule the roost but also by its suspicion of an institution of privilege in charge of the potentially powerful. Meanwhile, the counter-claim of autonomy has usually gone hand in hand with a well founded suspicion that governments which have to pay for virtually every note the piper plays are likely at any time to call a disagreeable tune. There is nothing very remarkable in that. Yet each side to this uneasy relationship in Ghana has changed substantially over the years. The university at Legon has grown larger and more 'African'. Governments have come and gone, and have altered their views—early Nkrumah to post-independence Nkrumah and late Nkrumah, to be followed by military control, Progress Party government, and back again to military rule. The story of the past twenty-five years has been an interesting one, full of variety: but the underlying tension has always been there, and does not seem likely to grow less.

The opening period, i.e. the late colonial period and the early Nkrumah period, was mild, a time of 'good will and optimism', since 'the country was prosperous and there was no difficulty in getting quite large funds for education'.[4] Cocoa prices had risen, the government was holding back substantial sums from the farmers, and in 1954-55 there was a doubling of £4 million of the provisional quinquennial grant (over and above the annual interest from the endowment fund of £2 million) for the removal of the teaching departments from Achimota to Legon. At no time since those early years had the university been quite so 'extraordinarily free to do as (it) thought best'.[5] Even in those happy days mistakes, of course, were made and misconceptions entertained. The colonial government was sometimes inclined 'to act the universal nanny' and to 'treat the university as a government department'—and it was sharply rebuffed.[6] The university, for its part, was often too closed in its councils, and had to learn to share its decisions with government. But it was a time of general hope, and the accession to office of the CPP in 1951 was only the most conspicuous evidence of a nationalist fervour which had already been exemplified in the establishment of a national university.[7]

The structure of the college proposed in the Elliot Commission was that of an English provincial university with a special relationship to the University of London. The first principal had different views. He was later to write that the London-provincial pattern had seemed to him 'singularly ill suited because of its autocratic constitution in which the vice-chancellor, with the connivance of the professors, makes absolute decisions. In a new country it was vital that our house should both be in order and be seen to be in order, and for this purpose the elective Oxbridge-type constitution is better'.[8] There was the attempt, therefore, to translate from 'Oxbridge' a collegiate-style university, its powers dispersed behind an elaborate screen of councils. They included, for example, convocation, representative of the whole body of the teaching staff and a useful device whereby the minority of young Ghanaian teachers could make their voice heard. In my own department there was a parallel effort to transfer a model of adult education from Oxford to Accra. However extraordinary it might seem in retrospect, it was with great zeal that we set about transferring a pattern of 'extra-mural studies' shaped by the industrial working class of Lancashire and the Potteries to the small towns and villages of Ashanti and Togoland. Again, changes were made. The Workers' Educational Association became the People's Educational Association; the nationalist and not the labour movement—it was argued—would become the vehicle of our success. But we copied closely the pattern of tutorial classes, summer schools, travelling libraries, weekend conferences, and an emphasis on 'liberal studies' among which, conspicuously, were economics and politics. It was as if a delegacy conceived on the banks of the Isis had suddenly taken flight and come to rest on the banks of the Volta.

I am much more doubtful today whether the structural adaptation of Oxbridge was as sensible in the long term as it seemed at the time. The system of residential halls, still in dispute,[9] created several points of tension: it gave partial autonomy to what in substance were dependent bodies, since, unlike Oxford or Cambridge colleges, the halls had no independent financial resources. The hedge of councils and committees did, however, form a protective screen against the extension of party power in the latter part of the 1950s. And Dr Balme was very conscious of the danger as political conflict spread across the country under the impetus of the two general elections of 1954 and 1956, for it was then that Dr Busia was enticed into politics; he was obliged to secure leave of absence from Legon, but many of the sins of the opposition were later transmitted via 'the Prof' to the university. As Dr Balme noted, 'The later troubles between our university and the Nkrumah government arose from Nkrumah's belief that the university was fomenting political opposition to him,'[10] and one could add that there was always sufficient ill will between the better educated of the university and the poorly educated of the CPP to foster the belief.

After independence, during the middle period of government by Nkrumah, the student body of the university at Legon grew, and the rate of Africanisation of its administrative and teaching staffs increased. The critical years were 1961-62 and 1962-63, when the student population rose from 682 to 1,174, of whom a little under 1,000 were in residence. By 1966 the 2,000 mark was reached.[11] Thereafter progress was very slow. It was not much more than two and a half thousand in the early 1970s, despite earlier predictions of a much higher rate of growth. The money ran out, and the accommodation ran out.[12] The academic level, however, was lifted—an average entry grade of two Cs plus one D at A level replaced the earlier two Es—and Africanisation proceded apace under very favourable ratios of staff to students. In 1960, after Dr Busia had gone into exile, there were no Africans among twenty heads of department, only five senior lecturers out of twenty, and twelve lecturers out of eighty-five, making a total of seventeen Africans out of 125. By 1966-67 Africans outnumbered expatriate staff (53 per cent); by 1969-70 the percentage had increased to 70 per cent of the administrative officers and 57 per cent of the teaching staff; in 1970-71 the percentage was 75. The effect of these changes, however, was probably to increase the sense of independence at Legon and the irritation of the CPP government over the university's claims to autonomy, not least because the 'localisation' of the university coincided with the growth of the regime as a 'single party' and of Dr Nkrumah's claim to be its 'Osagyefo'.

Precisely what it was that Dr Nkrumah would have wanted the university to become remained very unclear to the end. There was always the characteristic gap between the words and the deed. In September 1962, however, near the beginning of what might be called the 'last Nkrumah period', Dr Conor Cruise O'Brien became vice-chancellor at Legon. Thereafter the relationship of the two men, who were much inclined at first to like each other, grew worse until it broke out, in 1965, in public disagreement. It was a critical period, which the university survived—under attack—not least because Dr O'Brien was never an easy target for the kind of criticism aimed by the party at its opponents. The story of what happened is simple enough in outline, and it ended on 24 February 1966, with the arrival of the soldiers.

The university became independent of the University of London in 1961. On 25 November Dr Kwame Nkrumah, by now President of the new republic, was named as its chancellor; Nana Dr Kobina Nketsia IV became its interim vice-chancellor. A few days later there followed a similar ceremony for the Kwame Nkrumah University of Science and Technology at Kumasi.[13] Earlier that year the *Report of the Commission on University Education*[14] had appeared, a mouse of a report laboured over by two Ghanaians (Mr Kojo Botsio, chairman, and Mr Daniel Chapman, vice-chairman), one Russian, one Sierra Leonean, two African and three British members. In substance, notwithstanding its international authorship, it was in the long line of reports of the colonial and nationalist period, particularly in its emphasis on the need for greater Africanisation and for reform with safeguards—a characteristic which probably owed a good deal to its administrative secretary, Mr David Carmichael.[15] It also encouraged the establishment of an Institute of African Studies, which Dr Nkrumah believed might help to 'eradicate the colonial mentality which our contact with Europe has induced in us'.[16] However, early in 1963, on 24 February—a fateful date!— a more ominous if muffled note was sounded by the Osagyefo, the chancellor, in his address to the university:

> We know that the objectives of a university cannot be achieved without scrupulous respect for academic freedom for without academic freedom there can be no university. . . .
> Not only as Chancellor of the University, but also as President of Ghana, I would like to assure you of my readiness to defend at all times this right of the university. . . .
> There is, however, sometimes a tendency to use the words 'academic freedom' in another sense. . . .
> We know that academic freedom can be perverted and even abused. It can also become a dangerous cloak for activities outside the academic interests and . . . University staff and the students themselves

have a grave responsibility in maintaining this freedom since they themselves can also be a threat to academic freedom of the university. They must always be ready to expose those individuals in the university itself who abuse academic freedom.

The session of 1963-64 was full of darkness and doubt. It was also, one may note—since this is partly a personal memoir—a time when the People's Educational Association was declared to be dissolved and its place taken by a 'Public Education Association'—a chilling phrase—as 'an integral wing of the Institute of Public Education'. Much had happened in those early years of the republic. The widespread strike of harbour and railways workers had been suppressed in 1961, the first assassination attempt took place in 1962, the economy was in great difficulty and the CPP leaders had turned in on themselves—Gbedemah in exile, Krobo Edusei forced to resign, and Kojo Botsio demoted. They were supplanted by Tawai Adamafio, Ako Adjei and Coffie Crabbe until they too came under suspicion: they were first detained, then put on trial for their alleged part in the attempted assassination, acquitted but kept in detention. The court was presided over by the Chief Justice, Sir Arku Korsah, who had earlier been awarded—in the company of Dr Du Bois and Kofi Konuah—an honorary degree of Doctor of Law; Sir Arku Korsah too was dismissed at the end of 1963 by Dr Nkrumah, who was then shot at by a police constable early in 1964. Stirring times! And in his last address to congregation on 27 March 1965 Dr O'Brien explained that he too had had his differences with the Osagyefo.

Dr O'Brien defends the university from 'Nkrumaism'

The March meeting began with an address by Kwaku Boateng, Minister of Education and chairman of council, in a rambling speech which was part cajolery, part bullying, part lunacy, and which included a quotation from A. N. Whitehead—'the essence of education is that it be religious'—which was said to 'reflect the essence of our Nkrumaist Educational Policy here in Ghana'. Dr O'Brien replied in fine style: statistical, witty, indignant. It is the indignation which needs explanation. The vice-chancellor had been sorely tried. Deportation orders had been served on six of the expatriate members of staff, a Ghanaian lecturer and a student had been detained, and the grounds of the university invaded by a rowdy body of toughs led by a senior party member, breaking windows, shouting abuse, trampling about and the like. The session of 1964-65 had been relatively quiet and, said Dr O'Brien, 'We should be grateful for that'. He went on to observe—but the gist of what was said is best conveyed in his own words:

> My address last year followed a period of considerable disturbance culminating in an organised mass demonstration against the University. The events of the past year since my last address have been much less dramatic, and we should be thankful for that. Unfortunately, however, we cannot claim that during this period the University's position as a centre of critical and independent thought has become any more securely established. On the contrary, there are clear signs that influential elements in the community wish to turn the University from a centre of critical and independent thought into something quite different and that they are making some progress in the direction they desire.
>
> It was announced in the Press last November that a committee had been set up, under the Chairmanship of a professor of this University,

with powers to inspect publications in bookshops and in the libraries of schools, colleges and universities and ensure the removal from the country of all publications which do not reflect the Party's ideology or are antagonistic to its ideals. When I expressed serious concern about this matter and inquired how it affected the University Library, I received an official assurance that only public bookshops and public libraries are involved and that university libraries are 'not involved in this exercise'. This assurance is, of course, satisfactory as far as it goes, though the setting up of a committee with such vague terms of reference—which can already affect our bookshop even though not, or not yet, our library—is bound to cause grave concern in an intellectual community for whose activities the free circulation of serious and scholarly works and documents relevant to education is essential; nor were we reassured when we saw that an influential periodical published in Accra could reproduce on its front page a historical document borrowed from our Library—the manual of organisation in German of the German Nazi Party—and accompany this with the disgraceful insinuation that the University, through the Library, was instilling Nazi ideas into the students.

About the same time, that is to say, about the beginning of the present academic year, certain speakers and writers, enjoying a considerable measure of public favour, began to incite our students to 'watch out for' and 'expose' those of their teachers in whom they might think they detected unsuitable ideological tendencies. When I had occasion in my matriculation address to students at the beginning of this academic year to warn them against such behaviour, the sense of my words was distorted in the Press to make it appear that I was attempting to stifle a critical and questioning spirit among the students. . . .

. . . For a university, autonomy is not an end in itself. It is simply the guarantee and the protection of the freedoms of thought and of speech, of reading and writing, which are essential for the maintenance of high educational standards. As long as that autonomy is intact, critical and independent thought remains relatively secure; but if that autonomy is once breached, then elements inimical to such values may easily establish themselves in control and change the whole character of the University. Our students, and indeed our teaching body, may then be told—in words recently used by the influential periodical which I have already quoted: 'which views are official and right and which are unofficial and hence wrong'. Should that happen, critical and independent thought will not be ended—for happily it is not so easy to end it—but it will cease for a time to find open expression in the University.

. . . Now the autonomy of this University is on paper well established. The report of the 1961 Commission on University Education rests on two main principles: 'that Universities should be able to respond to the immediate and future needs of the community and that they should have the greatest possible autonomy in their organisation, teaching and research.' The principles of the Commission's report were accepted by the Government and are embodied in the University of Ghana Act. Unfortunately, autonomy on paper does not necessarily confer autonomy in practice. Events of this academic year have brought this home to the University in an unmistakable way. . . .

A decision to transfer the Institute of Education at Legon to the University College of Science Education at Cape Coast was taken last

August. The University was not in any way consulted in advance about
this decision. The decision was conveyed to me in the form of a Presidential Command and was made operative by executive decisions of the
Ministry of Education which treated the Government decision as in
force from the time of its promulgation irrespective of the constitutional processes of the University of Ghana of which at that time the
Institute was still a statutory part. . . .

It is with sorrow that I record that during this academic year the
spirit of the words I have quoted has not prevailed in all the practical
relations between the University and the authorities and that, in the
transactions to which I have just had to refer, the Constitution of the
University was not respected. The safeguards of academic freedom
at the University have suffered some diminution during this year.[17]

Dr O'Brien left in 1965 and the Nkrumah story was brought to an abrupt
end in February the following year. What might have happened had the
regime continued can only be conjecture. From October 1965—until
February 1966, when he was removed by the army—Professor Abraham
was appointed pro-vice-chancellor; he was a 'dedicated Party member and
intellectual *confidante*' of the President.[18] Despite its internal disarray,
the CPP was still very powerful and seemingly intent under Nkrumah on
extending its control over the civil service, trades unions, the judiciary,
voluntary bodies of one kind and another, and the university, whether by
instruction in 'Nkrumaism'[19] at the Kwame Nkrumah Ideological Institute
at Winneba or through the opening of branches within the institutions it
was eager to control. Outside help was offered. Early in 1965 a document
was sent by the Minister of Education to the university entitled 'Some
suggestions on the reform of the University of Ghana'. It had been prepared, so Professor Kwapong told the university in 1966, 'by a legal expert
from the Soviet Union who had been imposed by Nkrumah as Chancellor
on our Law Faculty', and it was concerned to effect changes in the structure
of the university and its curricula; to strengthen the role of party education; and to revise the methods of teaching. The document argued that the
role of the party branch of the university needed to be strengthened, and
suggested five ways whereby this might be done:

(1)   The party branch is to have sections in the faculties and departments
      in order to concentrate the most attention on questions of quality of
      teaching and education of students.
(2)   To determine the rights of the Party branch in the University of Ghana
      Act, namely, its rights in the personnel of leading organs, to give
      recommendations on all administration and all questions of academic
      life, including questions of staff and students.
(3)   The Party branch is to have its representative in all leading elected
      organs of the university, with a right to vote on the University Council,
      Academic Board, Boards of Faculties and an Appointment Board which
      is in charge of appointment of new lecturers.
(4)   Because of the big number of party members of the university, it is
      advisable that the post of all-time Party Secretary from the Head-
      quarters of the CPP should be established at the University.
(5)   The Secretary could be able to help the new vice-chancellor in the
      implementation of the progressive reforms of the University or to
      neutralise his actions if the new vice-chancellor does not justify re-
      sponsibilities entrusted to him for the realisation of these reforms.[20]

In a section on the revision of methods of teaching at the university the document also proposed the abolition of 'overseas reviewing of the examination works' ... and the introduction in all faculties and departments 'of compulsory courses of lectures in Marxist philosophy, political economy, scientific socialism and Nkrumaism'. It ended by advocating

> ... that the University of Ghana Act, 1961 should be revised by the introduction of a special article 11(a) which is to determine the role and rights of the Party branch of the University; the right of its members to advise the administration of the University on all questions and to have representatives on all elected organs; to abolish article 15 of the Act (empowering the university council to enact statutes for the general administration of the university) which places the University in a position of a 'state within a state' and ... to liquidate the independence of the University, having limited its autonomy.

Well, many such documents no doubt were presented to the Osagyefo by that small band of advisors who grouped themselves in competition around him. Not all were acted upon or even considered, although prior to the *coup,* changes in the university did begin to be introduced under the pro-vice-chancellor. The council was altered to include militant and eloquent 'Nkrumaists' such as Kodwo Addision, director of studies at Winneba, Kwaku Boateng and Dr Ekow Daniels, alongside more familiar faces. The soldiers intervened some months later, and the new vice-chancellor, Professor Kwapong, in his address to Congregation on 26 March, 1966, was able to declare that the university had been able 'to maintain our academic standards at the top relatively intact, and I am proud to say that this University has gone through the ordeal bruised but basically sound'. The fact is, however, that the *coup* followed so hard upon the attempt by the party to alter the university that one cannot say what might have happened had Dr Nkrumah continued in office.

Autonomy was preserved, therefore, and in the early days of military rule there was a free and close association between the university and the new National Liberation Council. Staff and students alike welcomed the soldiers, although by the time of the election in 1969 not only Dr Busia and the Progress Party but Mr Gbedemah and his National Alliance of Liberals found support at Legon. In those early days of February 1966 it was as if a heavy blanket of fear and doubt had been cast off. Journals and broadsheets began to appear, most notably the *Legon Observer* in July, under Mr B. D. G. Folson as editor. Ghana would not be Ghana, however, if the tolerance of the university had not stopped well short of allowing supporters of the former regime to continue in office. In his first 'address of welcome' to the congregation of the university on 26 March 1966 Mr Akufo Addo—the new chairman of council—expressed very eloquently what many in his audience must have wanted to hear. The country had suffered a 'monumental and sadistic indifference to the suffering and welfare of the people ... on the part of a consummate hypocrite' who had been, quite properly, 'left stranded and embarrassed in a glittering banquet hall in an oriental city (Peking)'.[21] The university was now free to develop its 'freedom and thought and expression', but Mr Addo warned:

> There may still be members of the staff whose intellectual faith in Kwame Nkrumah ... has not suffered a change in spite of recent events. Such men, if they exist, may not find the new going easy or congenial.... I say to them with all due respect: 'Be patriotic and leave the campus for the good of the campus.'[22]

Invective apart, Akufo Addo's speech to the university contained much that was sensible and thoughtful, as on the notion of 'academic freedom' and 'autonomy':

... To take a look back, the trouble seems to have been with our colonial past and the fact that we accepted from our colonial rulers a tradition, excellent in itself, of academic freedom. Our colonial rulers themselves had not really had this tradition for a long time; and when we took it over, its real meaning was not clear to anybody. Those in the University placed the emphasis on the word 'academic', so that to them it was natural to assume that they were free to do everything as long as they remained in what could be regarded as the academic world. Our notorious CPP Government put their emphasis on 'freedom' and so, again naturally, assumed that they were free to do anything however much it affected the academic community. Several generations of students took the phrase to mean that they were at liberty to do all sorts of selfish and destructive things provided academic reasons could be found for them.... [23]

Akufo Addo went on quite justly, as later events were to show, to argue that 'if the Government gives public money to any institution, University or otherwise, then (it) has the right to ensure that the money is properly used'.[24] At Legon, as at Kumasi and Cape Coast, 'all the funds are provided by Government and practically all the students are on Government scholarships'. And since 'the dependence of the universities on the State was balanced by the dependence of the State on the universities' the two sides had to act in consultation.

The restoration of academic freedom

It is clear that the university at Legon had taken a hard knock during these last years of Dr Nkrumah—and the early years of the NLC. A new chancellor, a new vice-chancellor, a new chairman of council, and a reconstituted council had to adjust to a new and military regime. The students were excited, the staff disturbed. During the year there were forty-five resignations and fifty-three vacancies which needed to be filled, including twelve Chairs. It had not been as bad as the new vice-chancellor, in the full flush of indignation, averred. But it had been bad enough, although the strength of the university could be seen in the way it very quickly returned to earlier ways. In my former sphere of interests, for example, the 'highly politicised Institute of Public Education', as recorded in the *Report* for 1967, was 'reorganised as the Institute of Adult Education (to become) an integral part again of the University of Ghana'.[25] The declared intention of the newly constituted university council was to return Ghana—the phrase echoes down the years from the great days of Achimota—'to the academic gold standard'. More prosaically, it was necessary to try and restore the finances of the university to good order. It would be—said the new vice-chancellor—'disingenuous if I were to pass over in silence the unfavourable report of the Auditor General on the University's accounts for the years 1963 to 1965'.[26] In brief, the university was heavily in debt and its accounts in poor shape; it had to borrow to make good a deficit which, by the early 1970s, came near a total of ¢5 million.

There were other problems in this dawn which followed the *coup d'état*. Students unrest began to grow, either as a vague local response to an almost global phenomenon, or from a sense of release from too much authority imposed by those in power:

> For the past six years, until the 24th February 1966, freedom of expression and conscience and, with this, freedom of the young to rebel, had been effectively silenced. Now there has been a tendency, evident since the return of freedom among some of our students, to mistake the new liberty for licence.[27]

The unrest persisted, derived not only from general considerations but also from practical grievances. Accommodation was tight, teaching facilities very poor. Financial reserves were inadequate, despite the *Report of the* [Ollennu] *Commission of Enquiry into the Situation of the University,* partly perhaps because the recommendations of the Vick report on the establishment of a university grants committee had yet to be carried out. The grounds of the university were lovely: they gave visitors to Legon the impression of great beauty and space, even a notion of luxury and extravagance. But these very aggreeable surroundings disguised the inadequacy of the site in relation to the growth—limited as it was—of student numbers. The buildings had been designed for a student population of 1,000, and not much had been done to extend them: between 1962 and 1970 the only new constructions were those of the School of Administration, and the biochemistry, nutrition and food science building. There were a lot of sketchy improvisations and makeshift arrangements, as Dr David Balme noted on his return for the twenty-first anniversary celebrations:

> You have the men ... and more to come. But where are the buildings? We left spaces for them, but the spaces are empty. Permit me, as a privileged visitor and old friend, to say that your teaching accommodation has become greviously inadequate.[28]

Here was one cause of discontent, although during the first period of military control between 1966 and 1969 student protest was sporadic rather than constant, if only because there was a general optimism about what would follow a return to civilian rule. Then the Progress Party won the elections, 'the Prof' became Prime Minister and in March 1970 received an honorary degree from the university. Some of the teaching staff had been rival candidates during the election, and political debate continued among both students and staff. Expectation was still high late in 1969 when I revisited the university, but there then occurred that early erosion of popular support for the new civilian government which was so marked a feature of the brief period of Progress Party rule. The expectation and the disappointment found outlet at Legon in noisy demands for 'participation' in the running of hall councils, the bookshop, the library, the estate organisation and so forth; demands too for a continuation of the subsidy for vacation residence and a bitter objection to the Progress Party government's proposal for 'student loans' to offset part of the cost of their fees and accommodation.[29] In 1970-71, the last year of Dr Busia's rule, there was a concerted attempt by the undergraduates to disrupt the proceedings of the university congregation.

The university under the National Redemption Council

The military seized power again in 1972, and as the National Redemption Council under Colonel Acheampong consolidated its rule, old accusations against the universities began to be renewed: they were not only 'elitist'

but troublesome, and if the unrest continued, said Colonel Acheampong, the
military would not hesitate to assert its authority.

The burden of the colonel's complaint was expressed strongly towards
the end of the NRC's first year in office in an address on 18 November
1972 to the first congregation of the University of Cape Coast, as it had now
become. The speech was a long one.[30] There was the customary bow to the
past—to the educational achievements of that impoverished city in which the
new university was placed; a fresh bow to the East—including quotations
from Confucius and Nehru—as well as to Western learning; but the main
text was borrowed from Lord Annan: 'What are our universities for, anyway?' Colonel Acheampong was not very certain about the answer, but he
was clear about what he disliked. There was, he complained, a certain
'lackadaisical attitude' in the universities, too little of the creative spirit
he had noticed in universities abroad and too little discipline among the
students. The universities cost a great deal of money, yet their privileges
were enjoyed by only 5, 000 out of a population of 8 million. He did not
wish even to imply that the NRC was against academic freedom, but such
virtues ought not to be the excuse for 'exception from constraints and
sacrifices required of the nation as a whole ... And here I must remind
you that in as much as our universities are financed from public funds it is
only fair that they should be accountable for the use of their funds'.[31] It
was a familiar theme, lifted out of the ordinary only by the soldierly advice
that perhaps both staff and students might benefit from 'formal military
training' in order to develop a conscious skill 'in the fields of discipline,
leadership, man management, motivation, sensitivity and so on'. Such
spurs—said the colonel—might have to be applied from outside the university if they were not to be found within its walls, a dictum repeated more
succintly at Kumasi the following year: 'I must state that if the Universities
will not seize the initiative the Government must make them move'.[32]

The temper of these disputes ought not to be ignored. It is true that the
opposition of the military and the university at Legon was mild, like most
public disputes in Ghana, compared with the ferocity of university life in
Asia, or even the noisy ebullience of Nigerian universities, which have
usually been more strident.[33] And yet, returning to Accra at the beginning
of 1974, it seemed to me that relations between the universities and the
government had slipped back to that earlier distrust between a displaced
elite and a newly ruling class which had been so marked a feature of the
Nkrumah years. Now, of course, the 'class' was the military class of
colonels and majors, and there were some among the university staff and
students who defended the overthrow of the regime of Dr Busia as the
welcome end of a bad regime. But the more general attitude was one of
regret at the demise of a civilian government which had been unable to
deliver either the promised cargo of goods or to bring the country into the
new land of progress. There were also many members of staff, and students
too, who were growing increasingly restless before the prospect of an indefinite prolongation of military rule. Articles began to appear at the end
of 1973, and the beginning of the new year, by members of staff in the *Legon
Observer* and by students in the *Forum*, which were critical of Colonel
Acheampong and the NRC in such outspoken terms that it needed only an
affray between students and soldiers to enforce the closure of the universities for several months in February 1974.

The tone of such comment is easy to recapture. In the *Legon Observer*
it took the form of an attack on familiar targets, including corruption and
newspaper censorship, the advocacy of some consideration of a future

civilian regime and of the need to uphold the freedom of the law and of
lawyers: 'when rulers begin to manifest autocratic tendencies' lawyers
should 'act as a pressure group to force them back to the path of righteous-
ness'.[34] The attack was 'from the left', in the sense of there being a dislike
of what was seen as a conservative alliance between the 'supposedly revolutionary government' of the NRC and the 'traditional elite' of chiefs; but it
was also a plea for the government 'to trust the intellectuals', notwithstanding the mistakes of Dr Busia's regime. Students, it was said, were more
conscious now of their obligations, universities were more aware of their
responsibilities:

> Hitherto the vast majority of people had considered [students] snobbish
> and aloof individuals who only cared about the maintenance of the
> privileged community in which they were bred. But people have now
> seen them sweeping out some of the streets of Accra. . . .
>   Since Ghana became self-governing the intellectuals in successive
> regimes have been estranged from the masses. . . . A new and more
> trusting relationship began to emerge when, following the collapse of
> the first Republic, the masses began to wonder if the national calamity
> could have been averted if they had listened to the intellectuals. . . .
> They swung behind the Progress Party therefore. . . but since the
> 13 January 1972 coup . . . there has been a re-surfacing of the old anti-
> intellectual feeling.
>   There were no grounds today for such antagonism since students
> in particular, either because of a lingering 'socialist orientation from
> their activities in the erstwhile Young Pioneers movement', or because
> of 'shrinking job opportunities', were more socially committed and
> morally mature. . . . [35]

The students' criticisms were less guarded. Many of them had
extended an almost enthusiastic welcome to Colonel Acheampong in January
1972, and they were particularly pleased when the student loan scheme was
abandoned by the NRC.[36] Now they were once more 'against the government'.
The closing number of the students' journal *Forum* for 1973 carried the
headlines 'Who is ordained to rule in Ghana ?' and argued that, whoever it
might be, there were no grounds for supposing that 'Chairman Ike the Great'
had an indefinite mandate to govern. He had 'come through a back-door
process of gun power' but—unlike the NLC—had begun to talk of 'staying on
the scene indefinitely'. To this end, the students complained, intellectuals
had been silenced and the press brought under control by the Newspaper
Licensing Decree (NRCD 161) and the earlier decree (NRCD 67) which gave
approval to government-controlled newspapers. 'It was now generally felt,'
wrote a student at Legon Hall in a letter to the *Forum,* 'that the twin concepts of Freedom and Justice . . . were better realised under the British
than under our own governments'—including the NRC. Early in 1974 there
was an ugly incident when a student was badly beaten by a group of soldiers:
the student body at Legon tried to 'march on Accra' but was turned back
from the city by a detachment of armoured cars. Towards the end of 1974
the *Legon Observer* was put out of business by NRC pressure on the
printers.[37]

Such was the general tenor of the complaints brought against the NRC
to match the warnings broadcast by the soldiers. The ground of the quarrel
was clear. To Colonel Acheampong the universities were extravagant and
claimed too many privileges with their 'autonomy'. In the eyes of many
of the staff and students at Legon the military were over-extending their

rule and outstaying any welcome they might have been given. But was the quarrel simply over rights and privileges or, more complicatedly, about the location of social and political power in a post-colonial State ? I turn now to the second theme of 'elitism'.

The status of the educated

In a general sense, at least until quite recently, virtually any educated person in Ghana could be seen as belonging to an elite. In the early 1950s, for example—and I turn briefly to my own recollections as an extra-mural tutor—it needed only a brief stay among my students to understand that even those who came irregularly to attend the evening's lectures were placed very advantageously in a largely unlettered society as teachers, clerks, storekeepers and skilled artisans. In a country instinctively observant of rank, the status of an educated person at that time was high simply by virtue of the fact that he could read and write English, particularly if he had passed the crowded barriers of the primary and middle schools. I used in these years to lunch frequently with the headmaster of the boys' middle school at Wenchi, a lunch followed by a somnolent half hour or so before we strolled through the town until the time when the lectures were scheduled to begin—but rarely did. It was invariably an excellent meal: a plain soup with mutton or goat, rice and fried plantain or yam, sometimes with *fufu* and palm soup, always with *kenkey* and ice-cold beer, reinforced with a bottle—which I grew a little to fear—of schnapps on the side table. We were served by schoolboys, lined up against the wall for orders, cheerful and willing and not at all resentful, so far as I could see, of being pressed into service. They fetched the beer, served lunch, consumed what was left, cleaned the pots, carried water, washed my car and, I suppose, were taught something or other during the late afternoon. But by four o'clock the headmaster and I were out into town. Great respect was shown all round, for although the headmaster was not very wealthy, he was powerful. He could in practice admit or refuse admission to a pupil, thus conferring on him, and indirectly his family, a profitable place in the educated ranks of this status-conscious society. He would gossip with the postmaster—another influential figure— the still more powerful local clerk to the council, the court registrar, the goldsmith, numerous storekeepers, local contractors and market traders. It was a leisurely progress, but not wholly devoted to leisure, since arrangements were made, transactions conducted and relations of mutual benefit maintained among the members of this 'modern' elite.

Visitors from Britain often missed this aspect of adult education. Fresh from Oxford or London, they were eager to translate what they saw into their own experience. They lectured to, and even talked with, a number of students, but found it hard to grasp that although the chairman, secretary, treasurer and librarian were commoners—the office of president being usually bestowed on the chief—they were certainly not 'levellers', except in the sense that they wished to level themselves up, when they could, to the status and wealth of that more established elite whose patron and leader was, pre-eminently, a lawyer. Many extra-mural students—among whom were numbered very often branch officers of the CPP, the NLM or the NPP (or, at a later date, Progress Party or NAL)—were ardent nationalists as well as locally important leaders. But they were not in any sense the 'cream of the cream'. Even after the coming to power in 1951 of the nationalist party whose leaders gained access to the full resources of the State, the 'true elite' were still thought to be the 'highly educated'—those who had been intra-mural students, particularly the graduates—and today, no doubt, the PhDs—of British and American universities. Wealth was not quite sufficient, by itself, to bestow the highest status. Hence the ambition which was openly proclaimed by several of my students, and quietly determined upon by many party leaders, to join the graduate elite *via* the hard road of a certificate of study in the United Kingdom.[38] Many of them tried painfully to climb the ladder of qualifications. Kwame Nkrumah was among the early pioneers when, in the 1930s, after leaving his teacher-training college and being appointed headmaster of a junior school in Axim, he 'took a private course to prepare ... for the London Matriculation but ... failed the examination in Latin and mathematics.'[39] Over the years the number of applications for such courses grew enormously, increased in time through similar attempts from London or Accra by former ambassadors, high commissioners, trade commissioners, ideological instructors, party journalists, opposition leaders in exile and retired army commanders—all stumbling in pursuit not of the millenium but of the LL.B. The stakes grew higher: in the inter-war years, primary and middle school; after the second world war, secondary school; now it is at least secondary school and, if possible, university.

The upward path through education

In those early years an extra-mural education could still provide a new path of opportunity if it were used skilfully to clamber towards the top of a social pyramid which narrowed very sharply as one drew closer to the summit. Even at that time, however, and much more so today, access to the higher slopes of the pyramid was becoming difficult. Since, when I was an extra-mural tutor, only about 13 per cent of the very large middle school population actually got to a secondary school, and since only about a quarter to a fifth of these succeeded in reaching the fifth or sixth forms, most of our adult students were from the middle schools, plus one or two years at a teacher-training college, or commercial academy, or not very good secondary school. I have said earlier that many of the ablest adult students were in search not of the millenium but the LLB, but of course for many the two were indistinguishable. And there was nothing new or reprehensible, according to local understanding, about such ambitions. To most Ghanaians they were simply translated from what was seen to be true of Europeans and of a 'European education'. It was an escape from the illiterate, restricted life of the peasant farmer. It is true that most of my students, and many university students, were the children of farmers. Many still had cocoa or food farms tucked away in the bush as an extra income, and they liked to watch over the progress of their labourers on these smallholdings. But that was not what education was about. The gentleman farmer, or even the educated farmer, has yet to appear in any great numbers in Ghana. There are some signs today of his appearance in food farming, but extremely few of my early students fell into such categories, and farmers were by and large excluded from 'adult education' by their illiteracy. That was the point of education—to escape from rural life. And the main purpose of the national movement—as of the extra-mural students who joined such parties —was to preside over the transfer of wealth from the agricultural sector, *via* the schools, to the new elite in government service, or politics, or the professions, or private trade.

That access to the commanding heights of the educated community was becoming yearly more difficult, as could be seen not only from the growing

number of adult students but from the rate of increase among the profes-
sionally qualified: for example—Dr Robin Luckham has plotted their growth—
from sixty lawyers in 1950 to 600 in 1970. The day of the 'prestigious
Standard VII certificate'[40] was almost over, although there was still a
direct if very narrow route to power which a few adventurous souls dared
to take. It is sometimes argued that the military in many new States should
be seen as 'the last of the pressure groups' to exert their strength in the
twilight of colonialism and the dawn of independence, and there is much to
be said for the argument. But some of the army leaders in Ghana can also
be seen perhaps as the last of the 'middle-school-leavers' to arrive in
office. For example, the Standard V pupil who helped Mr Agyemang in 1930
to 'collect his first firewood' was Asamoah Stephen, who became a soldier,
and was later Major General Stephen Otu, high commissioner in Delhi under
the NLC. At about the same time Emmanuel Kotoka was enrolled in the new
Roman Catholic primary school at Alakple, near Keta, before going on to the
senior school at Anloga. Having failed to gain a scholarship to a teacher-
training college, and being unable to afford the fees to go to a secondary
school, Kotoka became an adult education student. The extra effort proved
its worth, since after a brief period of work as a goldsmith he turned to the
army, being influenced, it is said, by a palmist who advised him to do 'white
man's work'. He joined the Education Corps and 'had an advantage over
other middle school leavers because he had continued his education after
leaving school by taking a Pitman's course in English'.[41] By 1953 he was at
the Regular Officers' Special Training School at Teshie; the following year
he was in England at Eaton Hall and well on his way, *via* the Congo and his
command of the Second Brigade at Kumasi, to the *coup* in 1966. A decade
later Ignatius Acheampong left the Ejisu Catholic middle school in Ashanti
in 1945 with his Standard VII certificate to enrol at the Central College of
Commerce at Agona Swedru; the GCE which he gained there enabled him to
teach at the Kumasi Commercial Institute in 1951—from which I drew a
number of extra-mural students; but he too, after working for a time as a
clerk and then 'as a labourer on a government farm', joined the army:
private, lance corporal, sergeant, the Officer Cadet Training School at Mons,
an officer in 1959, service in the Congo, a further period of training in the
United States, regional commissioner for the Western Region under the
NLC, and appointed by Dr Busia to be commander of the First Infantry
Brigade Group in Accra, from which it was an easy step to the new redemption of Ghana.[42] Thus it was that the middle school leaver-turned-army
officer arrived in office, not by the ballot as in 1951, but the gun. And after
a brief period in prison the Progress Party leaders of the intelligentsia are
back in the universities or more lucrative professions.

Recruitment into the officer corps has not always followed the Kotoka-
Acheampong route. The pattern is changing and may change quite fast as
the army begins to be seen as one of the permanent contenders for power.
I was told that the Officers' Training College at Tamale, recruiting from
secondary school level, was of good standard, and some of the more special-
ised junior officers can easily be matched in sharpness of mind with the
younger university teachers. I remember, for example, a triangular debate
in which I, a young army captain and a politics don sat over beer and
whisky one evening at Legon arguing the morality of army rule—a blurred
and inexact topic even in the calm light of day—and the soldier was by no
means the worse for academic wear when we parted company. Nor can the
officer corps as a whole be very dissimilar from those who once overthrew
the CPP and then turned to Busia. The contrast lies partly in the fact that

since 1972 the NRC has found itself very differently placed from the National Liberation Council of 1966-72, having put an end not to the People's Party of Dr Nkrumah but to the Progress Party of Dr Busia.

Is the anti-intellectual tone of the NRC simply a reflection, then, of its opposition to those it replaced? Up to a point, yes; and it can also be argued that the boundary between the university—and all it stands for—and the army —whatever it sees itself as representing—is still very uncertain. There are familiar links of a communal nature, and even of a generational kind, between some of the younger officers and students, as there are still between some of the retired NLC members and the more elderly university members. Nevertheless, such qualifications are only 'up to a point', for there is unmistakably an anti-intellectual stance to be discerned in the present attitude of the NRC, quite apart from the fact that the rank and file of the army are presently licensed to behave much worse today than in the liberating days of 1966.

The charge of 'elitism'

Running through the speeches by Acheampong, Selormey and others there is the old, almost populist assumption that the universities are too 'elitist', staff and students alike, and ought therefore to mend their ways. It is at best a puzzled irritation, at worst a vague yet menacing note of intimidation. It is proper, therefore, to consider more minutely the accusation that the universities are 'ivory towers'. A position of privilege which so many were anxious to try and share by correspondence courses, part-time degrees and study abroad can hardly be said to be wholly remote from society as a whole. But, allowing for a measure of external adoption into the university-trained elite, can one still say that they were—and are—'ivory towers'?

Physically all three universities are secluded amidst the flowering trees and mown grass of a cultivated landscape some miles distant from their respective cities. At Legon, in particular, a 'Chinese Cotswold' effect —if such a combination can be imagined—has been achieved by tiled roofs and white courtyards, fountains and reflecting pools: Nuffield College amidst the alien scrub which has been made to blossom.[43] Yet none of the three is so secluded as to suggest a monastic withdrawal from the active, busy life of the town. The more vexing question is that of their social isolation; has the university elite become almost a caste, self-perpetuating, recruited from families of similar background, and divorced from the community at large by too rigid a commitment to external values and customs?

At first sight, the social background of the students seems to offset the charge of 'elitism'. Indeed, the data are often puzzling in the sense that they tend to contradict one's own experience—a 'datum' which I do not pass over lightly. We can turn for help to Professor Jahoda, who has sketched the family occupations of students at Legon (table 21). Professor Klineberg's research, covering a slightly different period, shows that only 14 per cent of 291 students came from the professional classes; 31 per cent were the offspring of farmers, rich and less rich; and 26 per cent were the children of white-collar workers and schoolteachers.[44]

There has almost certainly been a good deal of consolidation of the 'educated classes' across the generations. Although the picture which emerges is that of a new educated elite for whom the rural and farming origins of their families have remained a strikingly dominant feature, a strong impression remains of the emergence of a new class with a sense of its own identity. Professor James O'Connell, who has studied Nigerian

Table 21

Parental occupations of 280 students at the University of Ghana

Father's occupation

Farming/ fishing 113	Crafts/ manual 27	Clerical 29	Lower com- mercial 26	Higher com- mercial 14	Lower profes- sional 40	Higher profes- sional 27

Mother's occupation

Trader 98	Farmer 77	Crafts 25	Professional 18	Other 62

Source. J. W. Berry (ed.), *Culture and Cognition: Readings in Cross-cultural Psychology,* London, 1974, p. 156.

students at Ahmadu Bello University, believes that the new educated elites in West Africa are beginning 'to harden into classes and to hand on generationally the advantages of earlier access to education'.[45] And certainly that is likely to become the case in Ghana, if only because of the financial barrier of entry into secondary school. University education is usually free—'to everyone that hath shall be given'. Secondary education is not free, and the aspirant to 'higher education' often fails at secondary level—'from him that hath not shall be taken away even that which he hath'. Wealth is thus a weighty determinant of higher education.

In so far as personal experience may be drawn upon, the writer would add his testimony to the recorded data. Visits to Legon in recent years have frequently been made agreeable by meeting the sons or daughters of those he once taught not very effectively. Mr Onipa, for example, an extra-mural class secretary early in the 1950s, was an able if scarcely literate clerk of the local native authority who early in 1974 confessed to the writer —confided, perhaps, is the better word—that despite his long interest in adult education he had been unable to read through 'a book': he could start one, but not finish one, whether in English or Twi. Yet such a handicap was of little importance to an energetic career which had carried him from local government via the opposition (Ashanti) NLM, and the National Assembly, to membership of the CPP and a district commissionership, until that fateful day in February 1966 when he put together a sleeping mat and toilet requirements in preparation for his entry into prison. When released he stayed in Accra, where he began—and who knows what unfulfilled desire prompted his choice?—a small printing plant in partnership with the de-stooled chief of his state, destooled, one should add, by the CPP in earlier years. The press flourished. It earned a sufficient income not only for himself, his wife, four or five sons and a maid but the secondary school fees of his daughter, whom I was able to entertain to lunch at Legon, where she was, as I was told, 'reading philosophy and maths'. The majority of her companions at university were not very differently placed socially, and it seems reasonable to conclude that many of the present generation of under-graduates are successfully and irreversibly consolidating the rise to fortune of their parents, by politics, or government service, or private business, or farming. They represent what was seen as a prudent investment in the golden coinage of a university education. But will the currency always be valid?

The charge of 'alienation'

I turn at last to the final charge levelled against many African universities —that they are not in effect, either in practice or theory, 'truly African'. Indeed, the 'Englishness', or in a broader view the 'Eurocentrality', of the universities has not only been part of the complaint against their 'elitism' but has been used, by extension, to question their claim to autonomy. They are, it is said, not home-grown but exotic, and if an 'ivory tower' is bad, when manned by 'imitative scholars' it is very bad. Such has been the assertion, although it was not said at the time of their foundation. The secretary of the Nigerian vice-chancellors' committee, Mr Ogbue, has noted in respect of the universities in Nigeria:

> They are now under quite severe and persistent criticism for being transplants of Western culture, [but] while there might be some truth in this allegation, the historical perspective must not be overlooked. Had the British government attempted to create a characteristically Nigerian university pattern and therefore different from the British, local opinion would have challenged it.[46]

That is absolutely true of the early foundation of the University of Ghana. But one must also recall that, in Ghana particularly, the nationalist party in its early years—that is, a little after the university was founded— was very much a homespun movement, and it was understandable perhaps that it should have looked suspiciously at the foreign origins and connections of a world which many of its members had been unable to enter. Since the party's leaders also claimed later to be in search of 'autochthony' by way of a single-party republic and the assertion of an 'African personality' through an 'African socialism', they were also—again understandably—eager to point to the 'Eurocentrism' of the universities to justify the need for party control.

A variation of this theme has reappeared under the NRC. Staff and students, it is being said, should be 'socially conscious' in their teaching, research and commitment: they should 'serve the community', and contribute to 'African scholarship'. What such phrases imply is very unclear, but one may reasonably assume that Colonel Acheampong, like his predecessors, would endorse the call by the vice-chancellor of Singapore, Dr Toh Chin Chye, for an 'academic decolonisation', and for the university staff 'to divest themselves of their Eurocentric attitudes and prejudices'.[47]

The extent to which the universities in Ghana and the criticism directed against them are both part of a residual, and indeed still active, colonialism of the mind may be debated at length, and interestingly. I have described earlier the commitment with which my own department of extra-mural studies set about importing a very idiosyncratic form of adult education, although it is proper to add—immodest as the claim today may sound—that we were extraordinarily well received by our students. Not, it has to be said, by those in authority; not if the official frown of recognition bestowed initially by the colonial government were taken at face value. I recall from my earlier months in the country a painful interview in Tamale, then administrative headquarters of the Northern Territories, when Thomas Hodgkin tried to explain to the Regional Commissioner that to give lectures in the community centre on 'democracy' was not necessarily the prelude

to revolution, and the reaction of His Honour, who observed—a little, I
thought, too indignantly—that no one in his region wanted 'radical change'.
The colonial case against extra-mural classes in the early 1950s was
interesting—it was that we were foisting on unwilling people a pattern of
education which was quite unsuitable for them, an argument which ran parallel to an earlier colonial advocacy of 'native authority' government instead
of Westminster parliamentary rule, and the much later nationalist defence
of control by a single party as authentically 'African'. The fact is, however,
that among the general run of our adult students in those early years the
gift of education from European hands, far from being suspect, was almost
certainly appreciated. Nor did it occur to any of us at the time that we might
be agents of a cultural imperialism. On the contrary. As we reached beyond the walls of the university we were sustained by the belief that our
instruction of a future elite would be balanced by popular education, intra-
mural studies would be balanced by extra-mural studies. In retrospect, I
rather think that we were not doing much more than satisfying and increas-
ing—often only marginally—the number of aspirants to an English or Euro-
pean-style education. We were helping to meet the demand within the adult
education movement for certificates in order to try and clear the hurdle of
entrance to the university. But what do those who succeed today find when
they arrive where they want to be, among the undergraduate and Westernised
elite ?
    It was interesting in 1974 to observe at all three universities an appa-
rent quickening of the erosion of the once overwhelmingly strong features
imprinted by their early founders: a 'divesting of their Eurocentric attitudes
and prejudices', not under compulsion from outside but through an impulse
from within. Many of the original appurtenances taken from Oxford and
Cambridge have gone. The visitor will also quickly be aware how common
is the use outside the lecture room, among staff and students alike, of one or
other dialect of Akan or Ga or Ewe or a northern language. And the most
cursory study of the instruction provided by the various faculties will show
how 'localised', or 'African', the teaching has become: King Prempeth or
King Chaka replacing Queen Anne, Chinuah Achebe and Ayi Kwei Armah
alongside Thomas Hardy, *corvus albus* replacing *corvus frugilegus,*
Ghanaian dances, music, drama and so forth. There is nothing, of course,
very remarkable in such changes. The university at Legon has been moving
in that direction for some time, and an account of similar attempts in the
nineteenth century in other formerly colonial territories can be found in
Lord Ashby and Dr Anderson's study.[48] One of the interesting questions
confronting Legon and Kumasi and Cape Coast in the 1970s and 1980s is not
whether they will continue to adapt the teaching content which they have
inherited—that is certain—but how far they can go and how close they might
come to some degree of qualitative change.
    Some of the recent innovations might very likely not be thought al-
together agreeable to an earlier generation of academics who taught there.
I was intrigued, for example, when I was told about the extent to which
interest in the occult had grown at Legon. There had been, it seems, a substantial increase in prophet-healing cults, and in the assertion of traditional religious beliefs, most notably among the students under twenty-five.
Caught between tradition and modernity, they have tried to strike a balance
between them, and some may have succeeded. According to Professor
Jahoda, it is now possible, on the basis of a good deal of detailed research,
to reach the 'tentative conclusion ... that the younger generation of
Ghanaian students have achieved what Barbichon called a "state of cogni-

tive coexistence" between modern ideas and values and some traditional African beliefs'.[49] Moreover their 'partial return to traditional West African cosmological notions and their declared concern with supernatural threats suggest that it has become an integral part of their cognitive structure, and is not merely a superficial national gesture'.[50]

I do not think it is possible to draw extravagant inferences from such subtle changes in attitude, or from what can perhaps be seen as the growing acceptance of 'traditional West African cosmological beliefs'. Nor does it seem very likely that such beliefs are evidence—proleptically—of any major shift in emphasis towards a traditionalist revival, or of a close correspondence between modernity and autochthony. That there is a sense of strain among the intelligentsia in West Africa—and it is tension rather than any easy 'state of cognitive coexistence' between tradition and modernity which I detect—may be seen in the extraordinary mood of disillusionment of many West African novelists. Mr Chinuah Achebe argues that the African artist 'has been left far behind by the people who make culture, and he must now hurry and catch up with them ... in that zone of occult instability where the people dwell'.[51] But in what possible sense can one offer such counsel to the universities?

The possibilities tried elsewhere do not seem available in Ghana. It is difficult, for example, to believe that there can be a Ghanaian equivalent to the Sinhalisation of education in Sri Lanka. The adoption of Akan might at first be thought to have parallels, as the language of the dominant majority, with that of Sinhala—Ewe, like Tamil, being placed in a subordinate position. But the pressure from middle school leavers and from those who look for employment, or some form of further education, is still within the English medium of instruction and the type of syllabus offered through it. There are no *swabasha* schools in the Ghanaian bush. Nor are the Akan put to a disadvantage in their access to 'English education' in relation to rival minorities. The upsurge of tradition, therefore, whatever it may mean in religion or custom, seems unlikely to affect the most potent instrument of 'academic colonialism'—language. The expansion of elementary and secondary education, lending 'powerful support to the modern status hierarchy',[52] seems likely to remain confined to English. The explanation of this marked difference between Akan and Sinhala, or Akan and Hindi or Malay, is no doubt a reflection of the difference between the force of Buddhist or Hindu or Muslim traditionalism and the power, in Ghana, of European rule. Colonialism in West Africa cannot be seen as a momentary episode, as it might be said to have been in the long history of Asia. It is fundamental; colonialism is the creator of a political artifact in which the use of English has been a dominant element and much of the erosion noted earlier has been the washing away of bric à brac. I suspect that Ghana is wedded indissolubly to its colonial past. Indeed, I am tempted to adapt Nirad Chaudhuri's imagery and say that the colonial world in West Africa was very much the island of Circe,[53] enchanting men's minds and turning them into—what? Well, into subordinate creatures of what was once an island empire and is now a global market economy.

Assertions of this kind come close to notions of a 'false decolonisation'. Very often, however, the demand for a stronger movement away from the colonial past is simply a hope of making institutions, like the universities, more effective. Arguments have been put forward recently, for example, to try and bring the universities a little closer to that broad stratum of aspirants to the elite for which they are examplars. The problem, it is said, is the danger not of over-expansion but of too restricted a view of their

function. Since there is no unemployment problem at graduate level—
vacancies are in pursuit of skills—and since there is little danger of over-
populated universities, the need, it has been argued, is for a broadening of
the range of teaching and the separation from the main work of the universities of institutes of research. The effect, so Sir Arthur Lewis has said,
would be to move the colonial university away from its absurd copy of the
British model—of 'teaching only for eight to ten hours a week' and the
enforcing of a 'gentleman scholar image' which becomes distorted into the
slogan of 'publish or perish'. It is the familiar and unsubstantiated case
against an unproductive elite in order, in a country which is short of middle-
level skills, to obtain value for money.[54]

> So many of our universities, clinging to the research ideal and its
> corollaries, get the worst of both worlds; they have to pay salaries
> competitive with Oxford and Cambridge and to limit teaching hours,
> without getting much creativity for money.
> This is a British trap; the United States is not caught up in it. The
> US has 1, 500 degree-granting institutions, of which less than a hundred
> expect to advance the frontiers of knowledge. The rest hire teachers
> at lower salaries and work them twenty to twenty-five hours a week. . . .
> India is travelling the same way. The money now goes increasingly
> into wholly post-graduate institutions, like the new Jawaharlal Nehru
> University, or into research institutes. . . .
> At the University of the West Indies I became convinced that we
> had started on the wrong track in adopting the English pattern. We
> would have done better to have had two separate institutions; one
> offering undergraduate degrees, and the other concentrating on grad-
> uate and professional studies. . . . The cost per undergraduate place
> in our university is much too high in relation to *per capita* income. . . .[55]

The NRC might very well see advantages in such changes, though it
might also hesitate a little before trying to persuade the staff at any of the
three universities to teach more for less salary than some of their
colleagues. The notion of 'service teaching', however, probably comes close
to the view which Colonel Acheampong has tried to set forth in his
speeches to convocation and council. And since the concept of 'service'
raises all three themes of autonomy, 'elitism' and identity, it is time to
bring them together by way of conclusion.

Some concluding reflections

Whether relations between the government and the universities will continue to be strained, become worse or grow better, is likely to depend as
directly on the view each has of the other as on the abstractions of ideology
or the opposition of rival interests. A distinguishing feature of relations
between universities and governments in the past is how large a part Legon
in particular has played in this relationship. The contrast with Nigeria, for
example, is sharp. Dr Okafor's detailed account of Nigeria's universities
looks briefly at the conflicts between the central government and the
universities of Ibadan, Ife, Lagos and Nsukka.[56] The impression conveyed
by his study, as in that by Pierre Van den Berghe[57] of Ibadan, is how much
less important any of the universities have been in relation to the government in Lagos—and, of course, against a more sombre background of vastly
more dramatic events—in contrast with the prominence of Legon *vis-à-vis*
Accra. The explanation is not only one of its familiarity within a much

smaller Ghanaian community, though it is partly that. It lies also in the
political history of Accra versus Legon, and the vexed question of the social
base of recruitment into politics. In retrospect it is possible to see how
disastrously the university was involved in the brief period of Progress
Party rule from 1969 to 1972: a former professor as Prime Minister; a new
President who was an uncle of the new vice-chancellor; Ministers, Junior
Ministers—and some of the opposition members of parliament—drawn from
the university staff. It began almost to look as if the old dream of the
intelligentsia of uniting social privilege with political power under an educated leadership had come true at last. Much of the political history of the
post-war years in Ghana had been concerned with problems arising from
the separation of social and political power and with attempts to bring them
into alignment. In 1969 it looked as if that happy time had dawned. But if
the triumphant days of the Progress Party brought Legon fully into that
apparent success, the downfall of that party brought a corresponding dismay
among those who had campaigned for 'the Prof'—to such a degree that it led
some of them into the dangerous underworld of plots and counter-*coups*.

An account of such intrigues has yet to be documented, and it must
necessarily be briefly treated here. As the NRC began its 'colonisation'—
I pick up the word from the beginning of this essay—and officers were
appointed to ministerial posts, public corporations and district offices much
in excess of the number who were placed in civilian positions under the first
military government, so opposition grew to this altogether more political
view of its role. For the present the NRC has warded off two attempts to
subvert its rule, one from the 'right', the other from the 'left'. In that first
attempt some members of the staff at Legon were implicated. George
Ofosu Amaah was senior lecturer in law at Legon when he was arrested,
brought before a military tribunal, found guilty of subversion and—with Staff
Sergeant Opon Nyantakyi and six other conspirators—sentenced to death.
These sombre events were repeated a year later when John Alex Hamah, a
former trade unionist turned businessman who had stood for election in
1969 as a United Nationalist Party candidate, was found guilty of trying to
subvert Colonel Kotei, commander of the First Brigade in Accra. At the
end of 1973 Imoru Ayarna, founder of the small People's Action Party, Kojo
Botsio, who had been chairman of the Commission on University Education
of 1961, John Tettegah, a trade union leader, Owusu Boateng, a journalist,
and Major Awuviri were also brought before a military tribunal and charged
with subversion.[58] The universities were by no means the sole location,
therefore, of opposition to the NRC; but when they were criticised, in the
phrase once used by the CPP, for behaving like 'a society for the preserva-
tion of ivory towers', it was also possible to detect not only scepticism
about 'What are universities for?' but suspicion—amidst such turmoil—of
what some of their members were doing.

Where will it end? If I thought such advice as I could offer to Legon and
its sister institutions would have effect, I would counsel the need for pru-
dence in the short term and confidence for the future. It is, alas, possible
that the NRC, from a nervous distrust of its own abilities, may one day
arrive at the point the CPP once reached if it is faced, or believes it is
faced, with a direct threat to its existence. It too may then begin to arrest
persons preventively by the score and bear down heavily on any institution
not under its control. For the present, however, one can take some comfort
from the fact that both in outlook and even politically the NRC is an excep-
tionally amorphous regime. It is sure neither who its friends may be nor
from what quarter its opponents will come, and, that being the case, the

universities can probably look with some assurance to their own strength
in the more distant future. As an enduring cultural redoubt they may seem
vulnerable today; but if one looks at the ranks of those who are going to do
the storming, their continued survival becomes plausible. Indeed, they might
do much more than simply survive if, while forfeiting any immediate
political goal, they began to address themselves firmly to their proper
task, which is 'to train the ruling class for the job it has to do'.
     That, after all, was the classic nineteenth-century duty assumed by the
British universities, and it raises the primary question of autonomy in its
fullest context. Perhaps too much may be made of its virtues ? When
African or Asian universities are seen to be 'losing their autonomy', or
appear to be in danger of becoming creatures of government, it is easy to
swing unrealistically to the other extreme. Comparisons are often made
with notional universities: the image of a protective 'ivory tower' of communal learning is presented for commendation, and we are back not in the
nineteenth century but in the age of a medieval monasticism. Yet such
analogies will scarcely do for Legon or Kumasi or Cape Coast. They are
very distant from the ideals of Oxford in the last century, which were
actively to serve both Church and State, not to sit isolated in contemplation.
Naturally, by its influence and standing, and through its 'colonising' of
government, including the Cabinet, parliament, judiciary and civil service,
the university expected to be left free to decide how it should serve; but
that Oxford, and even Cambridge, should 'train the ruling class for the jobs
it has to do' was never doubted.
     Pervasive influence in that order is not within the immediate reach of
the universities in Ghana as long as formal power remains with the military. But they could begin to draw close to its effects *via* the civil service
and all the auxiliaries of the State, including the professions, on which the
soldiers are heavily dependent. The post-colonial emphasis on administration is still very strong, and the universities are necessarily its beneficiaries. Autonomy might not need, therefore, to be so fiercely defended if the
universities' graduates were competently upholding the authority of the
State, whether it was military or civilian in form; and the universities themselves might do much to turn aside the charges of 'elitism' and 'Eurocentrality' if they also gave close attention to meeting some of the requirements of Ghanaian society in the 1970s. They might do so not necessarily
by switching resources so as to produce more doctors or engineers or
chemists or agriculturalists, though that may be needed, but by trying to
select from among a range of academically interesting projects those which
the NRC and future governments might think will supply them with answers
to some of their more pressing problems. The extent to which courses of
instruction in history, as in zoology and law and literature, have been
changed in 'an African direction' was noted earlier; but such redirection
also needs to be carried out in relation to Ghanaian needs. The problem is
not whether to teach 'African chemistry' or 'African sociology' or 'African
economics'—even supposing such fantasies exist—but how to use the body of
universal knowledge which is at the disposal of a university for quite local
and specific ends by teaching, research and training—the essential functions
of all universities wherever they be placed. There is clearly a danger in
commitment: serving interests may easily end up as being part of the
interests which are served. Yet to the more obvious threat of 'politicisation' there is added the less vivid danger of atrophy. The disloyal thought
has occasionally come to my mind at Legon that really the problem is not
that of the power of the State and how best to avoid the soldiers' grasp but

the university's social prestige and how to resist its charms. It is very tempting for teachers and students alike to succumb to indolence—to the 'lethargy of custom'—when the university simply ceases to act creatively and does not act at all.[59]

How easy it is to give advice at a distance! Were it to be accepted with even limited success, Jowett and Balliol and Oxford at large might indeed be translated to Ghana. But it is not at all simple at Legon or Kumasi, in the busy daily life of well established institutions, to know how to gain the respectful attention of a military government which is by no means certain of itself or of its needs in face of a slowly deteriorating economy. The earlier Oxford and Cambridge model, even if its overseas imitators try to preserve not the trappings but the substance of its 'service role', is unlikely to find life quite so manageable or its task so comfortably assured in twentieth-century Africa as in nineteenth-century Britain. In the long term, I am sure, the universities in Ghana will have to try to move towards that end, whatever regime exists in Accra, if they are to retain both academic and political credence. For the present, however, there is immobility rather than a search for new directions, and the suspicions which were being voiced when I was at Legon in 1974 seem certain to persist.

A quarter of a century has elapsed since I first heard such criticisms, but in no sense are they the abiding impression I retain from that time. My understanding of the university to which I once belonged is overlaid with memories not of the college at Achimota or of the university at Legon, but of those who thought that they too belonged there. I recall principally the students in my extra-mural classes. I remember those who enrolled and attended the weekly meetings, usually late, frequently bewildered, at times not fully sober, as in Bawku, in the north, where I lectured, talked and argued before a ragged class of adult students under the shade of a large 'flamboyant' in the hot afternoon, which grew agreeably cool towards evening as the sun set and the night drew on until only the stars lay beyond the hiss and glow of an inefficient pressure lamp. The students would bicycle in from stores and offices and schools, past the market place and the Bawku-naba's palace; they were eager to borrow books but reluctant to read them; they were very knowledgeable about the manoeuvres of local politicians and traditional office holders but almost ignorant of the world beyond Bolgatanga or Tamale or Accra, despite that fabled instrument of modernity, the village wireless set. But who, after all, learnt from whom? I do not think thay they learnt very much from me, except perhaps about what a young 'non-official European' might be like. But I learnt nightly from them. As soon as the class was over, the active spirits among us would go straight to the Hollywood Bar—the Bawku equivalent to the Kalamazoo-Shake-your-Head in Accra or the Kumasi Hotel de Kingsway—and then such talk!

Stories of legends, sorcerers, chiefs, of early education at primary and middle boarding school, views about marriage and politics, and death and immortality. I remember trying to retell stories from Shakespeare, and poetry from Yeats and T. S. Eliot. And I remember, too, how the moon came up and the stars were still bright when I climbed unsteadily on to a camp bed until my servant—companion of many such journeys—woke me at four in the morning with coffee, when we would drive the 150 miles back to Tamale over the Gambaga scarp, headlights at first and then sidelights, until the night faded and the sun began to warm the empty savannah country through which we travelled, very fast indeed, to reach the outskirts of Tamale and breakfast.

Other memories, always, it seems, of talking and drinking, very often

'political talk' about parties and leaders and programmes: the NPP in the
north, the NLM in Ashanti, the CPP throughout the country. But memories
also of trying to understand, in broken Twi, stories of unexplained mystery,
recounted in a little bar by the market. How farmers in the near-by village
searched during three days and nights in the forest for a child until they
were obliged to abandon him to the *mmoitia*—dwarfs who spoke to each other
by whistling and who, as in the stories of Persephone, would dangerously
offer food to the lost or straying child. And I remember, again, nights in
what is now known as the Upper Region, when the local secretary cancelled
the class at Lawra and we travelled out to a village to drink, sitting pillion
on a large motor bike until we reached Birifu, where the chief's son—one, it
was said, of thirty-four brothers—was a very active PEA member. His
father had pots of local beer—home-brewed—spread before us, and we drank
from calabashes on the flat mud roof while a little tinkling tune ran up and
down, plucked from an empty sardine can strung with wire. Once, I remember, there was a xylophone or dulcimer—and a Dagarti maid? If change was
in the nationalist air in Accra and Kumasi, or Tamale and Navrongo, it did
not seem of much consequence here. The sense of continuity—as, I suppose,
in medieval Europe and in most peasant societies—was very strong. There
was order and courtesy. It was very primitive and very civilised. Custom
and ceremony lay all about us, and, forgetful of the world, we were by the
outside world forgotten for a time.[60]
    If, therefore, I were asked what good or harm did 'adult education' do,
I should not be able to reply. I know only that I learnt a great deal about
myself and about a society so different from that of the industrialised West
as to make comparison meaningless. Were the classes 'academic
colonialism' ? Perhaps. But the changes which transformed the politics of
Ghana, with which the fortunes of the universities were so closely inter-
twined, were of much greater scope than the small compass of our activities. I know too that my adult education students were an elite among whom
I delighted to be, and that the Extra-mural Department, like the university
of which it was a minor branch, enjoyed an autonomy and freedom of which
I made full use until 1958. I then left Accra, shortly after independence, to
return only infrequently. I left the little airport beyond the Lisbon Hotel
and went by air to Rome, by train to Florence and Milan, and to Freiburg,
where I wanted to talk to colleagues in what is now the Arnold Bergstraesser
Institute. I walked into the Münster to look at the medieval glass, then out
across the square to the lovely Musikhaus. As I climbed that elegant stair-
case I could hear music—European music—coming from the piano room. I
stood and listened for a while to the little sonata in G major by Beethoven,
the first of the three of Opus 31: not 'great Beethoven', not the Waldstein
or the Appassionata or the Hammerklavier, but—how beautiful it was:
Allegro, Adagio grazioso, Rondo composed, I learnt later, in 1803, some
years before Bowdich thought of visiting Kumasi and while slaves were
still passing through Christiansborg Castle. Here in Freiburg, in this early
sonata, were a world and a civilisation quite removed from Ghana, very
different indeed from the densely stratified, closely organised rhythms of
Ashanti drum music. I had returned home to Europe. Not irrevocably: the
flight from London to Accra is easy and swift, and I know very well that the
friendly courtesies and warmth of Ghanaian society are a permanent possession. To return, however, to Accra in 1974, in the unheroic days of
military control, was also disquieting. There was a pessimism beneath the
gaiety, and an uneasy anxiety about what might come. It was not difficult to
share such apprehensions, particularly when looking back over a much

happier past, and no doubt I should have known that it would be so. Were we not told, many centuries ago, that it is always painful to recall past delights amidst present sorrows?

Nessun maggior dolore
che ricordarsi del tempo felice
nella miseria.

Notes

1   See W. J. M. Mackenzie's very interesting argument in Richard Rose (ed.), *Studies in British Politics,* London, 1969, 52.
2   Established by the National Liberation Council in June 1967 'to educate the public in democratic rights and possibilities', a task not easily accomplished by military rulers.
3   Quoted in International Association of Universities, *The Social Responsibility of the University in Asian Countries: Obligations and Opportunities,* No. 12, Paris, 1973.
4   D. M. Balme, 'Relations between university and government in the Gold Coast, 1948-57: points of friction' seminar paper No. UN/66/2, London: Institute of Commonwealth Studies, 1967, 40-7.
5   *Ibid.,* 41.
6   *Ibid.,* 43.
7   The University College was brought into being after the *Report of the Commission on Higher Education in the Colonies,* Cmnd 6647 (London, 1945) and the *Report of the Commission on Higher Education in West Africa,* Cmnd 6655 (London, 1945). The latter put forward a minority recommendation that there should be one university sited in Ibadan for all four colonies, with subsidiary territorial colleges. The Colonial Office endorsed the minority view; there was a public outcry in the country and a separate University College at Achimota followed in 1948. University classes (including engineering) had been started at Achimota College in 1932.
8   Balme, *op. cit.,* 47.
9   E. Boateng, *Report on the Hall System in the University of Ghana,* Legon, 1967.
10 Balme, *op. cit.,* 45.
11 Including 122 foreign students. Undergraduate numbers actually declined in 1970-71, the total of 2, 525 having increased only by twenty-four over the previous year. Postgraduate numbers increased, but there were now 210 foreign students, of whom Americans were the most numerous.
12 The forward projection of students in March 1965 had been: October 1965, 1, 855; October 1966, 2, 355; October 1967, 2, 955; October 1968, 3, 555. An early Balme plan had looked forward to a figure of 9, 000.
13 Founded in 1952 as the Kumasi College of Technology.
14 Ministry of Information, Accra; December 1960-January 1961.
15 The *Report* was enlivened by the occasional testy footnote of protest by Professor Torochesnikov; but the wonder is that such a committee produced a report at all. Shortly before it was constituted there was one of those characteristic and abrupt changes by Nkrumah, who decided that there should be separate universities at Kumasi and Legon in place of a single University of Ghana. It was also 'brought to the attention' of the committee that the government had finally decided to

establish a new University College of Cape Coast. (*Ibid.*, appendix III, 36.)

16   25 November, 1961, Speech as First Chancellor of the University of Ghana, in which he also noted that 'for the past thirteen years adequate care was taken to ensure that the standard of learning and scholarship ... was acceptable anywhere in the world. In this respect, Ghana is grateful not only to the University of London but also to other British universities ...' (University of Ghana, *Annual Report for 1961-62*, Accra, 1962, 11.)

17   University of Ghana, *Reporter*, IV, 21, 31 March 1964, reprinted in *Minerva*, III, 3, spring 1965, 343-55, particularly 350-5.

18   Professor Alex Kwapong's phrase in his 'Address to Congregation, 26 March 1966' (University of Ghana, *Annual Report* ... *1965-66*, 96), describing 'the determined effort (by the CPP) to storm, once and for all, the Legon Bastille' (a somewhat unfortunate phrase).

19   Described, adequately enough, by the late Tibor Szamuely, who was formerly a senior lecturer at the Institute, 'as a vast catch-all, an indiscriminate hotchpotch of sadly familiar concepts, usually ludicrously exaggerated and invariably unsuited to Ghanaian realities ... a grotesque caricature of totalitarianism both of the left and the right'. (Quoted by Kwapong, *op. cit.*, 99.)

20   *Ibid.*, 98.

21   University of Ghana, *Annual Report* ... *1966-67*, 90.

22   *Ibid.*, 91.

23   'Address of welcome to Congregation, 18 March 1967', in University of Ghana, *Annual Report* ... *1967-68*, 116.

24   *Ibid.*, 119.

25   *Ibid.*, 130.

26   University of Ghana, *Annual Report* ... *1970-71*, 16.

27   University of Ghana, *op. cit.*, *1967-68*, 32.

28   University of Ghana, *op. cit.*, *1970-71*, 30-3.

29   See Peter Williams, 'Lending for learning: an experiment in Ghana', *Minerva*, XII, 3, July 1974, 326-45.

30   I. K. Acheampong, *Speeches and Interviews by Col. I. K. Acheampong*, I, Accra, n.d., 290-302.

31   *Ibid.*, 298.

32   'Address to the University of Science and Technology, 16th June, 1973', in Acheampong, *op. cit.*, II, 150-4.

33   There is, of course, a simplified view of post-colonial Africa from the commanding heights of Marxist theory—a rather vulgar Marxism—which crowds such conflicts, including the relations of universities and governments, into one category. It is sometimes asserted that Ghana and similarly placed countries are governed by a new political class of soldiers who rule the State, for which universities are simply a pseudo-Western elite, in the interests not only of a growing number of local entrepreneurs (the 'nascent bourgeoisie') but their external masters. Terms so general as to encompass everything usually end by meaning not much, and I cannot fit the Legon story into so neat a box of tricks.

34   *Legon Observer*, IX, 1, 11-24 January 1974, 6.

35   *Ibid.*, VIII, 26, 28 December-10 January 1974, 611-14.

36   See Williams, *op. cit.*, 338-9.

37   See the 'special statement' on the *Legon Observer*, issued by the Legon Society on National Affairs, 3 October, 1974.

38   Such pressure had their effect. Over the years 'home grown' in extra-
     mural studies has tended paradoxically to place greater emphasis on
     certificate education, based on external standards of examination. The
     present Institute of Adult Education has begun a very large programme
     of correspondence courses; and it promises, through its classes and
     workers' colleges, tuition in (1) general certificate of education ('O'
     and 'A' levels); (2) professional courses leading to final certificates of
     recognised professional bodies; (3) liberal studies courses—(which are
     examinable but which provide certificates of attendance); (4) degree
     courses of the University of Ghana prepared for externally through the
     Accra Workers' College. Reversing the established order, *opera buffa*
     has given place to *opera seria*. To the early—largely expatriate—
     teachers of extra-mural studies such a programme would have seemed
     heresy, a perversion of intentions: Caliban has cast out Ariel. I do not
     doubt but that the change reflects the wishes of the students now and in
     the past.

39   Kwame Nkrumah, *Ghana: the Autobiography of Kwame Nkrumah*,
     Edinburgh, 1957, 21. Hence his decision to go to the United States?

40   See Fred M. Agyeman's interesting little book *A Century with Boys*
     (Accra, 1967). 'Thirty or more years ago the Standard Seven Certifi-
     cate was the golden key to employment in business houses, the civil
     service, teaching, nursing and the majority of the good jobs. . . . Not
     to have obtained the Certificate at the end of a school career of ten
     years was enough to give a boy a very difficult start in life' (p. 80).

41   L. H. Ofosu-Appiah, *Life of Lt. Gen. E. K. Kotoka* (Accra, 1972), 17.

42   Acheampong, *op. cit.*, II, 1-2.

43   Disfigured in recent years by buildings erected with the aid of American
     benefactions.

44   Otto Klineberg and Marisa Zavalloni, *Nationalism and Tribalism among
     African Students*, Paris and The Hague, 1969, 14-15.

45   Professor O'Connell observes that West Africa still has some way to
     go before it reaches a Latin American situation, as in Brazil, where it
     is said that in 1963 less than one per cent of a sample of students had
     fathers who were illiterate, despite adult illiteracy of 46 per cent.
     Paul A. Beckett and James O'Connell, 'University education and the
     sources of power: a Nigerian case study', seminar paper No. CP/73/5,
     London, Institute of Commonwealth Studies, 1973.

46   I. S. Ogbue, 'Innovations in Nigerian universities', *Report of the
     Conference of Overseas Vice-chancellors*, Ibadan, January 1974, 29.

47   *Ibid.*, report by Dr Seah Chee Meow.

48   Eric Ashby and Mary Anderson, *Universities: British, Indian, African*
     (London, 1966). Hearn and Wilson at Melbourne supported their pro-
     posals for reform of the curriculum in the 1850s with the plea that
     'In the Colonies the conditions of Society which gave rise to the English
     system never existed. The more closely, therefore, the Colonial uni-
     versities resemble those of the Mother Country, the greater the prob-
     ability of failure.' (Quoted by Ashby and Anderson, 43-4.)

49   'Supernatural beliefs and changing cognitive structures among Ghanian
     university students' in J. W. Berry (ed.), *Culture and Cognition: Readings
     in Cross-cultural Psychology* (London, 1974), 156.

50   *Ibid.*, 156-7.

51   *Africa Report*, XV, 3, March 1970, 12.

52   'Education enshrines many of the optimistic fantasies of Ahafo resi-
     dents and in doing so lends powerful support to the modern status

hierarchy.' See John Dunn, 'Politics in Asunafo' in Dennis Austin and Robin Luckham (eds.), *Politicians and Soldiers in Ghana, 1966-1972* (London, 1975), chapter 7; see Polly Hill, *Migrant Cocoa Farmers in Southern Ghana* (Cambridge, 1963), chapter 7.

53 See Nirad C. Chaudhuri, *The Continent of Circe,* London, 1966.

54 'In Africa and the Caribbean, where the demand for trained graduates still exceeds the supply, hardly any serious person doubts that one of the principal functions of the university is to train the middle class for the jobs it has to do'. Sir Arthur Lewis, *The Universities in Less Developed Countries* (New York, 1974), 14-15.

55 *Ibid.,* 19.

56 Nduka Okafor, *The Development of Universities in Nigeria,* London, 1971.

57 Pierre Van den Berghe, *Power and Privilege at an African University,* London, 1974.

58 They too were accused of attempting to suborn Colonel Kotei, who was later brought onto the NRC. On 19 December Ayarna, Botsio and Tettegah were sentenced to death, Owusu Boateng to thirty years' imprisonment; Awuviri was acquitted. On 14 January 1974, Alex A. Hamah was also sentenced to death. None was executed: all were sentenced to life imprisonment, but there were ugly stories during the trials of torture, including the death of the brother of the former Progress Party general secretary. For an excellent account of these intricate events see Simon Baynham, 'The military in politics: Colonel Acheampong's *coup',* thesis, University of Exeter, 1974.

59 For a sympathetic study of the paralysis of action of the colonial intellectual caught between tradition and modernity, whose 'fate destines him to provinciality, until his own modern culture becomes creative', see Edward Shils, *The Intellectual Between Tradition and Modernity: the Indian Situation* (The Hague, 1971).

60 Not, however, for long. By 1956 Birifu was a strong CPP outpost in a district dominated by the Northern People's Party. Below the ceremonies of innocence was a fierce communal rivalry between neighbouring towns and villages.

Index